Lutheran Theology and Secular Law

This collection brings together lawyers and theologians in the U.S. and Europe to reflect on Lutheran understandings of the political use of the law by secular governments. The book furthers the intellectual conversation about how Lutheran insights can be used to develop jurisprudence and specific solutions to legal issues in which there is strong conflict. It presents the basic theological and interpretive assumptions of the Lutheran tradition as they may inform the creation of legislation and judicial interpretation at local, national and international levels. The authors explore Luther's conception of the foundations of modern secular law and understanding of vocation. The work discusses the application of Lutheran theological principles to contemporary issues such as the war on terror, native land rights, property law, family law, church and state, medical experimentation, and the criminal law of rape, providing ethical insights for lawyers and lawmakers.

Marie A. Failinger is a Professor of Law at Mitchell Hamline University School of Law. She was editor in chief of the *Journal of Law and Religion* from 1988 to 2013, and has published dozens of law review and other articles, including several on Lutheran theology and law. She is also a co-editor of *Feminism, Law and Religion* (2013), *On Secular Governance* (2016), and *The Poverty Law Canon* (2016).

Ronald W. Duty served as Assistant Director of Studies at the Evangelical Lutheran Church in America. Among his published works are chapters in *Testing the Spirits* (Eerdmans, ed. Patrick Keifert 2009) and *On Secular Governance* (Eerdmans, eds. Ronald W. Duty and Marie A. Failinger, 2016) and articles in *The Journal of the Society of Christian Ethics, dialog, The Journal of Lutheran Ethics,* and *Word & World.*

ICLARS Series on Law and Religion

The *ICLARS Series on Law and Religion* is a new series designed to provide a forum for the rapidly expanding field of research in law and religion. The series is published in association with the International Consortium for Law and Religion Studies, an international network of scholars and experts of law and religion founded in 2007 with the aim of providing a place where information, data and opinions can easily be exchanged among members and made available to the broader scientific community. The series aims to become a primary source for students and scholars while presenting authors with a valuable means to reach a wide and growing readership.

Other titles in this series:

Law and International Religious Freedom
The Rise and Decline of the American Model
Pasquale Annicchino

Free Exercise of Religion and the United States Constitution
The Supreme Court's Challenge
Mark P. Strasser

Religious Freedom and the Australian Constitution
Origins and Future
Luke Beck

Islam, Law and the Modern State
(Re)imagining Liberal Theory in Muslim Contexts
Arif A. Jamal

Atheist Exceptionalism
Atheism, Religion, and the United States Supreme Court
Ethan G. Quillen

Lutheran Theology and Secular Law
The Work of the Modern State
Edited by Marie A. Failinger and Ronald W. Duty

For more information about this series, please visit:
www.routledge.com/ICLARS-Series-on-Law-and-Religion/book-series/ICLARS

Lutheran Theology and Secular Law

The Work of the Modern State

Edited by
Marie A. Failinger and Ronald W. Duty

Routledge
Taylor & Francis Group
LONDON AND NEW YORK

First published 2018 by Routledge

2 Park Square, Milton Park, Abingdon, Oxfordshire OX14 4RN
52 Vanderbilt Avenue, New York, NY 10017

Routledge is an imprint of the Taylor & Francis Group, an informa business

First issued in paperback 2020

British Library Cataloguing-in-Publication Data
A catalogue record for this book is available from the British Library

Library of Congress Cataloging-in-Publication Data
Names: Failinger, Marie A., author. | Duty, Ronald W., author.
Title: Lutheran theology and secular law: the work of the modern state / edited by Marie A. Failinger and Ronald W. Duty.
Description: Abingdon, Oxon [UK]; New York, NY: Routledge, 2018. | Series: ICLARS series on law and religion | Includes bibliographical references and index.
Identifiers: LCCN 2017059731 | ISBN 9781138245136 (hardback)
Subjects: LCSH: Religion and law. | Religion and state. | Law—Christian influences. | Secularism. | Church and state—Lutheran Church. | Lutheran Church—Doctrines.
Classification: LCC K3280.F35 2018 | DDC 340/.11—dc23
LC record available at https://lccn.loc.gov/2017059731

ISBN: 978-1-138-24513-6 (hbk)
ISBN: 978-0-367-59144-1 (pbk)

Typeset in Galliard
by codeMantra

But it is the work of the temporal power to protect its subjects, and to punish thievery, robbery, and adultery, as St. Paul says, Romans xiii: "It beareth not the sword in vain; it serves God with it, to the terror of evil doers, and to the protection of the good."

Martin Luther: A Treatise on Good Works (1520)

Marie Failinger dedicates this book to the many lawyers and pastors of faith who have taught her about her vocation as a lawyer and a person of faith, most especially her teachers at Valparaiso University and its School of Law and her colleagues from the Journal of Law and Religion Editorial Board/Council on Religion and Law. Steeped in many different faith traditions, they have served the community as lawyers and pastors interested in issues of law and justice from a religious perspective, and have powerfully influenced her own thinking.

Ronald Duty dedicates this book to his former colleagues on the Studies team in Church and Society at the Evangelical Lutheran Church in America: Karen L. Bloomquist, John R. Stumme, Kaari Reierson, Victor Thasiah, and Roger Willer. It was his pleasure to work with them as they helped the ELCA to discern, formulate, and adopt its official positions on a variety of ethical and social issues. Working with them, he learned the value and importance of doing Lutheran ethics as a corporate effort of the moral deliberation of the church by means of task forces working on specific issues, regular conversation among Lutheran ethicists and theologians, and the extension of that conversation digitally in the *Journal of Lutheran Ethics.*

Contents

Notes on contributors

About the principal authors

Dr. Ronald W. Duty served as Assistant Director of Studies at the Evangelical Lutheran Church in America. Among his published works are chapters in *Testing the Spirits* (Eerdmans, ed. Patrick Keifert 2009) and *On Secular Governance* (Eerdmans, eds. Ronald W. Duty and Marie A. Failinger, 2016) and articles in *The Journal of the Society of Christian Ethics, dialog, The Journal of Lutheran Ethics,* and *Word & World.*

Marie A. Failinger is a Professor of Law at Mitchell Hamline University School of Law. She was editor in chief of the *Journal of Law and Religion* from 1988 to 2013, and has published dozens of law review and other articles, including several on Lutheran theology and law. She is also a co-editor of *Feminism, Law and Religion* (2013), *On Secular Governance* (2016), and *The Poverty Law Canon* (2016).

About the contributors

Dr. H. David Baer is Professor in the Department of Theology, Philosophy and Classical Languages, Texas Lutheran University. He is the author of *The Struggle of Hungarian Lutherans Under Communism.* He has been on the executive board of the Forum for Religious Freedom Europe and the advisory board of the Central-European Religious Freedom Institute, and is the recipient of the 2013 Ambassador of Peace Award from the European Leadership Conference of Universal Peace.

Dr. Kelly Denton-Borhaug is Professor of theology at Moravian College and executive director of the college's InFocus Centers of Investigation. She has recently published *U.S. War-Culture, Sacrifice and Salvation* (Routledge, 2014); and has published numerous articles on war, peace and theology in such journals as the *Library of Social Science, dialog,* and the *Journal of Political Theology.*

Dr. Carl-Henric Grenholm was Senior Professor of ethics at the Department of Theology, Uppsala University, Sweden from 1992 to 2013. Recent published work includes *Beyond Humanism* (2003); *To Understand Religion* (2006); *Sustainable Development and Global Ethics* (2007); *Justification in a Post-Christian Society* (ed. with Gunner, 2014); and *Lutheran Identity and Political Theology* (ed. with Gunner, 2014).

Dr. Mary Jane Haemig is Professor of Church History at Luther Seminary, St. Paul MN. She has received Harvard's Frederick Sheldon Traveling Fellowship, the Regency

Advancement Award (PLU), and research support from the Herzog-August-Bibliothek and Evangelische Kirche Deutschland. She is an associate editor and book review editor of *Lutheran Quarterly,* associate editor of the *Dictionary of Luther and the Lutheran Traditions*, and member of the continuation committee of the International Luther Search Conference.

Dr. Stefan Heuser is Professor of ethics in the professions at Evangelische Hochschule-Darmstadt, and previously served in the Department of Ethics of the Theological Faculty of Friedrich-Alexander University, Erlangen-Nürnberg. Among his recent publications are *Human Dignity: A Theological Exploration* (2011), *Bonhoeffer and the Biosciences* (with Wüstenberg, 2010); and *Identity: Biblical and Theological Explorations* (co-edited with Deeg and Manzeschke, 2007).

Dr. Paul R. Hinlicky is Tise Professor of Lutheran Studies at Roanoke College and Visiting Professor of Systematic Theology at the Protestant Theological Faculty of Comenius University, Slovakia. Among his many recent publications are *Luther and the Beloved Community: A Path for Christian Theology after Christendom* (2010); *Divine Complexity: The Rise of Creedal Christianity* (2010); *Beloved Community: Critical Dogmatics after Christendom* (2015); and *Divine Simplicity: Christ the Crisis of Metaphysics* (2016).

Dr. Patrick R. Keifert is Professor of systematic theology at Luther Seminary and president of Church Innovations. His recent books include *But Is It All True: The Bible and the Question of Truth* (with Padgett, 2006); *We Are Here Now: A New Missional Era* (2007); *Testing the Spirits: How Theology Informs the Study of Congregations* (2009) and *Being Promised: Theology, Gift and Practice* (with Walter, 2013.) He has been the co-editor of the *Journal of Law and Religio*

Dr. Michael J. Kessler is Managing Director of the Berkley Center for Religion, Peace, and World Affairs at Georgetown University, an Associate Professor of the Practice of Government, and an adjunct professor of Law, Georgetown University Law Center. He has written *Political Theology for a Plural Age* (2013) and *Engaging Religion in U.S. Foreign Affairs* (2016), and co-edited *Mystics: Presence and Aporia* (with Sheppard, 2003).

Dr. Craig L. Nessan is Academic Dean and Professor of contextual theology at Wartburg Theological Seminary in Dubuque, Iowa. In addition to other articles, reviews, and books, Dr. Nessan is the author of *Shalom Church: The Body of Christ as Ministering Community* (2010); *Beyond Maintenance to Mission: A Theology of the Congregation* (rev'd 2010); and *Liberating Lutheran Theology: Freedom for Justice and Solidarity in a Global Context* (with Chung and Duchrow, 2011).

Dr. Ted Peters is Distinguished Research Professor Emeritus of Systematic Theology and Ethics at Pacific Lutheran Theological Seminary and the Graduate Theological Union in Berkeley, California, USA. He is former editor-in-chief of *dialog, A Journal of Theology;* and currently he co-edits the journal *Theology and Science.* He recently published *Sin Boldly! Justifying Faith for Fragile and Broken Souls* (2015) and the third edition of his systematic theology, *GOD—The World's Future* (2015).

Dr. Mary J. Streufert serves as Director of the Justice for Women program at the Churchwide Office of the Evangelical Lutheran Church in America. A theologian of the church, she is a regular lecturer and workshop leader. Her recent publications include

Transformative Lutheran Theologies: Feminist, Womanist, and Mujerista Perspectives (2010) and a number of scholarly articles on christology, salvation, power and theological method.

Dr. Deanna A. Thompson is Professor of Religion at Hamline University. Many of her publications, including her book, *Crossing the Divide: Luther, Feminism, and the Cross* (2004), focus on bringing Lutheran and feminist theology together in generative ways. She has also published the books *Hoping for More: Having Cancer, Talking Faith, and Accepting Grace* (2012); *Deuteronomy: A Theological Commentary on the Bible* (2014); and *The Virtual Body of Christ in a Suffering World* (2016.)

Dr. Michael Reid Trice is Assistant Dean for Ecumenical and Interreligious Dialogue and Assistant Professor of theological ethics and constructive theology at the Seattle University School of Theology and Ministry. He is a leader on the Interfaith Commission of the National Council of the Churches of Christ in the U.S.A., and serves on the executive board for Church World Service. His dissertation, titled *Encountering Cruelty: A Fracture of the Human Heart*, was published in April, 2011; and, among other work, he has published *Generosity: Reimagining the Core of Human Belonging* (2016).

W. Bradley Wendel is Professor of law at Cornell University School of Law, and previously taught at Washington and Lee Law School. Wendel has written or edited a number of books, recently including *Professional Responsibility: Examples and Explanations* (5th ed., 2016); *Torts: Cases and Materials* (with Twerski and Henderson, 4th ed., 2017); *The Law and Ethics of Lawyering* (with Hazard, Koniak, Cramton, and Cohen, 2017); and *The Law Governing Lawyers: National Rules, Standards, and Statutes* (with Martyn and Fox, 2005, rev'd annually).

Preface

The relationship between religion and law has become an important topic world-wide and especially in academic circles, including the American legal academy, over the past three or four decades. Scholars in other disciplines have also developed strong interests at the intersection of these two fields with their own. These concerns are both scholarly and practical.

Several academic journals specializing in religion and law have been founded, centers on law and religion have been created in various institutions around the world, and the International Consortium for Law and Religious Studies (ICLARS) and other international collaboratives have been formed around these issues. Courses on religion and law are being taught at numerous law schools and universities, and textbooks written by a number of scholars in this area have been published.

Much of the discussion so far has been carried on from Jewish, Catholic, Reformed, or Islamic perspectives. Lutherans have been relatively scarce in these conversations in English-speaking countries, although their absence has been little noticed. They have, however, participated in some national policy deliberations and written some important texts in social ethics. Lutherans, therefore, are not necessarily averse to joining in these discussions.

This collection of essays by Lutheran theologians and legal academics gives glimpses into the ways in which their heritage of thought, with its important insights and points of view, may address a range of public issues to inform those who shape or practice law. In Part 1 of this collection, Stefan Heuser brings Luther's well-known doctrine of the two kingdoms into play as support for the importance of secularization of politics and law-making, rather than for those identity-movements and ways of thinking that denigrate secularization of the law and call for reversing or transcending this secularization. He suggests that people should work for the re-secularization of politics, constitutional law, and deliberative political processes (where people of different political perspectives actually talk *with*—rather than *at* or *about*—one another) so that our inner persons can be subject only to God's rule.

In Part II, Carl-Henric Grenholm and Paul Hinlicky address the relation between Lutheran theology and legal philosophy. Grenholm compares legal positivism and natural law, noting their differences on questions of the legal validity and the moral basis of law, and shows how features of both are present in Lutheran social ethics. He argues that a Lutheran social ethic based only in a doctrine of creation, natural law, reason, and Luther's conception of the two kingdoms provides an inadequate basis for a moral critique of secular law if it is not informed by the gospel. Grenholm suggests ways in which Christology can be a basis for a moral critique of law as well as a foundation of the legislative process. Hinlicky maintains that Lutheranism is a conflicted tradition about the law, and explicates the implications of Lutheran antinomianism which uses the gospel to transform faith in Christ into a general divine acceptance and ethical permissiveness which dispenses on principle with accountability to God for the world and denies the need for justification. He suggests that the church's response should be to repent of a false gospel of all-is-grace and proclaim the gospel of Christ's law of love, in light of which the church can cultivate a culture of conscience in which the institution and its members take responsibility to God for that part of God's creation entrusted to them.

In Part III, Michael Kessler, Michael Trice, Craig Nessan and David Baer take up various aspects of the relation between the individual and the state. Kessler analyzes Luther's political theology and draws from his distinction between the proper work of both the church and the government the implications which this distinction has for individuals. He suggests that given Luther's understanding of vocation, this distinction calls for individuals to take up multiple responsibilities in family, church, and government, but to hold them as distinct aspects or spheres of individual life rather than depending on their separation as structural features of political and social institutions.

Trice characterizes both Luther and his contemporary Machiavelli as reformers, showing how each reimagined for his time the individual's private piety, public virtue, the relationship of religion and government, and the marks of personal and political duty in order to cast light on the nature and survival of humans in the midst of a radically changing world, and the regulatory power of religion and the government. He suggests that Luther and Machiavelli had different understandings of the role of Christian virtue and morality which stem from different understandings of the role of Christian quietism and the role and importance of government and individuals' relationships to it.

Nessan discusses how Luther's two strategies for God's ruling the world—through both law and gospel—free Christians for serving their neighbors in the world, in part, through the functions and activities of government. He suggests that this freedom includes the activities of Christians as political advocates for policies, programs, and actions that benefit others. Baer considers whether the right of conscientious objection extends beyond the traditional focus on an individual's active participation in combat during war to include other actions or activities to which they may object as a matter of moral conscience. He suggests that the right of religious freedom pushes beyond a universal core to civil recognition of rights of conscience about a variety of activities which a pluralist conception of the common good should recognize.

In Part IV, Ted Peters and Kelly Denton-Borhaug consider different aspects of the relationship between international law and human rights for vulnerable people. Peters draws on notions of human liberation which both the Church—in preaching the Gospel—and human rights advocates proclaim and promise, arguing that this liberation aims at conferring and protecting human dignity whenever it is not recognized. He suggests that the evident tension between the dignity assumed to be present but needing to be both conferred and protected can be resolved by trusting in God, and drawing dignity's immanent reality from God's imminent future.

Denton-Borhaug examines how official American policy rhetoric following the terrorist attacks on the United States on September 11, 2001 was used to empower, misdescribe, and justify significant abuses including the employment of torture, extraordinary rendition, and disregard of detainees' rights to avail themselves of legal processes. She describes how these practices flew in the face of international conventions on human rights and treatment of prisoners and combatants. Denton-Borhaug shows how the use of the Evangelical Lutheran Church in America's 1995 Social Statement, "For Peace in God's World", in conjunction with a rigorous description of the reality of U.S. war culture, can raise the consciences of Christians and embolden them to mount a challenge to this war culture.

In Part V, issues of domestic law, focusing on criminal and family concerns, are addressed by Mary Jane Haemig, Ronald Duty, Marie Failinger and Patrick Keifert, and Mary Streufert. Haemig considers the sermons that sixteenth century Lutheran pastors preached about the Seventh Commandment against theft to give sophisticated critiques of how all people and organizations of every station violated the commandment, often perpetrating economic injustice. She suggests that if pastors today were to preach with such directness and specificity, their audiences would be provoked to think about how law was intended to foster and uphold right relationships, and what proper conduct should be in any economic relationship.

Duty reviews the development of the doctrine of discovery over the centuries as it was utilized as a key foundation of American Indian law, and makes a Lutheran critique of the doctrine. He suggests that its various forms and uses consistently violate Lutheran understandings of the commandments against theft, covetousness and bearing false witness, as well as Lutheran understandings of the petition of the Lord's Prayer for daily bread.

Streufert analyzes the factors in U.S. rape law that effectively invalidate the moral authority of women's voices and bodies, focusing her critique on the gendered binary that assumes a hierarchy of men over women. She suggests that a Lutheran feminist critique of these factors reestablishes the moral authority of women and helps to critique recent reforms of rape law.

Failinger and Keifert offer a Lutheran critique of the common notions of contemporary marriage based either on status or on contract, showing both that these models are not consistent with lived reality and are not normatively desirable. They suggest that a Reformation model of marriage and divorce law provides "reality therapy" for family law based on two critical values—human freedom, which emphasizes consent, and responsibility, which emphasizes the public nature of marriage. Finding a right relationship between these two values can help legislators, lawyers, and jurists navigate the difficulties of marriage law in changing circumstances in order to foster trust within marriages and deal with the needs for both preservation and recompense from the law.

In Part VI, Deanna Thompson and W. Bradley Wendel consider the relationship between the roles of medical and legal professionals, law, and neighbor-love. Deanna Thompson discusses the strengths and weaknesses of bioethical requirements for informed consent and respect for patient autonomy, especially in medical trials for cancer research. She suggests that conventional understandings of those norms neglect the importance of the community of relationships patients have. In her argument, Luther's metaphor of neighbor and his ethic of neighbor love are more appropriate to the challenging calling of physicians to cancer patients who become participants in medical trials.

Bradley Wendel examines the moral dilemmas of lawyers' roles which require them to fulfill duties and responsibilities that seem to require them to do what others would consider wrong or morally ambiguous, or require them to participate in imperfect legal institutions which sometimes produce injustices. He employs a Lutheran paradoxical ethical understanding and a view of vocation that begins with the reality that lawyers must work in legal institutions that are imperfect and only partially just. Yet, this reality is held in tension with the promise that God continues to act through those institutions working to achieve justice, a promise that can empower lawyers both to continue to work for justice and to accept the moral qualms and unease of working in imperfectly just legal institutions.

Ronald W. Duty and Marie A. Failinger
November, 2017

Acknowledgements

We would like to thank the authors for tackling the difficult task of working across disciplines to find the intersection between law and Lutheran theology and ethics. We would also like to acknowledge the support of the Council on Religion and Law, which sponsored an October 2016 conference for the authors of this text to receive comments on their drafts, and our thanks go to United Theological Seminary in New Brighton, MN for hosting that conference, especially Brian Braskich who served as staff for that conference. Among the commentators and moderators whose questions and comments sharpened our essays were Thomas Berg, Mark Berkson, Deborah Cantrell, Paula Cooey, Perry Dane, Emily Albrink Hartigan, Stewart Herman, Suzann Hequist, Meg Hobday, Robert Kennedy, Mary Lowe and Howard Vogel.

We also wish to thank our research assistants, Megan Vincent and Alexandra Zabinski, for their careful and professional assistance with the technical aspects of this work.

Part I

Our secular age

At the same time, the outer rule of law establishes living conditions which safeguard the freedom of the inner man. Otherwise, war, oppression or other existential threats could make it impossible to receive and live on the inner freedom. The secularity of law, and its virtue, lies in the way that it blocks any human governance on the inner man, but yet orders outer human interactions so that the inner man can remain free. This means that the outer regime does not translate individual strength into a dominion over others, but that it remains bound through law to God's preserving power. Hence, genuine political power arises when people let themselves be ruled by God, inwardly through the Gospel, and outwardly through the law.[46]

According to Luther, the inner government by God's word and the outer government by law are categorically different, but they are *both* needed to create the "*status politicus*." Worldly—secular—government may never claim the human heart and it may not rule the inner man.[47] Hence, law—as the medium of government—is supposed to protect the inner freedom of the human being from manipulation. Law therefore has to be "secular" in the sense that it orders human interactions and the forms of human existence in a way that leaves the inner man subject solely to God's regime.[48] Politics can never draw its legitimacy from religion, but political leaders need to be ruled by God in order to be freed from transforming their economic, physical, rhetoric or whatever strength into dominion, and to be freed for practicing power on behalf of their subordinates. Whenever God governs the authorities, and whenever they let him govern themselves, they become secularized, and this means they become truly human, truly worldly, and stripped of divine pretense.

Luther thus inaugurates an understanding of secularization as a form of "*Weltwerdung*:" the process through which those who deemed themselves to be godlike become worldly.[49] Secularization is therefore the impact created by the preaching of the first commandment with its critique of idolatry. At the same time, it is part of Luther's theory of justification, with its emphasis on the simultaneity of "*iustus et peccator*," that the twofold truth of human beings cannot be derived from experience but needs to be revealed by God through Christ.[50] For Luther, a genuine part of God's work on human beings through the incarnation of Christ is to strip them of their Adamic pretension to be gods themselves, and to render them truly human, that is, to recognize them as sinners. Hence, Luther says that God must make "*ex infoelicibus et superbis diis homines veros, idest miseros et peccatores.*"[51] (*God must transform us from unhappy and arrogant Gods into true human beings, and that is: wretches and sinners.*)

Insofar as this rendering applies also to the worldly authorities, it means that they *receive* "secularity" through God's rule as it takes shape in the preaching of the first commandment: God's power frees them from their usurped divinity, from focusing on their own capacities, and God's rule empowers them to turn to the world not as gods, but as genuine human beings who search for power together with others, or vicariously for others. For Luther, law in its double use of *usus civilis* and *theologicus legis* is hence the decisive medium through which this secularization of the sovereign, his transformation from a faked god to a true human being, is effectuated. It decouples power from personal strength and autocracy; and it binds power to the exploration of political, joint action. In short, for Luther, the authorities can only be truly "*weltlich*" or "secular," when they let God govern them and free them from being lords to becoming servants.

Against the backdrop of this understanding of "secularization" as the world becoming truly worldly, human beings becoming truly human, and authority becoming transformed from force into power, "secularization" does not mean the transformation of religious into worldly power, but an exercise of worldly power that lets God rule. The point is not so much whether the conscience of the person in charge is dominated by God, as if justification were a state of mind that could be transferred into visible actions. In political practices, to let oneself be ruled by God first of all means not to act on account of the power that rests on one's own capabilities, but to beg for a wise, discerning heart, to let one's mind be transformed, to seek peace and welfare, and to let oneself be guided by a power that is bestowed upon oneself for the sake of others.[52] This does not presuppose a Christian "attitude," but rests only God's work on human beings.

For Luther, power hence cannot be "religious," since also the power that is exerted in the Church or other religious institutions is and needs to be "worldly" power. The question is whether rulers let God rule—and enter into cooperative, common modes of power—or whether they draw on other resources and apply force instead of power. God's proper work, his *opus proprium*, which human beings cannot influence, is the liberation of hearts from godless fetters, the transformation of lords into servants, and of force into power.

Luther's political thought hence bears affinities to the idea that power needs to be generated communicatively, as we find it in Hannah Arendt's and Jürgen Habermas' conceptions of the political. Here, "the political" has been transformed into the democratic political procedures and the practices of civil society, and finds its normative representation in democratic, constitutional law, leaving the concept of sovereignty metaphysically homeless. Habermas rightly asks: "Why shouldn't the political find an impersonal embodiment in the normative dimension of a democratic constitution?"[53] With Luther, we might agree, but we might also add: What about the inner man, then? Who will govern him? Should the heart of the human being then only be freed by discourse, and ruled by a morality of reciprocity?

The liberal state has no functional equivalent to God's spiritual regime that could offer an equally strong contradiction to any human power that tries to rule the inner man. Deliberative politics presupposes a freedom that it cannot produce without becoming illiberal. As the formerly German constitutional judge Ernst-Wolfgang Böckenförde has claimed: "*The liberal secularized state lives by prerequisites which it cannot guarantee itself.* This is the great adventure it has undertaken for freedom's sake."[54]

The secular liberal state cannot rule the inner man. But where should free citizens come from? Who will enter into legislative procedures with the experience that sovereignty does not result from the power to dominate the state of exception, as Carl Schmitt holds, but that the constitution of law answers to a justice which people are granted *sola gratia*, before their own efforts, and in which they are called to live together?

In regard to these questions, Lutherans have an important task to fulfill: besides all efforts and political practices that they engage in the field of civil society, they need to contribute to the re-secularization of politics, and of liberal constitutional law, by preaching and practicing God's Word, and by contributing to deliberative politics. The point is not to claim more influence for the Churches, but to witness publicly to God's justice in his twofold regime, e.g. by contradicting friend-enemy-patterns of thought, and by supporting political initiatives in which people explore how to find power together with others. If we follow Luther, we should not opt for Carl Schmitt and his political theology. Rather, Lutherans have strong reasons to join the ongoing task to secularize politics.

Let us finally return to the beginning: Is it correct to translate "*weltlich*" (worldly) as "secular?" It is possible, and even helpful. This translation indicates that from a Lutheran perspective, "secularity" is not the result of a history of decay, but an intended and at the same time highly contested mode of politics. So, secularity should indeed not be regarded as the result of a "subtraction story,"[55] but as a necessary dialectic of liberation and domestication of politics that has to be achieved in the dynamic processes mediated by democratic constitutional law.

Notes

1 Among the cornerstones of this research are: Steve Bruce, *God Is Dead. Secularization in the West* (Oxford: Blackwell, 2002); David Martin, *On Secularization. Towards a Revised General Theory* (Aldershot: Ashgate Publishing, 2005); Pippa Norris and Ronald Inglehart, *Sacred and Secular. Religion and Politics Worldwide* (Cambridge: Cambridge University Press, 2004).

2 See Peter L. Berger, "The Desecularization of the World. A Global Overview," in Peter L. Berger, ed., *The Desecularization of the World: Resurgent Religion and World Politics* (Grand Rapids, MI: Eerdmans, 1999), 1–18.

3 Detlef Pollack, *Wiederkehr der Religion? Studien zum religiösen Wandel in Deutschland und Europa II* (Tübingen: Mohr Siebeck, 2009) and "Religious Change in Modern Societies: Perspectives Offered by the Sociology of Religion," in Detlef Pollack and Daniel V. A. Olson, eds., *The Role of Religion in Modern Societies* (New York: Routledge, 2008), 1–22. See also Detlef Pollack, Christel Gärtner, Karl Gabriel, eds., *Umstrittene Säkularisierung: Soziologische und historische Analysen zur Differenzierung von Religion und Politik* (Berlin: Berlin University Press, 2012). See Friedrich Wilhelm Graf, *Die Wiederkehr der Götter. Religion in der Moderne* (München: Beck, 2004).

4 See Hans Joas and Klaus Wiegandt, eds., *Secularization and the World Religions* (Liverpool: Liverpool University Press, 2010).

5 Stanley Hauerwas, *After Christendom* (Nashville, TN: Abingdon Press, 1999); John Milbank, *Beyond Secular Order: The Representation of Being and the Representation of the People* (Malden, MA and Oxford, UK: Wiley Blackwell, 2013). See also John Milbank, *Theology and Social Theory: Beyond Secular Reason* (1990) (Malden, MA and Oxford, UK: Blackwell, 2006) (second edition); and Carl-Henric Grenholm and Göran Gunner, eds., *Justification in a Post-Christian Society* (Cambridge: James Clarke & Co, 2015).

6 Charles Taylor, *A Secular Age* (Cambridge, MA and London: Harvard University Press, 2007), 1ff. Taylor's otherwise thorough genealogy has some blind spots in regard of the contribution of the Reformation to secularization and may be complemented by Brad Gregory: *The Unintended Reformation: How a Religious Revolution Secularized Society* (Cambridge, MA: Belknap Press, 2012).

7 Taylor, *A Secular Age*, 774.

8 In regard of the highly problematic history of reception of Luther's doctrine, it is important to stress that Luther primarily uses the term "*Regierweisen*" (modes of regime, of governance or of government), not "*Reiche*" (realms, areas, or kingdoms), thereby indicating that he focusses on two ways God governs the world. See Ulrich Duchrow, ed., *Zwei Reiche und Regimente. Ideologie oder evangelische Orientierung? Internationale Fall- und Hintergrundstudien zur Theologie und Praxis lutherischer Kirchen im 20. Jahrhundert* (Geneva: Lutheran World Federation, 1977). See also Gerhard Sauter, ed., *Zur Zwei-Reiche-Lehre Luthers, Theologische Bücherei* 49 (München: Kaiser, 1973).

9 See Eric Gregory, *Politics and the Order of Love: An Augustinian Ethic of Democratic Citizenship* (Chicago, IL: University of Chicago Press, 2008). See also Oliver O'Donovan, *The Desire of the Nations. Rediscovering the Roots of Political Theology* (Cambridge: Cambridge University Press, 2003), 201ff.

10 For the present debate, see Matilda Arvidsson, Leila Brännström, and Panu Minkkinen, eds., *The Contemporary Relevance of Carl Schmitt: Law, Politics, Theology* (London: Routledge, 2016).

11 See Günter Frankenberg, *Autorität und Integration. Zur Grammatik von Recht und Verfassung* (Frankfurt/Main: Suhrkamp, 2003).

12 According to Decisionism, as proposed e.g. by Carl Schmitt, the validity of a legal norm does not rest on its content but on the power of the law-making authority. Hence "political" decisionism means that not legal procedures, but the de facto power of political authority grants validity to political decisions. For further analysis see the essays in Saskia Hufnagel and Kent Roach, eds., *Emergency Law, The Library of Emergency Ethics, Law and Policy*, vol. II (Farnham: Ashgate 2012).

13 On this debate in the aftermath of Amy Gutmann's and Dennis F. Thompson's *Democracy and Disagreement* (Cambridge: Harvard University Press, 1996), see the essays in Stephen Macedo, ed., *Deliberative Politics: Essays on Democracy and Disagreement* (Oxford: Oxford University Press, 1999).

14 See Barbara Bucknix, Jonathan Trejo-Mathys, Timothy Waligore, eds., *Domination across Borders* (New York: Routledge, 2015) and Hans Lindahl, *Fault Lines of Globalization: Legal Order and the Politics of A-Legality* (Oxford: Oxford University Press, 2013).
15 See William E. Scheuerman, "Emergency Powers and the Rule of Law After 9/11," *Journal of Political Philosophy* 14, no. 1 (2006): 61–84, reprinted in *Emergency Law*, vol. 2, Sakia Hufnagel and Kent Roach, eds. (Aldershot: Ashgate, 2013).
16 See Andreas Kalyvas, *Democracy and the Politics of the Extraordinary: Max Weber, Carl Schmitt, and Hannah Arendt* (Cambridge: Cambridge University Press, 2010).
17 See William E. Scheuerman, *Frankfurt School Perspectives on Globalization, Democracy and the Law* (New York and London: Routledge, 2008).
18 See John B. Judis, *The Populist Explosion: How the Great Recession Transformed American and European Politics* (New York: Columbia Global Reports, 2016).
19 See Tjitske Akkerman, Sarah L. de Lange and Matthijs Rooduijn, eds., *Radical Right-Wing Populist Parties in Western Europe: Into the Mainstream?* (Abingdon: Routledge, 2016). See also Johannes Kiess, Oliver Decker, and Elmar Brähler, eds., *German Perspectives on Right-Wing Extremism: Challenges for Comparative Analysis* (Abingdon: Routledge, 2016). For a classic analysis, see Hans-Georg Betz, *Radical Right-Wing Populism in Western Europe* (Houndmills: Macmillan, 1994).
20 See Carl Schmitt, *The Concept of the Political* (1932), trans. G. Schwab, (Chicago, IL: Chicago University Press, 2007). See also Carl Schmitt (1923), *Die geistesgeschichtliche Lage des heutigen Parlamentarismus* (Berlin: Nachdruck, Duncker & Humblot, 2010), 13–14. A brilliant analysis of Schmitt can be found in William E. Scheuerman, *Carl Schmitt: The End of Law* (Oxford, UK: Rowman & Littlefield, 1999).
21 See Ernst-Wolfgang Böckenförde, "The Concept of the Political: A Key to Understanding Carl Schmitt's Constitutional Theory," *Canadian Journal of Law & Jurisprudence* 10, no. 1 (1997): 5–19.
22 Samuel P. Huntington, *The Clash of Civilizations and the Remaking of World Order* (London: Simon & Schuster, 1997).
23 See Giorgio Agamben, *State of Exception*, trans. Kevin Attell (Chicago, IL: University of Chicago Press, 2005). See also Giorgio Agamben: *Homo Sacer: Sovereign Power and Bare Life*, trans. Daniel Heller-Roazen (Stanford, CA: Stanford University Press, 1998).
24 Chantal Mouffe, *On the Political* (Abingdon: Routledge, 2005). See also Chantal Mouffe, *Agonistics: Thinking the World Politically* (London and New York: Verso, 2013); articles in Chantal Mouffe, *The Challenge of Carl Schmitt* (London and New York: Verso, 1999).
25 See Andrew Norris, "Sovereignty, Exception, and Norm," *Journal of Law and Society* 34, no. 1 (2007): 31–45.
26 See Craig Calhoun, Mark Juergensmeyer, and Jonathan VanAntwerpen, eds., *Rethinking Secularism* (New York: Oxford University Press, 2011).
27 Jürgen Habermas, "'The Political': The Rational Meaning of a Questionable Inheritance of Political Theology," in Eduardo Mendieta and Jonathan Vanantwerpen, eds., *The Power of Religion in the Public Sphere* (New York: Columbia University Press, 2011), 15–32. See also Jürgen Habermas, "Secularism's Crisis of Faith: Notes on Post-Secular Society," *New Perspectives Quarterly* 25, no. 4 (2008): 17–29.
28 See Jürgen Habermas, "Religion in the Public Sphere," in Jürgen Habermas, ed., *Between Naturalism and Religion: Philosophical Essays*, trans. Ciaran Cronin (Cambridge: Polity, 2008), 114–147.
29 See Robert A. Markus, *Christianity and the Secular* (Notre Dame, IN: University of Notre Dame Press, 2006).
30 See Oliver O'Donovan, *The Desire of the Nations. Rediscovering the Roots of Political Theology* (Cambridge: Cambridge University Press, 1996) and O'Donovan: *The Ways of Judgement* (Grand Rapids, MI and Cambridge, UK: Eerdmans, 2005) (The Bampton Lectures, 2003). See also Luke Bretherton, *Christianity and Contemporary Politics: The Conditions and Possibilities of Faithful Witness* (Malden, MA and Oxford, UK: Wiley-Blackwell, 2010), 220.
31 Ibid., 220. See also, with an emphasis on the analysis of civic practice and community organizing, Luke Bretherton, *Resurrecting Democracy: Faith, Citizenship and the Politics of a Common Life* (New York: Cambridge University Press, 2015).

32 See Stefan Heuser, "The Public Witness of Good Works: Lutheran Impulses for Political Ethics," Part I–III, *Journal of Lutheran Ethics*, May 5, 2006. Accessed January 17, 2017. www.elca.org/JLE/Articles/598. For further conceptual elaboration see Stefan Heuser, "The Cost of Citizenship: Disciple and Citizen in Bonhoeffer's Political Ethics," *Studies in Christian Ethics* 18, no. 3 (2005): 49–69.

33 See Carl Schmitt: *Political Theology II: The Myth of the Closure of Any Political Theology*, trans. Michael Hoelzl and Graham Ward (Cambridge: Polity Press, 2008), particularly Chapter 2.1: "The Genesis and the Historical Limitation of the Matter," 60ff.

34 For the influence of Luther on the development of secular models of political legitimation (alongside Nominalism and Humanism) see Michael Allen Gillespie, *The Theological Origins of Modernity* (Chicago, IL: The University of Chicago Press, 2008), 101ff.

35 For Luther's description of the ruler who lets himself be ruled not just by the written law, but also lets himself be freed by Christ to handle the law rightly, see part three of Martin Luther's *Von weltlicher Obrigkeit* (1523), in J. K. F. Knaake, Karl Drescher, and Konrad Burdach, eds., *D. Martin Luther's Werke, Kritische Gesamtausgabe*, 65 vols, (Weimar: H. Böhlau Nachfolger, 1883), hereafter referred to as (*WA*, volume, page(s), line(s)); *WA* 11, 271ff., here: 11, 273, 8ff.

36 For Bonhoeffer's reception of Luther's doctrine of the two regimes, see Dietrich Bonhoffer, *Ethics*, ed. Clifford Green, trans., R. Krauss, C. West, and D. Stott, *Dietrich Bonhoeffer Works* 6 (Minneapolis, MN: Fortress Press, 2009), particularly the chapter, "Christ, Reality, and Good," 47ff. See also Ernst Wolf, "Königsherrschaft Christi und lutherische Zwei-Reiche-Lehre," in Ernst Wolf, ed., *Peregrinatio* Bd. 2, *Studien zur reformatorischen Theologie, zum Kirchenrecht und zur Sozialethik* (München: Kaiser Verlag, 1965), 207–229; Ernst Wolf, *Sozialethik, Theologische Grundfragen*, ed. Theodor Strohm (Göttingen: Vandenhoeck und Ruprecht, 1975); Ernst Wolf, "Politia Christi. Das Problem der Sozialethik im Luthertum," *Peregrinatio, Studien zur reformatorischen Theologie und zum Kirchenproblem* (München: Kaiser Verlag, 1962), 214–242; Ulrich Duchrow, *Christenheit und Weltverantwortung: Traditionsgeschichte und systematische Struktur der Zweireichelehre* (Stuttgart: Klett-Cotta, 1970). For a contemporary critique of globalization from a Lutheran point of view, see Ulrich Duchrow, Paul Chung, Craig Nessan, eds., *Liberating Lutheran Theology: Freedom for Justice and Solidarity in a Global Context* (Minneapolis, MN and Geneva: Fortress Press and WCC Publications, 2011); Hans G. Ulrich, "Wie Geschöpfe leben. Konturen evangelischer Ethik," *Ethics in Theological Discourse (ETHD)*, vol. 2 (Münster: 2005) (Second edition, 2007); Hans G. Ulrich: "The Messianic Contours of Evangelical Ethics," in Brian Brock and Michael G. Mawson, eds., *The Freedom of a Christian Ethicist: The Future of a Reformation Legacy* (London and New York: Bloomsbury T&T Clark, 2016), 39–63; Hans G. Ulrich, "The Future of Ethics within the Reformation Heritage," *Studies in Christian Ethics* 35, no. 2 (2012): 174–180.

37 Troeltsch focused on the formative power of Protestantism on the emergence of modern culture and individualistic religiosity. See Ernst Troeltsch, *Die Soziallehren der christlichen Kirchen und Gruppen, Gesammelte Schriften* Bd. 1 (2. Neudr. der Ausg.), (Tübingen: J. C. B. Mohr, 1922; Tübingen 1965); Ernst Troeltsch, *The Social Teachings of the Christian Churches*, trans. Olive Wyon, vols. I &II (Louisville: Westminster John Knox Press, 1992) (English version).

38 See Hans G. Ulrich: "On the Grammar of Lutheran Ethics," in Karen L. Bloomquist, ed., *Lutheran Ethics at the Intersections of God's One World* (Geneva: Lutheran World Federation, 2005), 27–48.

39 This "*status politicus*" is not identical with Friedrich Gogarten's praise of secularity (over against secularism with its negation of God) as "the necessary and legitimate effect of the Christian faith." Gogarten refers to a formative effect of the Christian faith on culture, a gradual process of making the world more autonomous, while I tend to think that Luther refers to God's actual and ongoing liberating work on the individual human being.

40 See Martin Luther, *Auslegung über die Psalmen*. "Der hundertsiebenundzwanzigste Psalm," in Joh. Georg Walch, ed., *Martin Luthers sämtliche Schriften* Bd. 4 (St. Louis, MO: Concordia Publishing House, 1940) (Groß-Oesingen 1987).

41 "Eins, das fromm macht, das andere, das äußerlich Frieden schafft und bösen Werken wehrt. Keins ist ohne das andere genug in der Welt." Martin Luther, *Von weltlicher Obrigkeit* (1523), *WA* 11, 252, 12ff.

42 Ibid., 11, 258, 1ff.

43 See Martin Luther, *Von der Freiheit eines Christenmenschen* (1520), *WA* 7, 20–38, here, 21.

44 For Luther, the institutions are places where human beings are transformed into instruments of God's twofold government. See Martin Luther, "Der hundertsiebenundzwanzigste Psalm," *op. cit.*
45 Roughly translated, "All created ordinances are masks of God." Martin Luther, *In epistolam S. Pauli ad Galatas Commentarius* (1531/1535), *WA* 40/I, 463.
46 Luther criticizes any exercise of power that claims God for its own legitimation instead of letting God rule. For Luther, every form of political power is under God's authority, but for him this does not mean that the monarch's power is fused with God's power or draws its legitimacy from some sacred origin. Luther's discourse is indeed not a legitimation discourse, but one on the renewal of the inner man and on the discovery of its ethical consequences. For Luther, any worldly use of power that claims a divine aura for itself or sets itself unauthorized into the position of the legislator, is godless. Power arises when a ruler lets himself be ruled by God. It is something that—for Luther in accordance with Romans 13—is essentially always granted by God, and delegated by him, or else it is a different sort of "power": one that rests on the capabilities of a ruler himself—a power that is always prone to transform into force.
47 See Martin Luther, *Von weltlicher Obrigkeit* (1523), *WA* 11, 264, 16ff.
48 For this basic insight, see also Thesis II of the Barmen theological declaration.
49 Dietrich Bonhoeffer has taken up this notion of Luther in his idea that the "world" needs to become "real", and that responsible action needs to be in accord with this reality. Dietrich Bonhoeffer, *Ethics*, 49ff. and 261ff.
50 Martin Luther, *Operationes in Psalmos zu Psalm 5* (1519–1521), *WA* 5, 128, 39–1299, 1.
51 Ibid., *WA* 5,128,38f. (*Operationes in Psalmos zu Psalm 5*, 2, 1519–1521). See also Hans Joachim Iwand, "'Sed originale per hominem unum:' Ein Beitrag zur Lehre vom Menschen," in Gerhard Sauter, ed., *Hans Joachim Iwand: Glaubensgerechtigkeit, Gesammelte Aufsätze* Bd. 2, TB 64 (München: Kaiser Verlag, 1980), 171–193.
52 See Luther, *Von weltlicher Obrigkeit, WA* 11, 272, 22ff.
53 Jürgen Habermas, "'The Political': The Rational Meaning of a Questionable Inheritance of Political Theology," in Eduardo Mendieta and Jonathan Vanantwerpen, eds., *The Power of Religion in the Public Sphere* (New York: Columbia University Press, 2011) 15–33, 21.
54 Ernst-Wolfgang Böckenförde, *Staat, Gesellschaft, Freiheit* (Frankfurt/Main: Suhrkamp, 1976), 60.
55 Taylor, *A Secular Age*, 22.

Part II

Lutheran theology and legal philosophy

2 Legal positivism in Lutheran ethics

Carl-Henric Grenholm

Within legal philosophy, there has been a vibrant discussion about the criteria of valid law and on the role of morality within the legal system. Legal positivism maintains that the criteria of legal validity must not include any reference to moral conceptions, while natural law theorists argue that there are certain moral principles with which law must conform if it is to be valid.

The purpose of this chapter is to present a critical analysis of attitudes towards legal positivism in Lutheran ethics. Is it possible to argue that Lutheran theology has made contributions to fundamental conceptions of law that have been important within later legal positivism? In what ways have theories of natural law been understood within Lutheran ethics? How should we today, within the framework of a reasonable conception of Lutheran ethics, evaluate legal positivism?

First, I will give a perspective on the disagreement between legal positivism and theories of natural law. I will analyze the definition of legal positivism given by H. L. A. Hart in *The Concept of Law*, and the natural law theory elaborated by John Finnis in *Natural Law and Natural Rights.* My thesis is that the disagreement between these theories concerns not only legal validity but also how we should understand the role of ethics as a source of critique of law and its role as one of the foundations for the legislative process.

With this in mind, I will examine what impact Lutheran theology has had on later theories of the relationship between law and morality. As John Witte Jr. argues in *Law and Protestantism*, the doctrine of God's two kingdoms has been an important framework for legal theory within the Lutheran tradition. One dimension of this doctrine is a natural law theory, but natural law has been interpreted in a particular way within Lutheran ethics. As Harold J. Berman demonstrates in *Law and Revolution, II*, Lutheran legal philosophy in certain respects has accepted the basic premise of contemporary legal positivism, namely that law and morality are to be sharply distinguished from each other.

How should Lutheran ethics today respond to the claims of legal positivism? In my article I will critically analyze the answers to this question given by the Swedish professor of ethics, Jarl Hemberg, and the German theologian, Martin Honecker. They both agree with legal positivism that morality is not a criterion of valid law, but they also agree with natural law theories that moral arguments influence and are foundations of the content in positive law. The ethical critique of law should rest on a normative position that is humane, without any particular Christian content.

Finally, I will argue in favor of a more comprehensive understanding of Lutheran ethics. I regard it to be an important task of ethics to give a critical evaluation of positive law and to examine whether it is morally justified. However, if Lutheran ethics would give a constructive contribution to this critique, it should not take as its starting point the doctrine of God's two kingdoms. A reasonable conception of Lutheran ethics is not based upon reason alone but also upon the gospel declaring God's love in Christ.

Legal positivism and natural law theories

Legal positivism claims that there is no necessary connection between law and morality. Rather, legal validity is ultimately determined by reference to certain basic social facts, such as the command of the sovereign or the rule of recognition. This means that it is not necessary that laws reproduce or satisfy certain demands of morality in order to be valid. In his seminal work *The Concept of Law* H. L. A. Hart gives the following definition of legal positivism:

> Here we shall take Legal Positivism to mean the simple contention that it is in no sense a necessary truth that laws reproduce or satisfy certain demands of morality, though in fact they have often done so.[1]

According to Hart, morality has an obvious influence on law. The legal system must rest on a sense of moral obligation, and the stability of legal systems depends in part upon a correspondence with morality.[2] However, this does not mean that laws must satisfy certain demands of morality in order to be valid. Particular laws are valid if they were enacted in proper form, are clear in meaning, and satisfy all the acknowledged criteria of validity in a legal system. The criteria are specified in what Hart calls "the rules of recognition" and it is not necessary that these rules include a reference to moral principles.[3]

Hart argues that there are two minimum conditions necessary and sufficient for the existence of a legal system:

> On the one hand, these rules of behaviour which are valid according to the system's ultimate criteria of validity must be generally obeyed, and, on the other hand, its rules of recognition specifying the criteria of legal validity and its rules of change and adjudication must be effectively accepted as common public standards of official behaviour by its officials.[4]

Hart distinguishes legal positivism from theories of natural law, which maintain that there are certain moral principles, awaiting discovery by human reason, with which law must conform if it is to be valid. Natural law theories are often associated with a belief in a Divine Lawgiver, and a teleological conception of human nature. A basic idea seems to be that laws that conflict with the principles of true morality should not be recognized as valid.[5]

The main difference between legal positivism and natural law theories concerns legal validity, according to Hart. Legal positivism implies a *wider* concept of law, which means that we should consider as "law" all rules which are valid by the formal tests of a system of primary and secondary rules, even though some of them offend against our moral convictions. Theories of natural law, on the other hand, imply a *narrower* concept of law, which means that we shall exclude from "law" such morally offensive rules. According to Hart, nothing is to be gained in the scientific study of law by adopting the narrower concept.[6]

The wider concept of law, which is proposed by Hart, allows a clear distinction between the *invalidity* of law and its *immorality*. It enables us to see the complexity and variety of these separate issues. This means that it would sometimes be possible to say, "this is valid law, but it is too iniquitous to be applied or obeyed." However, when a particular law offends our moral convictions we should not say "this is not valid law." Since it is difficult to decide whether a law is morally justified or not, it would be better for legal theory as a descriptive discipline to avoid this issue.[7]

An objection against legal positivism has often been that it seems to exclude the possibility of moral critique of law. It would be possible to read Hans Kelsen's influential *General Theory of Law and State* in such a way. He argues that the jurist ignores morality as a system of valid norms, just as the moralist ignores positive law as such a system. He also maintains that from the point of view of positive law as a system of valid norms, morality does not exist as such.[8] This view is critically evaluated by Hart, who takes the opposite position that a moral critique of law is both possible and necessary, since a good legal system must conform at certain points to the requirements of justice and morality. However, Hart regards such a critique as a task for individuals, citizens or politicians, not a task for legal theory. In his legal philosophy he does not make any contribution to the issue of what criteria should be fulfilled for a law to be morally justified.[9]

If we want to find instruments for an ethical critique of law, we can learn more from theories of natural law, which at least in part ground legal validity on whether a law is consonant with practical reason or whether a legal system is morally legitimate. This view implies that it is necessary to introduce some moral considerations into the process of legislation as well as into adjudication. It also implies that it is an important task of ethics to give a critical analysis of prevailing law.

One of the most interesting of these natural law theories is proposed by John Finnis in *Natural Law and Natural Rights.* It is inspired by Catholic moral theology and particularly by Thomas Aquinas, but it is a philosophical theory, free from any theological considerations. Finnis argues that nature is a norm for morality in the sense that we should act in accordance with rational principles. He also emphasizes the view that a theory of natural law is not just descriptive: its aim is to assist the practical reflections of those responsible to act in the capacities of judges, statesmen or citizens.[10]

What does it mean that positive law is founded upon a natural law? Finnis argues that natural law primarily clarifies the basic requirements of practical reasonableness, i.e. how we should know that a decision is practically reasonable. Principles of natural law that explain the obligatory force of positive law include (1) a set of basic practical principles which indicate the basic forms of human flourishing as goods to be pursued and realized, (2) a set of basic methodological requirements of practical reasonableness, which distinguish sound from unsound practical thinking, and (3) a set of general moral standards.[11]

A fundamental concern of a natural law theory, as proposed by Finnis, is to understand the relationship between the particular laws of a society and the permanent principles of practical reasonableness. This means that positive law is not a mere emanation from or copy of natural law. The integration of the requirements of practical reasonableness into the law is a rather complex and difficult matter.[12]

The intention of natural law tradition has been, according to Finnis, to show that legislation and adjudication should be guided by moral principles that are a matter of objective reasonableness, not of convention or mere subjective decision. Natural law theories also maintain that these moral principles justify the very institution of positive law, as well as the techniques within that institution and those institutions sustained by law. By determining what the requirements of practical reasonableness really are, these theories afford a rational basis for the activities of legislators, judges, and citizens.[13]

How should we understand the disagreement between legal positivism and theories of natural law? While it is quite obvious that they disagree on the issue whether the legal validity of particular laws must include a reference to morality, my thesis is that these theories also disagree how we should understand the role of ethics as a source of critique of law and its role as one of the foundations for the legislative process. Legal positivism does not give any instruments for such an ethical critique of positive law. Even if it admits that such a critique would be possible, this is not regarded as a task for legal theory. Natural law theories, on the other hand, take it as a major concern to elaborate moral principles and conceptions of practical rationality that can be used within the legislative process and a critical reflection on the issue of whether positive laws are morally justified or not.

These differences between the theories are related to their various understandings of the task of legal theory. Legal positivism regards legal theory as a pure descriptive discipline, while natural law theories are normative and justificatory from an ethical perspective. These theories are also associated with different ethical theories and interpretations of moral judgements. Legal positivism denies that moral judgements have truth value, and thus it is not a task within a scientific discipline to give a critical evaluation of moral principles. Natural law theories maintain that a rational deliberation in order to justify moral judgements is possible and necessary. Therefore, it can be regarded as an important task within a scientific discipline to develop a theory of moral justification of law.

Legal theory in Lutheran theology

What impact has Lutheran theology had on later theories on the relationship between law and morality? Is it possible to argue that Lutheran theology has made contributions to fundamental conceptions of law that have been important within legal positivism? In his study on *Law and Protestantism*, John Witte Jr. has provided a careful analysis of legal theory in the Lutheran reformation. He argues that the doctrine of God's two kingdoms was an important framework for the Lutheran theories on law in the sixteenth century. According to this doctrine, God has ordained two kingdoms in which humanity is destined to live. The earthly kingdom is governed by the Law, and here a person operates primarily by reason. The heavenly kingdom is guided by the Gospel, and here a person operates primarily by faith.[14]

The doctrine of the two kingdoms is closely related to Luther's sharp distinction between law and gospel. Luther maintains that God is acting in the spiritual realm through the Word and the gospel in order to promote justification by faith (*iustitia fidei*). In the secular realm, God is acting through the law and the sword in order to promote political justice (*iustitia politica*). Human deeds belong to the secular realm, while faith is relevant in the heavenly kingdom. The state should be governed by reason and the natural law, which anyone can understand independently of God's revelation in Christ. This means that the gospel does not inform the content of ethics.[15]

John Witte argues that the Lutheran doctrine of the two kingdoms had important implications for theories of law, politics and society. According to this doctrine the law is part of the government of the earthly kingdom. This means that only the state has legal authority, while the Church should no longer be a law-making authority. Martin Luther attacked the canon law and the jurisdictional claims of Church officials. In the earthly kingdom it was the task of those in political power, the *Obrigkeit*, to use the sword and to enforce positive laws.[16]

One dimension of the doctrine of the two kingdoms is a natural law theory. According to Luther, law is given by God in creation and written by God in the hearts of all people. This natural law, as it was set at the creation, continues to operate after the fall into sin, and it provides the foundation for all positive law. This means that both moral insight and our understanding of positive law are based upon human reason. The gospel does not make any contributions to the content of law, and the revelation in Christ is not necessary in order to get moral insight, but a summary of natural law is given in the Decalogue.[17]

In *Law and Protestantism* John Witte Jr. analyzes the legal philosophy of Philip Melanchthon and the Lutheran jurists Johannes Eisermann and Johann Oldendorp. He argues that these sixteenth-century legal theorists shared Luther's basic understanding of the two-kingdoms framework but that they emphasized, more than did Luther, that the Bible was an essential source of earthly law. They regarded the Ten Commandments as the clearest expression of natural law, and thus the Decalogue came to play an important role in Lutheran jurisprudence.[18]

Philip Melanchthon regarded political rulers as God's mediators in the earthly kingdom, and their task was to promulgate rational positive laws for the governance of both the Church and the state. To be rational, positive laws should be based on the general principles of natural law, into which all individuals can gain insight by using their reason. However, he also argued that human reason is "darkened" due to sin and therefore the law of nature is often misunderstood. Melanchthon emphasized the view that the best summary of natural law is given in the Ten Commandments, and therefore the Decalogue can be regarded as a model for the positive law enacted by the earthly rulers.[19]

According to Witte's analysis, Melanchthon used the Decalogue to organize the various systems of positive law, looking to the state, instead of the Church, to promulgate these positive laws:

> The magistrate was God's vice-regent, called to enforce God's law in the earthly kingdom through positive laws. God's law was most clearly summarized in the Ten Commandments. The magistrate therefore had to pass positive laws for each of these Commandments, superseding other laws that might have existed.[20]

In his impressive study *Law and Revolution, II*, Harold J. Berman gives a similar analysis of the legal teachings of Luther and Melanchthon. Like Witte he makes clear the impact of the two kingdoms theory for Luther's understanding of law. In the earthly kingdom, law is needed—including the moral law of the Decalogue and the positive law of the secular ruler. This means that the secular political authority, the *Obrigkeit*, must undertake the lawmaking responsibilities that previously were within the jurisdiction of the Church.[21]

The doctrine of the two kingdoms, according to Berman, made possible an attack on the prevailing legal order in the German principalities and in the empire by authorizing the political power, the German prince, to promulgate positive laws that should be obeyed by subordinates. Berman emphasizes that Luther not only made the prince the ultimate source of law but also imposed limits on the right to disobey when the ruler commanded subordinates to act in ways that were evil.[22]

Like Witte, Harold Berman maintains that Philip Melanchthon characteristically interpreted natural law theory in line with the two kingdoms theory. He argued that certain moral principles are inscribed in the hearts of all people and accessible to human reason, but since human reason is "darkened" we need guidance from the Ten Commandments. Thus, the Decalogue is both the ultimate source and summary of natural law, and hence a model for positive law.[23]

According to Berman, the Lutheran reformation exerted enormous influence on the transformation of the Western legal tradition from the sixteenth to the early eighteenth centuries. Lutheran reformers undermined the canon law and the entire jurisdiction of the Roman Catholic Church. This gave to civil rulers the ultimate prerogative of legislation and adjudication.[24]

Interestingly enough, Berman argues that Lutheran legal philosophy is a primary source for both contemporary legal positivism and contemporary natural law theory. Lutheran theology helped to lay the foundation for modern theories of legal positivism, since it regarded written laws as necessary because of the excessive generality of natural law. Thus, it was the source of the positivist's definition of law as the will of the state expressed in rules and enforced by coercive sanctions.[25] Berman writes:

> Thus Lutheran legal philosophy accepted the basic premise of contemporary legal positivism, namely, that law and morals are to be sharply distinguished from each other, and that the law that *is* should not be confused with what the law *ought to be*. To identify law with morality is to foster uncertainty and instability in the law, and hence disorder; it is also to make the civil law the source rather than the object of moral criticism, and thus to foster injustice.[26]

On the other hand, it is quite obvious that Lutheran legal theory is associated with a kind of natural law theory, holding that there are some general moral principles, summarized in the natural law and given by God in creation, which should be the foundation of the rules within positive law. As a natural law theory, Lutheran legal philosophy postulates that every person has within herself certain moral sentiments relating to legal justice. Lutheran theology underlines that the content of natural law is best understood from the perspective of the Decalogue, since reason often fails due to human sin. However, the basic idea that the positive law of the state should be consistent with natural law remained the same after the Lutheran reformation as it was before.[27]

How should we understand this complex relationship between Lutheran theology on the one hand and contemporary theories on legal positivism and natural law on the other hand? I have argued that the disagreement between legal positivism and natural law theories concerns both legal validity and the role of ethics as a source of critique of law. A reasonable conclusion is that Lutheran theology would agree with legal positivism that it is not necessary that positive laws satisfy certain demands of morality in order to be valid. It is enough that these laws are promulgated by those in political power.

However, Lutheran theology would certainly agree with natural law theories that morality is an important foundation both in the process of legislation and in adjudication. A basic task for legal theory is therefore to deal with the issue of moral justification of existing laws. Natural law, understood as a set of general moral principles and a methodology for rational reflection on moral issues, is also a starting point for an ethical critique of positive laws. Traditional Lutheran ethics would regard the Decalogue as an instrument to clarify the content of natural law, but the gospel does not give any contribution to ethics.

A theory of ethics and legislation

How should we today, within the framework of a reasonable conception of Lutheran ethics, evaluate legal positivism? An interesting answer to this question is given by the Swedish theologian and philosopher Jarl Hemberg. In his study *Etik och lagstiftning* (*Ethics and Legislation*) he gives a careful analysis of the debate between legal positivism and natural law theory, primarily within Scandinavian and German legal philosophy.

Hemberg argues that it is important to make a distinction between "valid law" (from a legal perspective) and "morally justified law" (from an ethical perspective). Legal validity does not presuppose that positive law is morally justified, and from an ethical perspective, it might be necessary to criticize prevailing laws. This means that Hemberg agrees with legal positivism that morality is not a criterion of valid law. From a legal perspective the criteria of validity should be "internal," which means that they should not refer to any extra-juridical factors. At the same time, Hemberg agrees with natural law theories that moral arguments should be foundations of the content in positive law. This also means that moral considerations should have an important influence in the process of legislation.[28]

In his study, Jarl Hemberg elaborates a theory of ethics and legislation that deviates from natural law's view that the validity of law is dependent on extra-juridical factors. It is not necessary that criteria of legal validity refer to any moral principles. At the same time, Hemberg does not accept the view of legal positivism that it is not a task for legal theory to give an ethical critique of law and a moral foundation for the legislative process. This view often rests upon an emotivist theory of moral judgements, which claims that these judgements cannot be justified by rational arguments, and this theory is false.[29]

Hemberg proposes a "legal theory based on humane ethics" with five conceptions. The first is that moral considerations influence the positive law in an important way, which is not only an empirical fact but also a normative statement. It is a central task not only to examine criteria of valid law, but also to consider the conditions for law to be morally justified. Legal theory should specify what moral principles should be the foundation of positive law.[30]

Hemberg's second claim is that moral arguments are not just subjective. He does not accept a traditional emotivist theory, according to which moral judgements are expressions of emotions and therefore cannot be justified by rational arguments. His position is that even if we defend a non-cognitivist theory, it is possible to give criteria for a moral conception that are reasonable. Arguments in favor of a moral statement can be rationally evaluated.[31]

Third, Hemberg argues that the moral arguments that should be the foundation for the legislative process must be related to what he calls "humane ethics." This is a normative position which includes such principles as we can agree upon in a pluralistic society, independent of our various ideologies and world views. One example is a principle of benevolence, according to which we should promote what is good for all human beings. Another example is a principle of justice, according to which we should strive for a just distribution of social goods.[32]

Fourth, Christian ethics can, like other traditions, contribute to the development of such principles in humane ethics. However, Hemberg is critical of the idea that Christian theology can give any unique contributions to the content of ethics. The revelation in Christ does not give us any unique Christian ideals that can be the basis for a critique of prevailing law in society. Theologians should not claim that there is a particular ideal of sacrificial love that should be guidance for the state.[33]

Finally, Hemberg argues that it is a task of legal theory to study the relationship between law and morality. Legal theory should not simply study the issue of legal validity, leaving the issue of moral justification of law to politics. Instead, legal philosophy should learn from moral philosophy in its critical reflections on the content of humane ethics. Within moral philosophy there is an ongoing discussion on the meaning of a principle of benevolence, as well as a vibrant debate on theories of distributive justice. This ethical discourse is of high relevance also for legal philosophy.[34]

German professor of theological ethics, Martin Honecker, proposes a similar theory in his important introduction to social ethics, *Grundriss der Sozialethik*. He also makes a clear distinction between legal validity and moral justification of law, arguing that law cannot be identified with morality, but that it is necessary that positive law has a moral foundation. Thus, law is not independent of morality, and sometimes valid law can be said to be immoral.[35]

Honecker agrees with Hart that it is not necessary that the criteria of valid law include references to moral principles. In this sense he does not accept a natural law theory. At the same time, he argues that law is not quite independent of moral considerations. Christian ethics cannot be accepted by all individuals in a pluralistic society as a foundation for positive law, but this does not exclude the possibility that prevailing law is based upon some general moral ideals. The main issue is then: What kind of morality should be the basis for law in such a pluralistic society?[36]

In his legal theory, Honecker refers to the doctrine of God's two kingdoms in Luther's theology. According to this doctrine law belongs to the earthly kingdom, and it is the task of the political power to promote positive law. Reason is the criterion of positive law, and every human being can understand what reasonable law is. This doctrine is closely related to the distinction between law and gospel, which implies that even if positive law is based on moral considerations, the gospel about justification by faith alone does not make any contributions to the content of ethics and law.[37]

From a Lutheran perspective, Honecker argues that Christology cannot be regarded as a foundation for positive law. All laws in society are promulgated by human beings, and they are not given directly by God. Honecker regards law as a mediator between ethics and politics. As a part of culture, law is created by political decisions, but at the same time law needs ethical legitimacy and it should be critically evaluated from an ethical perspective. A presupposition for law is therefore a dialogue between politics and ethics, and this is possible when legislation is part of a democratic process.[38]

So, what kind of morality should be the basis for law in a pluralistic society? There is a distinction between law and morality according to Honecker, but they should also be related to each other. The difficulty is, however, to reach consensus within a pluralistic society about what moral considerations are reasonable. From a Lutheran perspective, law belongs to the secular realm, and this means that particular Christian moral ideals cannot be the basis for law. Instead we should try to find a normative position that humans with different world views can have in common. A principle of human dignity might be an important part of such a common morality.[39]

Lutheran ethics as critique of law

How should we evaluate the theories on morality and law that are proposed by Jarl Hemberg and Martin Honecker? In what way should a reasonable conception of Lutheran ethics today evaluate legal positivism? First, I regard it as reasonable to accept the thesis of legal positivism that morality is not a criterion of valid law. From a legal perspective the criteria of validity should be internal in the sense that they do not refer to any extra-juridical factors. It is not necessary that these criteria refer to any moral principles. This means that we should make a clear distinction between legal validity and moral justification of law.

Second, I regard it to be an important task of ethics to give a critical evaluation of positive law and to examine whether it is morally justified. A critical reflection on moral conceptions should be a foundation for the legislative process as well as for critique of prevailing legal rules. In this respect, I agree with a natural law theory. It is important to notice that it is also a task for legal theory to deal with the issue of moral justification of law. A strong argument in favor of this position is that it is possible to justify moral judgements by rational arguments, even if we accept a non-cognitivist ethical theory. Moral arguments can be rationally evaluated, and therefore it is possible to argue that legal theory is not just a descriptive discipline.[40]

However, I have a different opinion than Hemberg and Honecker concerning what kind of moral considerations should be the basis for an ethical critique of prevailing law in a pluralistic society. I would regard it as important to elaborate a more comprehensive understanding of Lutheran ethics, where the gospel gives some contributions to the content of ethics. My argument is that it is not possible to elaborate a common morality in pluralistic society. Moral conceptions are always related to a variety of cultural and religious traditions, which means that we cannot reach consensus about a common "humane ethics." We could agree that principles of benevolence and justice are important, but we have different interpretations of these principles.

A Lutheran contribution to the ethical critique of law would take into consideration the relevance of Christian faith for our moral conceptions. This is not accepted by all members in a pluralistic society, but it would be one of many contributions to a common dialogue on morality and law. From this perspective Christian ethics is not only based upon reason but also upon the revelation in Christ. All humans have capacity to get at least a partial moral insight through rational considerations and human experiences. However, human sin means that we often fail and therefore need the guidance of God's revelation in Christ to get a comprehensive moral insight.

Traditional political ethics in Lutheran theology have often been related to the doctrine of God's two kingdoms. As a result, Lutheran political ethics can be characterized by three important ideas. First, it is based upon reason and the natural law, as it is expressed in the Decalogue. The gospel does not give any contribution to the content of ethics. Second, Lutheran theology often defends an ethical dualism, according to which the content of political ethics is different from the Christian ideal of sacrificial love, which is relevant only within private morality. Third, it is related to a patriarchal view of society, which means that it is our duty to obey superiors. In this view, the equality between humans before God has no relevance for the meaning of social justice.[41]

Ethics in Lutheran theology have been based on the doctrine of creation, not on Christology or eschatology. This kind of Lutheran ethics is often combined with a political ethic that is uncritical towards the *Obrigkeit*. Lutheran political ethics have frequently taken a legitimizing position, in support of existing society and the authorities in power. My thesis is therefore that Lutheran ethics cannot be based upon creation and reason alone, if this ethics would take a critical position towards political authorities. A more reasonable ethical theory in Lutheran theology should also be based upon Christology and eschatology.[42]

This means that if Lutheran ethics would make a constructive contribution to a critical evaluation of law, Lutheran ethicists should not take their starting point in the doctrine of God's two kingdoms and the sharp distinction between law and gospel. A reasonable conception of Lutheran ethics is not only based upon reason and natural law. It should also be based upon the gospel about God's sacrificial love in Christ. This gospel gives a new perspective on what love and equality should mean. Thereby it is often combined with a strong critique of established authorities in society, which also can inspire a critique of prevailing positive law.

Christology can contribute to ethical reflection in several ways. The message about God's love in Christ is related to an idea of equality, according to which all humans have an equal worth before God independent of their merits. This means that justice is not only equal opportunity or a distribution in accordance with desert—it means an equal share of the good life. The gospel is also related to an image of God's sacrificial love in Christ, which gives a unique understanding of love between humans. In order to satisfy the needs of others and to promote liberation from oppression we should be prepared to suffer and abstain from promoting our own interests.

In what ways can this Christological perspective contribute to an ethical critique of law? One concrete example is that it objects to the current policy in Europe on immigration and the refugee crisis. A Christian understanding of human love and equality implies a generous immigration policy, characterized by hospitality and support of people who have been forced to flee from their country due to war and oppression. From this perspective the closed borders in European countries, the refusal to respect the right to seek asylum, and the policy to deport refugees to countries where their lives are in danger is a scandal. In such a situation, when authorities implement laws that cannot be morally justified, Christians do not have a duty to obey these laws. Sometimes civil disobedience is necessary, which can imply concrete actions to prevent deportation of refugees.

My thesis is that ethics are not only a source of critique of law, but also one of the foundations for the legislative process. What does this mean? Obviously, it is not possible to argue that Christian ethics should be the only foundation for legislation in a pluralistic and post-Christian society. Since there are different moral convictions, related to various religious and cultural traditions, legislation should be the result of a deliberative process, where contributions from different traditions are respected. In a pluralistic society it is not possible to legislate in all controversial issues—sometimes the authorities should leave it to the individuals to make their own moral choices. This explains why ethical critique of prevailing law will always be necessary. In all societies there is always a tension between valid law and the Christological perspective on ethics.

Notes

1 H. L. A. Hart, *The Concept of Law*, 3rd ed. (Oxford: Oxford University Press, 2012), 185–86.
2 Ibid., 202ff.
3 Ibid., 108–09, 185–86 and 207–08.
4 Ibid., 116.
5 Ibid., 156, 186, 188–89 and 207–08.
6 Ibid., 209.
7 Ibid., 210–11.
8 See generally Hans Kelsen, *General Theory of Law and State* (Cambridge: Harvard University Press, 1945).
9 Hart, *The Concept of Law*, 205–06, 240–41; and H. L. A. Hart, *Essays in Jurisprudence and Philosophy* (Oxford: Clarendon Press, 2001), 301–02.
10 John Finnis, *Natural Law and Natural Rights*, 2nd ed. (Oxford: Oxford University Press, 2011), 18. This philosophical interpretation of natural law is different from the interpretation given by many Catholic moral theologians. Jean Porter argues that natural law is part of a theological tradition, and based upon nature, reason and Scripture. See Jean Porter, *Natural and Divine Law. Reclaiming the Tradition for Christian Ethics* (Grand Rapids, MI: Eerdmans, 1999), 48ff, 85ff, and 164ff.
11 Finnis, *Natural Law and Natural Rights*, 23, and 28.
12 Ibid., 281, and 284.
13 Ibid., 290.
14 John Witte Jr., *Law and Protestantism: The Legal Teachings of the Lutheran Reformation* (Cambridge: Cambridge University Press, 2008), 5 and 105.

15 Ibid., 91f, 99f, 102. I have given a similar analysis of Luther's doctrine of the two kingdoms in Carl-Henric Grenholm, *Tro, moral och uddlös politik. Om luthersk etik* (Stockholm: Verbum, 2014), 59ff.
16 Witte, *Law and Protestantism*, 39–40, 53ff and 109–10.
17 Ibid., pp. 113f. See also Grenholm, *Tro, moral och uddlös politik*, 62–63.
18 Witte, *Law and Protestantism*, 10 and 168–69.
19 Ibid., 76–77, 123–24 and 125ff.
20 Ibid., 133.
21 Harold J. Berman, *Law and Revolution, II: The Impact of the Protestant Reformations on the Western Legal Tradition* (Cambridge, MA: Harvard University Press, 2006), 6–7.
22 Ibid., 40–41, 43–44, 62–66.
23 Ibid., 79–80, 81–82, 85.
24 Ibid., 94–95, 97.
25 Ibid., 76, 98.
26 Ibid., 98.
27 Ibid., 76, 98–99, 374.
28 Jarl Hemberg, *Etik och lagstiftning. En studie av rättsfilosofisk teoribildning och konkret lagstiftningsarbete* (Stockholm: Verbum, 1975), 9–10, 15–16.
29 Ibid., 68ff.
30 Ibid., 71–72.
31 Ibid., 73–74.
32 Ibid., 79.
33 Ibid., 82ff, 85ff.
34 Ibid., 93ff.
35 Martin Honecker, *Grundriss der Sozialethik* (Berlin: Walter de Gruyter, 1995), 567ff.
36 Ibid., 572–73, 575–76.
37 Ibid., 578–79, 580.
38 Ibid., 581ff, 584–85.
39 Ibid., 586–87, 588–89.
40 A plausible ethical theory is an ethical construction which is combined with a non-cognitivist interpretation of moral judgements. Such a theory can accept certain criteria of a rational justification of moral judgements, even if these cannot be verified. See Carl-Henric Grenholm, *Etisk teori. Kritik av moralen* (Lund: Studentlitteratur, 2014) pp. 266ff, 272ff.
41 These three ideas are expressed quite clearly already in Martin Luther, *Von weltlicher Oberkeit, wie weit man ihr gehorsam schuldig sei* (1523), in *D. Martin Luther's Werke*, Kritische Gesamtausgabe, J. K. F. Knaake, Karl Drescher, and Konrad Burdach, eds., 65 vols. (Weimar: H. Böhlau Nachfolger, 1883) hereafter referred to as (*WA*, volume, page(s), line(s)); *WA* 11, 251,1–31; *WA* 11, 253,17–32; *WA* 11, 254:27–255, 21.
42 This thesis is elaborated in Carl-Henric Grenholm, *Tro, moral och uddlös politik*, 258ff and 275ff. See also Carl-Henric Grenholm, "Law and Gospel in Lutheran Ethics," *Justification in a Post-Christian Society*, ed. Carl-Henric Grenholm and Göran Gunner, 102ff (Eugene, OR: Pickwick Publications, 2014).

3 Antinomianism—the "Lutheran" heresy

Paul R. Hinlicky

Is Edward Snowden a hero or a villain? Is disclosure of the secrets of the National Security State an act of conscience or an act of treason? Where can ethical conscience stand in the "plane of immanence" described by Deleuze,[1] which seems to allow no appeal to a higher court than the political sovereignty which de facto presides in this region or that? We debate these questions today. I mention them at the outset and without prejudice to indicate the *kind* of questions about Christian theology and positive law that are under scrutiny in what follows. What follows is a theological study, which does not directly intervene in the contemporary question in that it instead forces reflection on matters usually taken for granted as settled in "secular" regimes, though I will indicate in conclusion the posture which in my own judgment follows from the presentation.

The Lutheran heresy

The classical idea of a "heresy" is of a deviation in Christian doctrine that thinks outside of the theological circle of revelation and faith and so leads faith away from its abiding source in God's Word. To speak of a "heresy" in this classical way is a serious matter, to be sure, but the concern in what follows is a distortion internal to developments within Christian theology in Luther's tradition. Antinomianism—rejecting the law as God's law or demoting its role in teaching and preaching as superseded by the gospel—is an exaggeration of the distinction of law and gospel at the heart of Lutheran theology. It is a subtle but ultimately injurious distortion that not only does a disservice to civic life but undermines the gift nature of the gospel. To be sure, Lutheranism, as an historical phenomenon, is a *conflicted* tradition, such that what "antinomianism" is or could be as a Lutheran "heresy" is itself a hotly disputed matter, usually formulated as contestation over a so-called third use of the law. But it is a fact that Luther himself acknowledged the "heresy" of Lutheran antinomianism and this fact can orient our deliberations.

A prefatory comment. Simply put, Augustine's idea of "ordered love" (*ordo caritatis*) is that the love owed supremely to the Creator norms the loves owed to the range of fellow creatures, so that creatures are loved fittingly and not idolatrously. Such love can thus take the strange form of a word of judgment against them, as well as the proper form of a word of blessing and approbation. I will defend *ordo caritatis* in what follows as the backbone of Luther's own doctrine of law against critics like Anders Nygren who have influentially argued that in Christian understanding, love for creatures is to be unconditional.[2] But in speaking of the law of love as, first of all, *God's* law, "You shall have no other gods before me," law in Luther's usage is not to be equated either with secular law or autonomous conscience, as we conceive of these today.

Just because of this possible confusion in our minds, appropriation of Luther's doctrine of law today requires a genealogy that does not shrink from the fact that law, even the law of love, is, qua law, a reflex of a *fallen* creation, always then a *coercive* mechanism enforced by a regime that in principle *exempts* itself from the very ethical behavior it requires of those under its protection—as Giorgio Agamben has acutely analyzed.[3] An illustrative anecdote: when Roland Bainton, Luther biographer of *Here I Stand* fame,[4] heard criticism of the magisterial reformers for sanctioning violence on religious grounds to preserve the status quo, he pointed out that contemporary national security regimes do not hesitate to sanction violence on secular grounds to preserve the status quo. The state of exception is operative in either case. Recognition of this painful paradox is at the heart of Luther's Christian realism. *Quis custodiet custodes?* Luther's answer: the divine law of love in the custody of the prophetic Church of the Word. This custodianship, let alone its urgent political work in public theology, is forfeited, however, by antinomian Lutheranism for which everything is grace and blessing. But let us look and see.

In his antinomian writings from later in life, Luther conceded that what I am calling a "Lutheran heresy" based itself on his own writings from early in the Reformation period. Responding to the antinomian thesis that "not the law, but the Gospel must be taught. For the law, by terrifying us, does not bring about anything other than the hatred of God[,]" Luther replies, "It is true, at the beginning of this matter, we began to teach the Gospel vigorously and we also used the very words the Antinomians are now using." These "charming theologians retain our words, our doctrine, that joyful promise concerning Christ ..." But they have not noticed the change in times and audience. In the beginning, "it was not necessary to inculcate or teach further the law to those consciences which were thus already oppressed, utterly terrified, miserable, anxious, and afflicted." But now "we have become and are secure and evil, inconsiderate, unjust robbers, indeed, also Epicureans who respect neither God nor men ..."[5] Note well: Luther's theology is rhetorically oriented to particular, hence shifting audiences in the fog and friction of social life, even if the ultimate audience is the judgment of God.

Thus in the place of first principles or abstract ideas of the philosophers, Luther's reference is to conscience, to a culture of responsibility to God for the world as opposed to a culture of irresponsibility to God, or a culture of responsibility to this world *in place of* God—which would be a *conscientious* idolatry. This is the problem I wish to get at. So far as law functions in this way as responsibility to God for the world, it presupposes an ethical culture which can subsequently defend but hardly generate. Let me explain.

The issue is not only the pastoral one, then, of discerning one's audience so that Christian teaching knows to comfort the afflicted conscience and afflict the comfortable one. Such discernment depends on clarity about the "justification" in "justification by faith." The very words of the early Luther that the Antinomians are using have materially to do with the nature of justification, whether by works or by faith. Justification denotes satisfaction or fulfillment of God's justice; it speaks of God in the office of judge prosecuting the whole world as Luther depicts, as we shall see, by His law of love. It is true that the early Luther wrote that his soul "hates the word, satisfaction."[6] It is also correct to understand that his reference there was to the idea that by natural human powers one could satisfy God's contract with creation by doing one's little part—(1) as if this minimal effort truly satisfied the law of love, and (2) as if satisfying the law of love were in the power of a fallen humanity. In the first case, thinking in terms of one's natural and self-interested effort to acquire reward and avoid punishment, conscience is anesthetized; in the second case, awareness of being trapped in a subjectivity of self-seeking, conscience is tortured. Self-justification leads either to pride or despair. But this hardly means that either conscience or the doctrine of justification is to be abolished from theology.

For the good news of the gospel of the grace and glory of God, according to Luther, is that Christ in the power of God has satisfied the law of love, indeed, so to say, over-satisfied it by loving the loveless in loving obedience to God's uncanny will that led Him to their place on the cross. Moreover, this satisfaction of the law by Christ's obedience is vindicated by God and given as a gift to the penitent; it is the very righteousness of Christ, won by his obedience to death on the cross on behalf of the conscience stricken before God with its real, not fictitious, guilt of irresponsibility to God for the world, beginning with one's own self. This righteousness is given by imputation or attribution or credit, so that it becomes the believer's own, not by virtue of having performed this work of satisfaction as one's own performance but by virtue of having received it as a genuine gift. This reception of a putative gift communicated in language is thus possessed solely by faith. It is not money you can put in your hands, but a promise you can have—as in "having not" (cf. 1 Cor. 7:29–31)—in your "heart," the seat of conscience, for Luther.

So by faith the penitent believer unites herself to Christ in His gift and so entrusts herself to God. And further, given as a genuine gift and received as one's own by faith, this satisfaction of the law by Christ for us becomes in us by the Holy Spirit the believer's own satisfaction of the law by Christ active in us, purging sinful desire and cultivating conscience in the new relation of responsibility to God for the world that Augustine named the *ordo caritatis.*

The basic idea of Luther's anti-antinomianism can now be sketched immediately. There are constructions or developments of the chief article of justification by faith alone that can undercut the doctrine itself by destroying in our understanding the very need for *justification* before God, *whether* it be by works *or* by faith *or* by anything else. How will you answer to God for your stewardship of His world, beginning with your own body-and-soul? That is the question of justification. It is the question of conscience. When this specific question of conscientious responsibility to God for the world is eclipsed, however, the teaching on justification by faith in Christ transforms into general ideas of divine acceptance and ethical permissiveness. This subversion occurs when in the name of *unconditional* grace—that is, a grace *not* conditioned by the cross of Christ where the Son of God took conscientious responsibility for sinners before His God and Father, that is, *not* conditioned as accountability to the law *of God* by which, in Paul the Apostle's words, *God "judges* the world" (Romans 3:6)—it is dispensed with on principle.

In tandem with this subversion, the theological diagnosis of our root human predicament shifts away from the radical sinfulness of irresponsibility before God. In its place, new enemies are depicted: outmoded ideas of society, or culturally retrograde moral codes, or legalistic logic-chopping casuistry, or ecclesiastical authoritarianism, or the Old Testament with its representations of a wrathful deity, or pharisaical self-righteousness. But these new enemies, real and imagined, at their worst are but symptoms of the radical, that is, root irresponsibility before God that is sinfulness.

There is a further irony to antinomianism. The retooling of the gospel *without* the law and the prophets that bear witness to it makes the event of divine grace in Christ into a new idea of God or ideal of divine justice, that is, *into a new law* standing in judgment over such bad old ideas or ideals as enumerated above. But for Luther, it does not help the loveless one to hear that God is love, true though it is. If I am to be helped in the sense of being changed into a loving person, the God of love must find the way to love me, the loveless sinner who has learned to justify himself in order to fend off God's call to responsibility, "Adam, where art thou?"[7]

Truly to help Adam who flees just judgment in this way, and so misses the very possibility of the mercy of love, God must—conscientiously, so to say—fulfill His own law of love in a surpassing and surprising way, precisely on behalf of the one judged unworthy by that same law of love that summons us to responsibility to the God of love for the blessing of His creation. The Christian message, in Luther's understanding of Paul, is just this right kind of help: at the right time, Christ died for the ungodly (Romans 5:6) so that, incorporated into His death, believers might die to sin and rise to walk in newness of life (Romans 6:4). So they are liberated both from the guilt of irresponsibility by imputation of Christ's obedience and the power of self-justifying desire by Holy Spirit purification.

Key concept: in Christ the law is fulfilled *for us* and then also by His Spirit *in us*. Antinomianism as a "Lutheran heresy" undercuts this key theological concept by denying the need for justification, that is, the need for fulfilling or satisfying the law by representing God the judge as a terrorist, as a human idea, then, unworthy of God who should instead be represented as an indulgent father welcoming home all his prodigal children.

One final remark on Luther's anti-antinomianism. For Luther, the faith which justifies does not merely keep an outward observance of the law out of servile fear of punishment or calculating hope for reward. That is mere civil righteousness and social conformity. But justifying faith *fulfills* the law inwardly out of new-born filial love of God above all and all creatures in and under God. Antinomianism as a "Lutheran heresy" undercuts this unitive and transformative understanding of faith as Christ in us by keeping Christ and His righteousness extrinsic to the believer, ever alien and only imputed. As such, believers may sin on the calculation that grace abounds.

But for Luther, what is alien and imputed becomes really our own by faith which personally appropriates it, not of course in the first place as the doer who did righteousness but as the receiver of righteousness given as a gift. Just so, however, in the second place, the receiver, being loved by God in her state of lovelessness, is therewith recreated and arises to walk in newness of life. Faith, for Luther, is this Spirit-wrought new birth, a new subjectivity such that sin has no more dominion over believers now led by the same Spirit who led Jesus to the cross for them. Consequently, in them the just requirement of the law is satisfied step by often painful step on the way to the hope of righteousness.

So the law is not abolished but fulfilled in several senses. First, in Christ, it is more than satisfied in His extraordinary obedience in the place and for the sake of the disobedient. Second, it is being satisfied by His Spirit in the new lives of the just who live by this faith. The terror of law as condemnation is ended because the claim of the law on conscience is not cancelled but rather fulfilled.

I wish now to return to my opening comment that historically Lutheranism is a conflicted tradition. From the very beginning, it is not only the heresy of antinomianism but the predominant response to the heresy of antinomianism in Lutheranism that puts an obstacle in the way of our understanding and re-appropriation of the doctrine of law embedded in Luther's doctrine of justification as a culture of conscientious responsibility to God for the world. This obstacle is Melanchthon's understandable, but all the same flawed, attempt to impose socially with the backing of the state what can only be received freely and joyfully as a gift. His was an attempt to secularize Luther's inalienably theological account of divine law. Secularism in older or new forms has prevailed since Luther's time as a moral and legal ideology that holds conscience responsible to this present world in place of God—even when the ideology sounds oh-so-religious, but in fact is using God to sanction the exceptional authority of the self-seeking state. My disturbing suggestion in conclusion will be that retrieval of Luther's anti-antinomian doctrine of justification puts the believer into a state of profound and conscientious objection to secularism's conscientious disavowal of responsibility to God in its idolatrous demand on conscience to love this age instead of the promised age to come.

Witte on Melanchthon's Protestant political theory

John Witte's marvelous study, *Law and Protestantism*, tells how the sixteenth century Reformation turned to secular society as the place of sanctification, and to law as ordered there toward serving the neighbor, and how this turn profoundly and for the good effected the future. "A good deal of our modern Western law of marriage, education, and social welfare, for example, still bears the unmistakable marks of Lutheran Reformation theology."[8] Moreover, we learn from it, Witte claims, that

> the state has a role to play not only in fighting wars, punishing crime, and keeping peace, but also in providing education and welfare, fostering charity and morality, facilitating worship and piety ... law has not only a basic use of coercing citizens to accept a morality of duty but also a higher use of inducing citizens to pursue a morality of aspiration.[9]

Witte calls this early Lutheran project for the reform of society "Christian republicanism." He traces this project of a Protestant theology of culture and jurisprudence back to Melanchthon's role as *praeceptor Germaniae*, especially in the years after Luther's death.

To understand Witte's argument, however, we have first to step back to the way Luther negotiated untenable claims to institute Old Testament law in a theology that claimed to work by Scripture alone. For Luther, the civil, religious and ceremonial legislation of Moses for ancient Israel has, qua positive law, no abiding significance for Gentile Christians. Not only is it outmoded, it was never addressed to them and so does not speak to them as law, although historically and critically interpreted, it may have heuristic value illuminating how positive law can be informed by the moral law of love. It is the law of love, as the law of creation itself, which abides for Luther. In his writings against the Antinomians, indeed, we find the statement, *Solus decalogus est aeternus*—a claim that is intelligible when we take the Decalogue, as Luther did with Augustine, as the *ordo caritatis*. Otherwise, one wonders, why should the moral law of Moses in the Decalogue transcend its historical context unlike the other forms of Mosaic law?

In his formative work, *On Christian Doctrine*, Augustine had identified the double-love commandment of Jesus in the gospels as the heart of Christian doctrine. In keeping with this tradition of theology, Luther takes the Decalogue as "natural" law spelling out the dimensions and scope of love in the Creator's intended world. We should not be misled by the language of "natural" law, however, to imagine an autonomous human thinker discerning, by reason alone and unaided, the rational and universal moral core behind the manifold formulations of positive law. Luther is not a Thomist, let alone Kantian. His theology of law as epitomized in the double love commandment, understood with Augustine as an *ordo caritatis*, holds by faith that it is written universally on the human heart. It is not an empirical generalization. Although platitudes like, "Do no harm," or, "Don't treat others as you would not be treated," can be found in the *ius gentium*, crucially what is lacking there, following Augustine, is the *crucial* ordering of love so that creatures are loved in and under God their creator, never above or in place or instead of the love which is owed to the Creator. It is the first table of the Decalogue that is decisive for understanding the proper sense of the second table. This understanding of "natural" law is revealed *theology*, doctrine of the living Creator who actively, albeit hiddenly, governs the world by the law of love. This hidden governance is known from revelation (Romans 1:18ff).

Moreover, God's law as "natural" works as governance in the dark experience of retribution. It is to be sought and found in the actual unfolding of events, in human experience of karma, so to speak, or nemesis, the exceedingly rough justice of experience. Here faith affirms that all things work together for good to them that love God, that is, to those who are called *according to God's purposes.* But to make this affirmation, faith brings to experience its knowledge of God's calling to God's purpose in the ordering of love. The Decalogue is thus needed for Luther as the clearest formulation of natural moral law just because it grounds the second table in the first. As such, it works as a hermeneutic of actual human experience. As clear divine instruction, it works to interpret experience, both political and spiritual, as blessing or curse, as God creating, preserving, punishing, healing, re-creating so that believers may know sin and cease to collaborate with it but rather know righteousness and come to cooperate with the cause of God. In other words, the Decalogue works to inform judgment.

So, arguably, in American history Lincoln used the law of God to interpret the catastrophe of the Civil War and discern in it the hidden purpose of God in ending slavery. As he concluded with the psalmist, "so still it must be said "the judgments of the Lord are true and righteous altogether."" Following upon this affirmation of divine judgment on the nation's original sin of a race-based slave system now requited by the shed blood of the fallen of both North and South, Lincoln was thus able to summon the judged to mercy:

> With malice toward none, with charity for all, with firmness in the right as God gives us to see the right, let us strive on to finish the work we are in, to bind up the nation's wounds, to care for him who shall have borne the battle and for his widow and his orphan, to do all which may achieve and cherish a just and lasting peace among ourselves and with all nations.[10]

This, I think, illustrates how Luther conceives of the Decalogue working as a hermeneutic, clarifying the actual lawfulness of chaotic events under God's governance of a fallen world.

To be sure, Luther universalized and radicalized the Decalogue. He dispensed with the biblical preface regarding the Exodus. He omitted the commandment against images, spiritualized the Sabbath commandment and generalized the promise of prosperity in the land of Canaan to all life on the earth. As per the Sermon on the Mount, he looked through external action to the motives of actors, anchoring obedience in fear, love and trust in God above all things. All nations, he asserted, with their religions know that God is to be honored and that society is to be governed in structures of accountability. Yet such governance cannot adequately be prescribed in a written code and left to its impersonal application, as in the notion of "blind justice." Indeed, such ideals of "blind" justice working like an algorithm appeal when confidence in God's seeing, as Jesus proclaims in the Sermon on the Mount, has been lost. It is rather the conscience formed by the moral law which can judge wisely, applying the written code with equity amid a virtual infinity of unique and complex circumstances.

Wisdom is the humane understanding of happy creatures, not the cunning of unhappy gods. This understanding of our ineradicable finitude, and its goodness, includes the insight that human circumstances are unlimited in variety and complexity and that multiplying law in a vain attempt to cover all cases only multiplies the rule of the bureaucrats, legal and otherwise. In the process, the application of law is depersonalized where personhood is fundamentally at stake in matters of guilt or innocence, that is, of responsibility and conscience. What would repair of an offender mean other than restoration of the ability to respond truthfully? Instead of the multiplication of laws, then, what is needed for Luther is wise judges using the rational insight of imagination that comes about as a judge puts herself into the place of the judged. This is a practical principle of equity provided by the Golden Rule of loving others as ourselves, alike creatures of the same Creator, of equal value though otherwise diverse in talent, opportunity and need. It works to temper the written law's strict logic by the reparative and sometimes also retributive purposes of love. For love is the fulfillment of the law according to the Creator's intention, as the Sermon on the Mount makes unmistakably clear. So the wise judge judges the letter of the law by the spirit of the law. But the Spirit of the law is known from the first table of the Decalogue.

So the Decalogue is needed. For not only is God's governance hidden. The law has been obscured by sinfulness whenever law is used for one's own advantage and at the expense of others. The law without knowledge of God is vulnerable to self-justifying abuse, even tyrannical abuse. *Quis custodiet custodes*? asked the early Marx. Abuse of the legal system solely for the assertion of one's own rights in turn undercuts the moral authority of law in a downward cultural spiral of conscienceless litigation, barely disguised bribery and partisan contests for power. Conscience and the sustenance of a culture of conscience thus become decisive—which is one way of formulating the unique and indispensable political work of the church as creature of the gospel. Checking the danger of caprice and abuse in commending honest but risky reliance on the wisdom of judges is the further principle for Luther, as Piotr Malysz has acutely argued, *nemo iudex in sua causa*.[11] The one who is justified by the gracious intervention of Another, who believes that Other's promise of grace even against the testimony to his own guilt resounding in his own conscience, knows this principle best of all. From this ecclesial center laying out social structures of mutual accountability, radicalized by the Sermon on the Mount's preaching of the heavenly Father who sees in secret and knows in secret so that actors are made transparent before God as the person who acts in the world, Luther's Decalogue serves to expose the universal lawfulness of human society and to clarify and purify it by resituating law and its performance within the Creator's purpose of a good world intended for blessing, not curse. In such a social organization, the fear of the Lord is the beginning of wisdom, binding the conscience of judges to God's ultimate judgment. Thus, the guards are guarded.

Although Luther said all these things about law and justice and conscience, in his lifetime he could and did dodge the question of the institutional reform of jurisprudence because of his conviction that the world was about to end. Melanchthon, left with the task of reforming society on a new Protestant basis, could not and did not dodge that problem. He followed Luther's lead. He solved the problem of the reform of jurisprudence "by subordinating the natural law that is discerned but distorted by reason to the biblical law that is revealed and understood by faith" above all, in the Decalogue.[12] Following Luther's Christianization of the Decalogue, he wrote that it is not enough to grasp negatives, the prohibitions in which the Decalogue is largely formulated.

> Rather one must know who God is and know that God earnestly wants us to be like Him, and that he assuredly rages against all sins … so that we know that they are not only our thoughts but that they are God's law … human reason, without God's word, soon errs and falls into doubt ... about what God is, who He is, about what is right and wrong, what is order and what is disorder.[13]

So the full-blown *ordo caritatis* is even more pronounced than in Luther, if that is possible. Witte rightly observes that

> Melanchthon, building on Luther, transformed traditional legal theory by making not reason but the Bible, and more particularly the Ten Commandments, the basic source and summary of natural law in the earthly kingdom .... a model for the positive law enacted by the earthly rulers.[14]

The Decalogue becomes the model of positive law in the new Protestant regime. Melanchthon, in Witte's reading, grasped the pedagogical meaning of Torah, indeed to such an extent that he virtually

> folded the civil use of the law into the pedagogical use .... [T]he multitude must be instructed, ruled, and coerced in this manner even now by laws and by certain offices ... This political pedagogy, which is justice, forms morals and includes both religious rites and human and civil offices. Through teaching and exercise it accustoms children [of God] to the proper public worship of God, and it restrains foolish people from vices.'[15]

As a preacher and theological teacher by vocation, Luther thought pastorally about his political interventions. He restricted himself to counseling the consciences of Christians, whether rulers or ruled, instructing them in divine law and advising them in conduct that pleases God. But Melanchthon's idea—undoubtedly necessary in his circumstances, after Luther, of rebuilding a reformed Christendom—went further than Luther in commending a "divinely imposed task of Christian magistrates to promulgate what he called 'rational positive laws' ('*rationes iuris positivi*') for the governance of the earthly kingdom."[16]

Melanchthon started from the position that the Christian magistrate is the "custodian" of both tables of the Decalogue, "a voice of the Ten Commandments" within the earthly kingdom ...

> [M]agistrates must pass laws against idolatry, blasphemy, and violations of the Sabbath—offenses that the First Table prohibits on its face. Magistrates are also, however, to pass laws to "establish pure doctrine" and right liturgy, "to prohibit all wrong doctrine," "to punish the obstinate," and to "root out the heathen and the heterodox."[17]

Needless to say, as Witte too points out, this move toward institutionalizing reform moves a long way beyond the early Luther's emphatic teaching on the freedom of faith and its correlate about the incompetence of secular rulers to decide matters of faith. With Luther, it was the theologians of the gospel who instructed rulers and ruled in their responsibility to God; but now, after Melanchthon, it is the rulers who determine what theology will prevail in their fiefdoms. Biblical theology becomes the ideological instrument of court theology on the grounds that the rulers are the custodians of the Decalogue. But that means the rulers can decide which religion fulfills the first table. Thus with Melanchthon, we witness the first movement in principle towards the *cuius regio eius religio* doctrine; Witte goes so far as to say that "the Peace of Westphalia (1648) rested ultimately on Melanchthon's theory that the magistrate's positive law was to use the First Table of the Decalogue to establish for his people proper Christian doctrine, liturgy, and spiritual morality"[18]—that being, again, whatever version of Christianity the ruler decrees. In sum:

> the Ten Commandments, instead of the seven sacraments, [were used] to organize the various systems of positive law. And [Melanchthon] looked to the state, instead of the Church, to promulgate and enforce these positive laws on the basis of the Ten Commandments.[19]

The reform of jurisprudence was a change—but a change *from within*—the centuries-long European project of Christendom, of a *holy* Roman Empire, going back to Leo III's coronation of Charlemagne as emperor.

I take it for granted, and will not further argue it here, that this project is kaput today and that we have a new and unprecedented cultural situation in the West for theology and law in post-Christendom.

Christian conscience under secularism

The flaw in Melanchthon's reform of society was the theocratic turn, as Witte laconically observes in conclusion: "Ever since, Germany and other Protestant nations have been locked in a bitter legal struggle to eradicate state establishments of religion and to guarantee religious freedom for all …"[20] It is no accident, in the light of this history, that the achievements in human equality attained by modern secular law which derive from the Lutheran Reformation's turn to equity in secular life as the place of sanctification have had to kick away the ladder on which they climbed to this enlightened place. Ironically, as I will now conclude, this loss of the Decalogue puts the secular state in the self-absolutizing posture that Thomas Hobbes first theorized, when he supposed that the rule of law is always instituted, not by God for the sake of a conscientious obedience according to His purposes, but rather by a violent "state of exception" described by Agamben.[21] What an irony! Having given the princes the authority to determine how the first table of the Decalogue is to be fulfilled, the princes took the authority but abandoned the first table. Or rather, they consumed it. They became Hobbes' Leviathan, the early modern state as the incarnate god on the earth.

Abandoning the Decalogue, however, the secular state cannot acknowledge any higher power to which it is accountable; it become the judge of its own case without exception. Coupled with the disestablishment of religion under the principle of equity, the perception of the pluralism of religions emerged in secular modernity which ipso facto permits no social consensus on what higher power might require accountability or sustain a culture of conscience. The ad hoc adaptation to this state of affairs is the return in the churches to the antinomianism according to which all is grace, as H. Richard Niebuhr captured in the nineteenth century preaching in mainline American churches (and which today again predominates) of a "God without wrath who brings men without sin into a kingdom without judgment through the ministrations of a Christ without a cross."[22] A sharper sketch of the Lutheran heresy could not be drawn. Judgment is abandoned. Justice, however passionately advocated, reduces to intense fighting over rules of procedure—as if equal opportunity in a secular culture of greed were the righteousness of God!

If the case I have been building succeeds, then it will have put theology in the tradition of Luther on the horns of a dilemma. I hope I have shown that Luther's view of "natural" moral law as *ordo caritatis* cannot be secularized coherently, beginning with Melanchthon's own fatally flawed attempt to enforce the Decalogue. The reason for this is not simply social tolerance. But also, on Lutheran terms itself, faith in God, if it is to be justifying faith, can in no sense be coerced without falsifying it. It must be filial, free and joyful, not servile, forced and fearful. To this extent, the rise of secularism against Protestant religious establishment is theologically justified and indeed a piece of poetic justice. Religious freedom is the first of all freedoms, the one higher principle to which secularism still (pretends to) bow.

The law that must be fulfilled theologically is the law of love, first by Christ for us and then by Christ in us. This is the message of the church regarding justification also today, and it is the only message which can subvert the self-absolutizing temptation of the secular state of modernity and *force* it—I used the word advisedly, thinking of Romans 12:20 and Martin Luther King's ministry of non-violent resistance—to a posture of responsibility to God for that piece of His creation entrusted to its care. If that is so, the urgent theological task is for the church to regain confidence in just this gospel message which does not "take sides" in the partisan politics of the secular state, but "makes sides" by cultivating a culture of conscience. It does this just by showing forth the fulfillment of God's law in Christ's obedience to death on the cross when He took responsibility for us while we were yet sinners. On this basis, a public theology of a public church demands a conscientious response in turn—call it Luther's lifelong repentance. It is by proclaiming the gospel in this way, that is, on its own theological terms of justification before God, that the church makes a true and helpful contribution to secular political life and the performance of law in it. With conscience bound to this word of God revealing righteousness in Christ, Christian living satisfies the justice of God in the hope of righteousness. What this witness of conscience means for life under secularism, and for law according to secularism, I leave for others to imagine. But I suspect it means, as it meant in Luther's own time, *resistance*.

Notes

1 For a discussion of this term, see "4.3 What Is Philosophy, Gilles Deleuze," *The Stanford Encyclopedia of Philosophy*, ed. Daniel Smith and John Protevi (2012). Accessed November 5, 2017. https://plato.stanford.edu/entries/deleuze/.
2 See, e.g., Anders Nygren, *Agape and Eros*, trans. Philip S. Watson (New York and Evanston, IL: Harper & Row, 1969), 92.
3 See generally Giorgio Agamben, *Homo Sacer: Sovereign Power and Bare Life*, trans. D. Heller-Roazen (Stanford, CA: Stanford University Press, 1998).
4 See Roland Bainton, *Here I Stand: A Life of Martin Luther* (New York: Meridian Books, 1995).
5 The quotations in this paragraph are taken from *Solus Decalogus est Aeternus: Martin Luther's Complete Antinomian Theses and Disputations*, ed. Holger Sonntag (Minneapolis, MN: Lutheran Press, 2008), 356–357.
6 See, e.g., Martin Luther, *Preface to Latin Writings* [1545], American edition of *Luther's Works*, ed. Jaroslav Pelikan and Helmut T. Lehmann, 55 vols. (Philadelphia, PA: Fortress Press and St. Louis, MO: Concordia Publishing House, 1955–1986), 34, 336–337.
7 For an example of this reference see, e.g., Martin Luther, *Two Sermons upon the Fifth Chapter of Luke* ("Here you see how poor and miserable conscience is when it really begins to feel its sins. How it trembles! How it runs to escape from God when he draws nigh, as if it would run across a hundred worlds! Thus Adam in Paradise thought to hide himself when God kindly asked: "Adam, where art thou?"). Accessed November 5, 2017. www.covenanter.org/reformed/2015/7/27/martin-luthers-two-sermons-upon-the-fifth-chapter-of-luke.
8 John Witte Jr., *Law and Protestantism: The Legal Teachings of the Lutheran Reformation* (Cambridge: Cambridge University Press, 2002), 295.
9 Ibid., 296.
10 Abraham Lincoln, Gettysburg Address. Accessed November 5, 2017. www.abrahamlincolnonline.org/lincoln/speeches/gettysburg.htm.

11 Piotr J. Malysz, "*Nemo iudex in causa sua* as the Basis of Law, Justice, and Justification in Luther's Thought," *Harvard Theological Review* 100: no. 3 (2007): 363–386.
12 Witte, *Law and Protestantism*, 125.
13 Ibid., 126 quoting Phillip Melanchthon, *Corpus Reformatorum*, 28 vols. *Philippi Melancthonis Opera Quae Supersunt Omnia* (Halle and Brunswick: C. A. Schwetschke, 1834–1860). (Hereafter, CR.) CR 22, 256–257.
14 Ibid., 127. Melanchthon "defined a good deal of the content and character of Lutheran theories of law, politics and society … Generations of students thereafter studied his legal, political, and moral writings, many of which were still being printed two centuries later and used as textbooks in universities throughout Germany and well beyond." Ibid., 139.
15 Ibid., 129, quoting Philip Melanchthon, CR 1, 706–708.
16 Ibid., (referring to Melanchthon's views).
17 Ibid., 131, quoting Philip Melanchthon, CR 22, 617–618.
18 Ibid., 132.
19 Ibid., 133.
20 Ibid., 296.
21 See discussion of Hobbes in Agamben, *Homo Sacer*, 106–109.
22 H. Richard Niebuhr, *The Kingdom of God in America* (New York, Evanston, IL and London: Harper Torchbooks, 1959), 193.

Part III

The individual and the state

4 Separability as distinction

The individual subject of the civil law

Michael J. Kessler

Introduction

James Madison offers a spirited argument for separating the civil or legal sphere from ecclesiastical government in his 1785 *Memorial and Remonstrance against Religious Assessments.* He provides many related justifications for holding religious life and moral claims in some tension with, and distance from, the political sphere. Following Locke's lead, Madison claims that each citizen enjoys an inalienable right: "the Religion … of every man must be left to the conviction and conscience of every man."[1] No legislature, judge, or executive can manage what it is exclusively the province of the divine sovereign to manage: the interior disposition of the individual. In refuting the legitimacy of a proposed Virginia bill for religious assessments, Madison also provides another powerful argument, best described as the *incompetency* of civil government over matters of religion:

> [T]he Bill implies either that the Civil Magistrate is a competent Judge of Religious Truth; or that he may employ Religion as an engine of Civil policy. The first is an arrogant pretension falsified by the contradictory opinions of Rulers in all ages, and throughout the world: the second an unhallowed perversion of the means of salvation.[2]

Yet, Madison tells us little about *why* the civil magistrate is incompetent in these affairs, though he offers a clue when he asserts that, historically, religion has been stymied rather than helped by civil governmental control. To say that the Christian religion needs civil support

> is a contradiction to the Christian Religion itself, for every page of it disavows a dependence on the powers of this world: it is a contradiction to fact; for it is known that this Religion both existed and flourished, not only without the support of human laws, but in spite of every opposition from them, and not only during the period of miraculous aid, but long after it had been left to its own evidence and the ordinary care of Providence.[3]

Madison points to the long and bloody historical experience of sectarian violence and strife created over discordant views about theological and liturgical matters and offers a pragmatic assessment: religion is better off when left alone by government. God has managed just fine thus far without governmental assistance.

Yet we can identify a more robust justification for separability and the incompetency argument, even if Madison only offers a faint gesture toward it. In a letter to F. L. Schaefer dated December 3, 1821, after Schaefer addressed a cornerstone-laying ceremony at St. Matthew's Church in New York, Madison pointed to Luther as his main influence for the idea of separate ecclesiastical and civil governments:

> [Your address] illustrates the excellence of a system which, by a due distinction to which the genius and courage of Luther lend the way, between what is due to Caesar and what is due to God best promotes the discharge of both obligations. The experience of the United States is a happy disproof of the error so long rooted in the unenlightened minds of well-meaning Christians, as well as in the corrupt hearts of persecuting usurpers, that without a legal incorporation of religious and civil polity, neither could be supported. A mutual independence is found most friendly to practical Religion, to social harmony, and to political prosperity.[4]

The citizen, *qua* human, inhabits both God's and Caesar's realms simultaneously and gives to each realm that allegiance which is due—invoking Augustine's definition of justice as rendering to each their due—which makes thriving religion, social harmony, and prosperity possible. "Distinction" is the key word here. It has positive connotations: we hold the civil and religious realms distinct and in tension so that each can maximize their potential. Separation channels our individual allegiances through "due distinctions" so that *we*, the subject-citizens, fulfill the appropriate duty to the appropriate sovereign in order that each can accomplish its distinct goals.

Following Madison and Madison's guide, Luther, this chapter will explore how Luther's political theology laid out multiple, distinct modes of the social order while imposing a robust responsibility on the faithful citizen. Understanding Luther's argument that separation is primarily a task of faithful citizenship rather than a structural feature of political and legal institutions can illuminate more richly what is sometimes obscured in later attempts to build theories of separation like Madison's.

Luther's political theology: politics as a distinct structure of the kingdom of man

Quentin Skinner has argued that the chief political task driving the Reformation was distinguishing the legislative duties that descend from the Divine upon the ruler from those duties incumbent upon the ruler's subjects.[5] This chapter does not adopt Skinner's view that Luther's political model is absolutist.[6] Rather, Luther's two-kingdoms typology and his concept of vocation raise a more profound issue: what duty lies *within* the Christian to relate her moral and religious identity in the private realm to the public realm, given the tension between both realms? The privatization of religion under the evangelical reformation requires an answer to two questions: first, how do private imperatives become public actions, while remaining grounded in the private realm; and second, how can public institutions host actions motivated by citizens with multiple intentions—natural and religious—while protecting the secularity of the public realm as sufficient in itself? Unmasking Luther's subtle—and very modern—theological resolution of this question has profound implications for connecting the liberalism of later political theologians to the historic tradition of the Christian faith.

Luther's political theology begins with the evangelical *sola fidei* tradition of Christian life.[7] By rejecting the central authority of the Church as the sole mediator of God's grace, Luther places the locus of God's gracious activity directly within the human person. The bondage of the sinner is transformed into freedom to love God and the neighbor through the unmerited salvific grace of God. Without grace, all good works are selfish and done in the hope of attaining salvation. However, unburdened from the task of trying to merit salvation, the Christian "may serve and benefit others in all that he does, considering nothing except the need and advantage of his neighbor."[8] Genuine love for the neighbor arises only through freedom from the bondage of sin and can only emerge "out of spontaneous love in obedience to God."[9] In this way, Luther paradoxically argued, the Christian, totally free, is bound to "take upon himself the form of a servant … and serve, help, and in every way deal with his neighbor as he sees that God through Christ has dealt and still deals with him."[10]

Christian freedom is responsible freedom, requiring work for the betterment of others, Thus "the Apostle Paul has prescribed this rule [Phil. 2:1–4] for the life of Christians, namely, that we should devote all our works to the welfare of others."[11] This is the paradox of Christian freedom: one is simultaneously the perfectly free lord of all and the dutiful servant of all.[12] It lives alongside the paradox that a Christian is not fully re-created but is rather *simul iustus et peccator*, simultaneously sinner and saint. For Luther, these good works are the task of all believers (the so-called priesthood of all believers), not merely a few ecclesiastics; the distinction between priest and regular believer is merely one of order and function, not of hierarchy or ontology. The satisfied life asks: through what channels of the social order might the actual work of neighbor love be accomplished?

For Luther, the activity of the Christian in loving the neighbor goes *beyond* the Church into the secular world and attends to matters of "the things below." Like Christ, who stepped out of heaven, as it were, ministering to humans through the mechanisms of the sinful world, the Christian pilgrim takes on "temporal human form" and, in the company of the communion of saints, the individual enters the social order *as a minister to serve the neighbor in love and simultaneously to achieve the basic natural ends of the social spheres.*

Luther's account of the political realm unfolded from his conception of the civil use of the law as a mechanism of controlling the material harms brought about by the reality of sin in a world where most of its inhabitants were not Christians renewed by God's grace. Besides the law's theological use (to chastise and weaken the inner part of the human), the law functions at an external, material level to restrain wickedness and transgressions that harm others, to preserve everything in creation from destruction, and to institute a proximate peace among fellow citizens. The political and legal sphere achieves security and social stability by using the blunt instrument of the sword, restraining "a savage wild beast … bound with chains and ropes so that it cannot bite and tear as it would normally do, even though it would like to …"[13] A sign of the world's unrighteousness, "every law was given to hinder sins. Does this mean that when the Law restrains sins, it justifies? Not at all."[14] The political order will not increase salvation or moral virtue but can promote material stability and prevent harm to the world.[15]

This simple account of civil law created a problematic tension with the seeming nonviolence of the gospel imperative to love the neighbor unconditionally. Luther acknowledged this tension between Biblical acknowledgement of secular authority, as in Romans 13:1ff. ("every power is ordained by God") and I Peter 2:13–14 ("be subject to every ordinance"), and the pacific exhortations of the Gospel, as in Matthew 5:38–39 ("a man shall not resist evil, but if any strikes you on the right cheek, turn also the left cheek to him") and Romans 12:19 ("defend not yourselves, but leave it to the wrath of God.")[16] If outward works are to be reordered according to divine grace acting internally to reform the individual, why work to transform or participate in the social order at all? Many times, in fact, Luther suggested an antithetical relationship between being a Christian and being a state:

> [B]eing a Christian is something quite different from holding and administering a secular office or position. Therefore He [Jesus] intends to say: "Leave the resistance of evil, the administration of justice, and punishment to the one who holds a position in the secular realm, as the lawyers and the laws instruct you to do. But to you, my disciples, whom I am not teaching about ruling outwardly but living before God, I say: You shall not resist evil."[17]

Luther responded to this apparent contradiction by arguing that perfectionism is indeed about the heart inclining properly towards God: though the faithful are to respond in forgiveness to those evildoers who offend, this does not mean that Christians are "obliged to let your whims run riot all over him if he can prevent it by appealing to the law and by seeking help from the government."[18] Retributive action, enacted through the justice of the state, is an acceptable response to the evildoer. In his political theology, Luther resolved this tension by co-opting the Augustinian doctrine of the two-kingdoms—the temporal kingdom of the world and the spiritual kingdom of God—two distinct and separate authorities.[19] Both realms were ordained by God and both were necessary to the divine plan for the human good.[20] This theology of the two kingdoms specified the relation of the Christian to the world, and argued against the subordination of the temporal order to the spiritual order.[21] The members of the Kingdom of God are all true Christians, believers in Christ born of the Spirit by faith where the Gospel is the governing principle. The Church, the invisible communion of these faithful bonded together through love, aims at the redemption of humanity back into the divine fold. The visible Church is the temporal correlate to this invisible communion, but in itself is part of the sinful world and is not a perfect institution, mixing elements from both kingdoms.

The kingdom of the world, on the other hand, is composed of all material human beings—all flesh.[22] This kingdom produces civil laws that govern external actions, keeping people obedient and maintaining some bulwark against evil run rampant: "These divine stations and orders have been established by God [so] that in the world there may be a stable, orderly, and peaceful life, and that justice may be preserved."[23] Because the temporal realm is fallen, characterized by human abuse of freedom, self-interested actions, and the egoistic exertion of power over others, all fallen humans need the sword and the civil law to externally coerce their compliance with natural laws of harmony and order. Without these external constraints, the wicked would destroy each other and all good people alike, even harming the mission of the Church.

At a structural and institutional level, this distinction between kingdoms requires that the secular order must remain secular. The Church can encourage Christians to be dutiful members of society, to take up the tasks of magistrates, judges, barbers, and farmers, but the Church for Luther is specifically enjoined from *Christianizing* politics, law, haircutting, or farming. These vocations are part of natural orders—secular and worldly—which are outside of the salvific ends of the kingdom of God. Yet they participate in the creation of God and have a holy task within the secular order.

Natural reason and legal promulgation as secular yet "holy" work

In Luther's schema, the prince, or magistrate, holds a central political position to ensure this external and material stability.[24] The magistrate is responsible to God for the citizens' well-being and is thus subject to citizens as an agent of a directly-instituted "holy estate."

Luther argued that "on earth [there is] no better jewel, no greater treasure, nor richer alms, no fairer endowment, no finer possession than a ruler who makes and preserves just laws. Such men are rightly called gods."[25] In this manner, Luther effectively baptized the political order with the sanctity that had before been held only by the *ecclesia*.[26] To the claim that the pope could hold this princely power, Luther answered an emphatic no.

John Witte explains that for Luther, "God's natural law, set at the creation, continued to operate after the fall into sin, and ... provided the foundation for all positive law and public morality in the earthly kingdom."[27] Secular rulers were to formulate the positive law using reason and divine law: "wise rulers, side by side with Holy Scripture, would be law enough."[28] By divine law Luther meant the natural law, the Mosaic law, the teachings of conscience, and the created order. The prince was designated the interpreter of the divine law and the maker of human law; thus, "the ideal of Christendom with Pope and Emperor at its head gave way to the notion of the godly prince, through the legitimacy of the law was not dependent on the prince's faith or virtue."[29] Luther argued that the secular should reflect the general aims of the divine law, and the central role of wisdom in determining the content and shape of the law. The idea that secular law would be based on principles of utility directed for the common good that squared with the revealed divine law was not a contradiction for Luther, who believed that humans were created to organize the social order in the most expedient forms and to evaluate its consistency with divine law:

> God has subjected such matters to reason and has ordered that [reason] may deal freely with them; Genesis 2[2:8]. For it is worldly matter and earthly existence which are subjected to reason through the word, 'Have dominion over the earth.' Since secular government is reason's highest product, [the government] is able to be creative and give orders in these matters.[30]

But ultimately, he followed nominalism in declaring that its validity depended only on the will of the sovereign:[31] "we should keep written laws subject to reason."[32]

This understanding of secular lawmaking meshes with the Lutheran concept of vocation. For Luther, God's creation is extended as the individual takes up his vocation to shore up the world's affairs and the well-being of its members even if there is no explicit theological content to the vocational activities. The three orders of family, state, and church are directly instituted by God to satisfy certain human needs and to achieve stability in the material order so that creation, not chaos, can reign as a holy work of God:

> All fathers and mothers who regulate their household wisely ... are engaged in pure holiness ... Moreover, princes and lords, judges, civil officers, state officials, notaries, male and female servants and all who serve such persons, and further, all their obedient subjects—all are engaged in pure holiness and leading a holy life before God. For these three religious institutions or orders are found in God's Word and commandment; and whatever is contained in God's Word must be holy, for God's Word is holy and sanctifies everything connected with it and involved in it.[33]

For Luther, the vocations are holy work and extend the reign of God. The fact that family, Church, or political activity are pronounced holy in the Scripture does not mean that these activities obey explicit commands of God. From the perspective of the temporal and material world, God is the *deus absconditus*, and reveals God's self only through "mask[s]."[34] "[The Word of God] is not given to the secular and unregenerate man ... but only to the spiritual man. He alone can distinguish the position from the Word, the divine mask from

God Himself and the work of God."[35] One such mask is the product of the proper use of natural reason, which can achieve effects that refer to the Divine law, yet are not perfectly correlated to it. For Luther, biology, culture, and reason lead humans to participate in the social structures of family, communal orders, and political rule, and to work to the good of the world. In this way, nature acts according to the divine plan, whether or not that divine action is explicit, because it fulfills God's intention. Thus, humans construct these holy orders not by being good obedient Christians, but simply by following their nature—i.e., when they are rational in planning state organization, biologically satisfied in family rearing and sociality, emotionally fulfilled in marriage and cultural association, and so forth. To summarize, for Luther, the political implication of this view is that the gospel does not make any claim about the structure or content of the social order; this is a matter left entirely to reason:

> God made the secular government subordinate and subject to reason, because it is to have no jurisdiction over the welfare of souls to things of eternal value but only over physical and temporal goods, which God places under man's dominion, Genesis 2:8ff. For this reason nothing is taught in the Gospel about how it is to be maintained and regulated, except that the Gospel bids people honor it and not oppose it. Therefore the heathen can speak and teach about this very well, as they have done. And, to tell the truth, they are far more skillful in such matters than the Christians; Christ himself says (Luke 16:8) that the children of this world are wiser than the children of light.[36]

Reason alone can manage and organize the civil-political realm, in the same manner as other reason-directed activities of our natural well-being:

> In temporal affairs and those which have to do with men, the rational man is self-sufficient: here he needs no other light than reason's ... Therefore God does not teach us in the Scriptures how to build houses, make clothing, marry, wage war, navigate, and the like. Here the light of nature is sufficient.[37]

This use of reason, in its proper sphere, is a good use of a divine gift, since "it was God himself who implanted reason in man."[38]

It followed for Luther that the vocation of magistrates was to apprehend the situation at hand and fashion rules that simultaneously upheld the needs of the community, the demands of reason, and the general import of the divine purpose. As an adjunct to reason, Luther argued that the magistrate should rely on the precedent of the canon law and Roman law, as known through the *Corpus iurius civilis.*[39] While not of distinct Christian origin, Roman laws were, according to Melanchthon, the product of more than "human ingenuity," as they were "derived either by firm demonstrations of, or at least by solid arguments from the solid principles" of natural law, of "the rays of divine wisdom poured into us."[40]

Since the order of creation bears a hierarchy of skill—some are better at discerning rationally than others—the best ruler must be found among those who are the most rational: "One has to speak, the other must listen."[41] However, because the natural law was not "encased in [the] head" of the ruler, but was the product of the magistrate's sometimes flawed reason, the resulting law *resembles something of a patchwork, which must constantly be re-evaluated and corrected by reason and wisdom.*[42] The natural law thus exceeds the ruler's capacity to fully carry it out, and for this reason the laws are not permanent but in flux.[43] But for Luther, "it is enough, however, that laws and kings try to hit the mark so that they do not miss it altogether."[44]

A deeper theological account of the purposes of reason and legal regulation implies that because the criteria of justice within the legal system are rational, laws are *morally valid* if they achieve stability and keep order in the social sphere. They are especially likely to do so when rulers, using reason and exercising their particular virtues, help the wretched and needy to get justice and suppress violence and crime.[45] Yet, because of sin, Luther makes it quite clear that unjust laws must be disobeyed (even though one must also accept the punishment for disobeying them) and that God will hold rulers accountable for the sins in their rule.[46]

Importantly, Luther's insistence on this separation of the two kingdoms would yield a limitation on cross-sphere dogmatism: the true Church could attend to its business of salvation without the state interjecting and forcing its hand and the state would be exempt *a priori* from control by a Church that was misguided in its attempts to reform social structures rather than human wills.[47] Luther did think that the ideal harmony would be found by the Christian prince who paid attention to both, but his enthusiasm for this ideal should not obscure his insistence that law and morality were two very distinct phenomena of human life.

Politics as a vocation of subjective distinction

For Luther, although true Christians do not need external constraints of civil law, for they will act out of love for the neighbor and God, they nevertheless bear the law for the sake of others: "the law was not given for the righteous but for the unrighteous." (I Tim. 1:9).[48] The true Christian does acts of love toward neighbors through his or her temporal and material body. The secular civil law, a direct application of the second table of the Mosaic Law pertaining to interpersonal relations, is one *channel* through which the Christian might profitably manifest love for the neighbor.[49] Every Christian is required to support the government by paying taxes, and possibly providing military or civil service so that it may be sustained and honored.

It might seem to modern sensibilities that love for neighbor could be enacted in many ways and that political activity would be a sub-optimal path at best. Luther argued, however, that each of the three distinct modes of the order of creation is part of the basic and necessary structure of human existence in time and matter:

> You must be part of a family, a father or mother, a child, servant, or maid. Second, you must live in a city or in the country as a citizen, a subject, or a ruler. Third, you are part of the Church, perhaps a pastor, an assistant, a sexton, or in some other way a servant of the Church, if only you have and hear the Word of God.[50]

These three spheres, or *Regimente*, are specific and distinct orders of creation and realms of responsible "vocations" that compel humans to look beyond their own immediate self-interest toward the responsibility they owe to others.[51] Entry into the world's affairs is done through specific "callings" (*vocation, Beruf*) in each of these *regiments*. All humans have both a spiritual calling and a temporal calling into the vocations. These are spheres of influence, demarcated from each other, functioning to achieve specific tasks and ends in the order of creation. These realms are directly instituted by God to achieve natural, that is, created and intentional ends or goods.[52]

A crucial development emerges from Luther's analysis of these three regiments: the idea that *the subject must act across many different competing spheres of influence, none of which operate under a unifying worldview*.[53] Luther developed the Augustinian notion of the Christian as *simul iustus et peccator*, a pilgrim navigating both the temporal and the spiritual worlds. For Augustine, this division was unified under the grace of God; the pilgrim awaited final reconciliation only in the life to come. Luther expanded this idea into a more complex notion of a socially-divided self.[54] In negotiating the affairs of humans in the temporal sphere, one needs "to employ your secular person, to be prudent in your contacts with other people, to recognize the poor, to see the kind of people with whom you are dealing and those to whom you should or should not give."[55] The fact that Luther speaks here of the "secular" person, which is distinct from the spiritual, domestic, or ecclesial person, indicates that he intended the Christian to understand her role in the social order as one of multiple layers of competing interests, divided among various responsibilities that do not necessarily correlate one with another or resolve into a final synthesis for this life.

This bi-polarity of service and faith splits the Christian into a subject with distinct responsibilities, simultaneously working toward multiple ends that reunited only ultimately at the level of the Divine. For the human in time and space, these vocations remain in unresolved tension. In her spiritual person, she may suffer the wrongs others inflict without retribution, recognizing that they originate from the evil operating in the world. However, in her responsibility as a secular authority, she is required not to let any transgression of the law slip by unpunished, for the sake of the social order and the suppression of evil. Under the grace of God, the human subject might be unified in the life to come, but on earth he or she will live a fractured life. *It is the task of the Christian himself or herself to maintain these distinctions despite the fractures.*

Given these multivalent responsibilities, Luther claimed, the sword should never be used to coerce the inner life or conscience of an individual, but only to regulate external affairs for the secular good of another, as determined by the public authority.[56] "Faith is free, and no one can be compelled to believe," says Luther, which places the burden, the anxiety, the responsibility, precisely and exclusively on the individual's own soul to respond to God, or not. Only God can incline the soul and capture it from wickedness. The ruler's proper province is only over the outward things of "tribute, custom, honor, and fear."[57] However, if a prince commands an act that clearly violates conscience, then he should be disobeyed even at the cost of suffering and punishment.[58] Rulers should be reminded bluntly that

> I owe you obedience with my life and goods. Command me what lies within the limits of our authority, and I will obey. But if you command me to believe, or surrender my books, I will not obey. For then you [will have] become a tyrant and overreach[ed] yourself commanding where you have neither right or power.[59]

By contrast, if the subjects cannot clearly know if the prince is right or wrong (as is often the case), then it is not a sin but in fact a duty to obey the prince, even if the subject's obedience turns out to be objectively wrong.[60] Thus, the Christian is the clear-headed, grace-filled keeper of the distinction between the earthly and the heavenly kingdom, particularly when the sovereign has forgotten his wits and blurred the boundaries.

Conclusion

Luther's theological ontology described the human creative capacity to use reason toward our natural ends as holy work. In our vocations, we exercise natural capacities exactly as the Divine intended; our work is not a violation of divine will or a humanism with intrinsically sinful ends. The work of politics and law, sanctioned by theological accounts of justice, is possible precisely through rational freedom, the primary natural human way of both manifesting holy concern for the neighbor and fulfilling natural political duty.[61]

Luther's impact on the development of the separability of law from religion and moral culture was crucial. Implementation of his political theology shifted the authority of the government and its vast network of social institutions from the ecclesia to temporal powers.[62] His even-more-revolutionary view of the relationship between the subject and the law emerged in this notion that Christians had multiple vocations, multiples selves in differentiated spheres which the Christian was to both recognize and maintain. In articulating a vision of the separation of legal from religious moral culture, Luther was not advocating the disenchantment of law but merely the transfer of its enchantment through the mechanism of the natural order (a mechanism of the hidden God), the natural rational capacity of the creative subject, and its ultimate foundation in the natural goodness of the created order. But his enchantment was not ultimate in the sense of forging a New Jerusalem, for Luther's vision of the political order limited its role to the creation of a secure and stable mode of interactive justice. Creating a New Jerusalem was a religious matter between the human and the divine.

What united these two spheres was the need to secure the conditions of existence for human life and the demand to create structures that might insure respectful interaction. That the Christian might create temporal structures motivated by infused neighbor-love was a necessary component in Luther's understanding of the sanctification process. Indeed, as this chapter has noted, Luther argued that participation in the three temporal social spheres is mandatory for each Christian subject and an extension of the creation of God through the natural creative capacities of the human subject. All are called to service of others in the natural order.

In this way, Luther's focus on the individual as the subject and operator of this distinction represents a substantial step toward the kind of modern view of separation espoused by Madison. Where the medieval world gave the individual her place in the cosmos, Luther insisted the Christian must find her own conditions through the *vocatio*, or calling, and create this life out of given conditions. Christians participate actively and creatively in their callings, responding to the world's rational demands for their help as well as in obedience coerced by the state. But whatever else the Christian might do out of obedience to the reigning authorities, she alone is responsible to the Divine for enacting her neighbor-love in the natural world and secular institutions, simultaneously as a parent, a congregant, a political participant, and a Christian. Even if the political institutions maintain the separation and distinction upon which Luther and Madison insisted, ultimate responsibility remains with the individual subject. This is a difficult task—indeed interminable in this temporal horizon—that demands that one's heart and eyes must look and act in multiple directions at once. This is surely an uncomfortable and difficult life, but one that Luther thought achievable through grace, humility, and indeed, in a person's created natural capacities.

Notes

1 James Madison, "Memorial and Remonstrance against Religious Assessments," 20 June 1785, in Philip B. Kurland and Ralph Lerner, eds., *The Founders' Constitution*, vol. 5 (Chicago, IL: University of Chicago Press), 82–84.

2 Ibid.

3 Ibid.

4 Madison to F. L. Schaeffer, 3 December 1821, in *Letters and Other writings of James Madison, in Four Volumes*, Published by Order of Congress, vol. 3 (Philadelphia, PA: J. B. Lippincott & Co., 1865), 242–243.

5 Quentin Skinner, *The Foundations of Modern Political Thought*, vol. 2, *The Age of Reformation* (Cambridge: Cambridge University Press, 1978), especially, 15–19, 81–90, 349–354.
6 The author fully acknowledges that some of Luther's political decisions lack liberality, particularly in his reprehensible abandonment of the peasants. It seems that in some matters Luther had not fully driven to consistency in the implications of his own positions.
7 For general historical information about political thought in Germany at this time, see John Witte, *Law and Protestantism: The Legal Teachings of the German Reformation* (Cambridge: Cambridge University Press, 2002) and Ralph Keen, *Divine and Human Authority in Reformation Thought: German Theologians on Political Order 1520–1555* (Nieuwkoop: De Graaf Publishers, 1997).
8 Martin Luther, "The Freedom of a Christian," in John Dillenberger, ed., *Martin Luther: Selections from His Writings* (New York: Anchor Books, 1961), 73.
9 Ibid., 68.
10 Ibid., 75.
11 Ibid., 74.
12 Ibid., 53.
13 Martin Luther, *Temporal Authority: To What Extent It Should Be Obeyed* (1523), American edition of *Luther's Works* (hereafter *LW*), ed. Jaroslav Pelikan and Walter A. Hansen, 55 vols. (Philadelphia, PA: Fortress Press and St. Louis, MO: Concordia Publishing House, 1955–1986), *LW* 45, 10.
14 Martin Luther, *Lectures on Galatians* (1535), *LW* 26, 308.
15 Unlike, for instance, in Calvin, where the civil law is a "bridle." See John Calvin, *The Institutes of the Christian Religion*, ed. John T. McNeill (Philadelphia, PA: The Westminster Press, 1960), 2 vols, especially, vol. 2, book IV, chap. 20, and vol. 2, book IV, chap 10, nos. 5–8.
16 See Luther, *Temporal Authority*, *LW* 45, 87.
17 Martin Luther, *The Sermon on the Mount (Sermons)* (1532), *LW* 21, 114.
18 Ibid., 116.
19 For a helpful account, see Erling T. Teigen, "Two Kingdoms: Simul Iustus et Peccator: Depoliticizing the Two Kingdoms Doctrine" (paper presented at the Lutheran Free Conference, New Ulm, MN, November 7–8): 8–9.
20 See Augustine, *City of God*, *op. cit.* XIV:1:261 and I:16–18:353–63; see Luther, *Temporal Authority*, *LW* 45, 88–89. For Luther, the main purpose of the temporal sphere was simply to stop people from killing each other so that the Church could do its work and creation was not destroyed.
21 This term was used, not by Luther, but by Harald Diem in 1938. See William H. Lazareth, *Christians in Society: Luther, the Bible and Social Ethics* (Minneapolis, MN: Fortress Press, 2001) pp. 20–21. Diem's book is *Luther's Lehre von den Zwei Reichen* (Munich: Kaiser Verlag, 1938).
22 See Martin Luther, "Preface to the Epistle of St. Paul to the Romans," in Dillenberger, *Martin Luther*, 25: "Flesh, according to St. Paul … means everything that is born from the flesh, i.e. the entire self, body and soul, including our reason and all our senses."
23 Martin Luther, *Psalm 111*, *LW* v. 13: 369.
24 It was easy for Protestant reformers to misuse this argument to establish, and support, the legitimacy of, absolutist monarchies. See Skinner, p. 114, showing Luther's influence on the Scripturally-based absolutism of Jacques-Bénigne Bossuet (1627–1704), as in *Politics Drawn from the Very Words of Holy Scripture*, ed. P. Riley (Cambridge: Cambridge University Press, 1990), and Robert Filmer (1588–1653), *Patriarchia and Other Writings*, ed. J.P. Sommerville (Cambridge: Cambridge University Press, 1991).
25 Luther, *Psalm 82*, *LW* 13, 54.
26 J. N. Figgis, *Studies of Political Thought: From Gerson to Grotius, 1414–1625* (Bristol, UK: Thoemmes Press, 1998), 81.
27 Witte, *Law and Protestantism*, 113.
28 Martin Luther, *To the Christian Nobility of the German Nation Concerning the Reform of the Christian Estate*, *LW* 44, 203.
29 Figgis, 60.
30 Martin Luther, Letter "To Elector John [Coburg,] August 26, 1530," *LW* 49, 411; Martin Luther, *Psalm 101*, *LW* 13, 198.
31 Luther, *Psalm 111*, *LW* 13, 160. For Luther's reference to Aristotle, see Aristotle's *Politics*, III:13.
32 Luther, *Temporal Authority*, *LW 45*, 88.
33 Martin Luther, *Confession Concerning Christ's Supper* (1528), *LW* 37, 364–365.

34 Luther, *Lectures on Galatians*, *LW* 26, 94–95. For an excellent discussion of the hidden God in Luther and the epistemological crisis of uncertainty, see Susan Schreiner, "'Are You Alone Wise?' Unmasking the Angel of Light," in Michael Kessler and Christian Sheppard, eds., *Mystics: Presence and Aporia* (Chicago, IL: University of Chicago Press, 2003).

35 Luther, *Lectures on Galatians*, *LW* 26, 94–95.

36 Luther, *Psalm 101*, *LW* 13, 198.

37 Martin Luther, "Postil for Epiphany on Isaiah LX 1-6," in Brian Gerrish, ed. and trans., *Grace and Reason: A Study in the Theology of Luther* (Oxford: Clarendon Press, 1962) 12.

38 Ibid., 22.

39 Witte, *Law and Protestantism*, 114–115.

40 Ibid., 77.

41 Luther, *Psalm 101*, *LW* 13, 161. Much of Luther's articulation of authoritarian political structures can be traced to this anthropological assumption: a hierarchy of skills exists, and most humans are not that skilled in the arts of politics. Reason, cleverness, sharp wits, and perseverance are required for political rule and so few manifest these character traits. The vast majority should follow the few rational Hannibals and Solomons that God raises up amidst the horde of humans. See ibid., 160–165.

42 Ibid., 160, 164.

43 Luther, Psalm 111, *LW* 13, 369.

44 Martin Luther, *Psalm 45*, *LW* 12, 238.

45 Luther, *Psalm 82*, *LW* 13, 51–58. Luther emphasizes three virtues of the prince: securing justice for the god-fearing and suppressing the godless; helping the poor, orphans, and widows get justice and furthering their cause; and, protecting and guarding against violence and force.

46 Ibid., 41–72.

47 See Harold Berman, *Faith and Order: The Reconciliation of Law and Religion* (Atlanta, GA: Scholars' Press, 1993), 183. Berman emphasizes only the avoidance of confusion, and overlooks the anti-dogmatism to which Luther's position aims.

48 Luther, *Temporal Authority*, *LW* 45, 89.

49 Martin Luther, *Against Hanswurst*, *LW* 41, 248.

50 Martin Luther in George Forell, *Faith Active in Love: Investigation of Principles Underlying Luther's Social Ethics* (Minneapolis, MN: Augsburg, 1954), 123; cf. Luther, *Treatise on Good Works*, *LW* 44, 80ff. Luther articulates this three-part social order based on three levels of obedience to the commandment to "honor thy father and mother;" see Luther, *Confession Concerning Christ's Supper*, *LW* 37, 364–365.

51 Luther, *Confession Concerning Christ's Supper*, ibid.; the classic English study of the *vocatio* is in Gustaf Wingren, *Luther on Vocation*, trans. Carl C. Rasmussen (Philadelphia, PA: Muhlenberg Press, 1957); cf. F. Edward Cranz, *An Essay on the Development of Luther's Thought on Justice, Law, and Society* (Cambridge: Harvard University Press, 1959), pp. 153ff.

52 Luther, *Psalm 111*, *LW* 13, 364–365. The third realm, which I have not yet discussed, is the domestic sphere, responsible for marriage, procreation, the education of children, economic activity, and the order of private affairs. Due to Luther's understanding, Reformation countries removed the exclusive province of the canon law over marriage, family, and education and they became the business of the state. See Witte, *Law and Protestantism*, 199–292.

53 The notion of functional differentiation of social spheres, as described by Max Weber, means that in modernity, with the lifeworld no longer capable of producing social cohesion, complex and differentiated (and increasingly isolated) forms of bureaucratic structures emerge with a monopoly of power to regulate activity, social functions, and interaction. See Jürgen Habermas, *The Theory of Communicative Action*, vol. 2, *Lifeworld and System: A Critique of Functionalist Reason*, trans. Thomas McCarthy (Boston, MA: Beacon Press, 1985); cf. Niklas Luhman, *A Sociological Theory of Law*, trans. Elizabeth King-Utz and Martin Albrow, 2nd ed. (New York: Routledge, 2014). These bureaucratic structures of modern societies became rationalized and specialized with each sphere defined by specific processes of social reproduction. Thus each social structure that organizes and manages a different social function (e.g. law, education, land management, welfare, economy, etc.) utilizes a different set of rules, processes, purposes, reasons, and powers. This differentiation emerged from the social division of labor that changed the basis of social solidarity and social integration. See Emile Durkheim, *The Division of Labor in Society*, trans. George Simpson (New York: The Free Press, 1933) 41–46; cf. Max Weber, *The Protestant Ethic and the Spirit of Capitalism*, trans. Talcott Parsons (London: Routledge, 1992), I:2.

54 For an excellent assessment of Luther's understanding of subjectivity, see Mary Gaebler, "Luther on the Self," *Journal of the Society of Christian Ethics*, 22 (Fall, 2002), pp. 115–132.

55 Martin Luther, *The Sermon on the Mount (Sermons) and the Magnificat*, *LW* 21, 118.

56 Luther's reluctance to use coercive power over consciences is unlike Thomas Müntzer, who preached that a ruler was obliged to eradicate heresy or unbelief: "The weeds must be plucked out of the vineyard of God in the time of harvest," Thomas Müntzer, "Sermon before the Princes: An Exposition of the Second Chapter of Daniel" [1524], in George Williams, ed., *Spiritual and Anabaptist Writers* (Philadelphia, PA: Westminster Press, 1957), p. 68. For more on radical and militant religiosity, see Norman Cohn, *The Pursuit of the Millennium*, rev. ed. (New York: Oxford University Press, 1970).

Luther, however, shared a similar view of the responsibilities of public authorities with Erasmus, who writes, "The first and chief concern of the prince must be to serve the state to the best of his ability: he can do it no greater service than to ensure that the magistrature and its duties are entrusted to the most upright men, those most devoted to the common good. What is the prince but a physician to the state," Erasmus Desiderius, *The Education of a Christian Prince*, in Lisa Jardine, ed., trans. Neil M. Cheshire and Michael J. Heath (New York: Cambridge University Press, 2011).

57 Martin Luther, "Secular Authority: To What Extent It Should Be Obeyed," in Dillenberger, *Martin Luther*, 387.

58 It was on this point that Luther received much later critique. See, e.g., William Montgomery McGovern, *From Hitler to Luther: The History of Fascist Political Philosophy* (Cambridge: Houghton, Mifflin, 1941), arguing extensively that claiming simple obedience to the prince and removing the religious institutional check against the state set up the conditions for the modern fascist movement. See the helpful essays by Heinz Schilling "The Reformation and the Rise of the Early Modern State," and Eric Gritsch, "Luther and the State: Post-Reformation Ramifications" in James D. Tracy, ed., *Luther and the Modern State in Germany* (Kirksville, MO: Sixteenth Century Journal Publishers, 1986) 21–30, 45–60.

59 Luther, *Temporal Authority*, *LW* 45, 112.

60 Ibid., 125.

61 For the latter view, see especially Ernst Troeltsch, *Protestantism and Progress: A Historical Study of the Relation of Protestantism to the Modern World*, trans. W. Montgomery (Eugene, OR: Wipf and Stock Publishers, 1999) and *The Social Teachings of the Christian Churches*, 2 vols, trans. Olive Wyon (Louisville, KY: Westminster/John Knox Press, 1992).

62 See Witte, *Law and Protestantism*, pp. 177–292, where he carefully shows the conversion of civil, marriage, and education laws to secular governmental control.

5 Luther and Machiavelli—the human subject, religion and the state

Michael Reid Trice

Introduction

Martin Luther and Niccolò Machiavelli were both reformers in their own right. Contemporaries, although they lived in unique early Modern worlds, Luther and Machiavelli re-imagined the qualities of private piety, public virtue, the relationship between religion and government, and the specific markers of personal and political duty. Popular images depict Luther constructing his views with colleagues and students over a beer in Wittenberg, and Machiavelli meeting with his humanist colleagues at Cosimo Rucellai's gardens on the outskirts of Florence. Even so, they never met in person. If they had met, history might record protracted conversations about the central challenges of personal and political governance, the irascibility of a utopian political order, and the dangers of unchecked coercion in government, even as both differed by degree on these themes of early modern concern, and much more.

Their educations were distinct but not inseparable: Machiavelli, ten years Luther's senior, was trained in a climate of Italian Humanism, whereas Luther completed his education as an Augustinian friar. They both knew the Roman humanist philosophers. What they ultimately held in common included a belief in the power of the public voice, and a trust in their own capacities to enact change during a time of immense societal disruption; at this time, Europe was drifting from Feudalism to early Modernism, the seismic shudders of which are still heard in their respective thought. Amid this disruption, in their own ways, Machiavelli and Luther resisted the strictures of Scholasticism and went on to reconsider compelling notions of anthropology, the greater workings of society, and the proper function of the political sphere at large. This chapter will examine some of these specific notions, with a particular emphasis upon two pervasive themes: the nature and survival of the human subject amid the travails of the world, *and* the regulatory power of religion and government in relation to the human subject.

What is the human subject?

Martin Luther's theology of the human subject is evident in his *Lectures on Romans* (1515), his *Freedom of a Christian* (1520), and his *Lectures on Genesis* (1536). In the arc of his professional life, Luther wrote consistently, and persuasively for his time, about the corrupted psychological operations of the human subject, degenerated from an original state of perfection.[1]

Luther draws heavily upon Augustinianism and the theological formulation of original sin.[2] From birth to the grave, the fall of humankind in the Garden reveals the breadth and depth of sin upon human consciousness.[3] Luther describes in varying prose the *sin* within the human fall; his most memorable ruminations describe human consciousness as curved inward, akin to the ancient Egyptian icon of the *ouroboros*—the etching of a snake eating its own tail. "The most serious loss consists in this, that not only were those benefits [of pure insight of self and perfect union with God] lost, but man's will turned inward and [became] hidden from God."[4] At later moments, Luther crafts in detail the first pretentious blush of the progenitors, Adam and Eve, in Eden.[5] In both cases, the *esse* of sin spells calamity in two distinct ways: First, humanity has lost the benefit of God's original image or righteousness in creation; and second, the human subject devolves into something of a gray-eyed amnesiac, unaware of its current status and without recollection of how it arrived in this new place.[6] "What an ocean of knowledge and wisdom there was in this one human being! But [the knowledge] gradually became fainter in his descendants and has almost been blotted out."[7] Luther's sense of humanity's irretrievable hiddenness from both God and itself is evident in human ignorance of both God *and* its own interiority. Loss from sin is thus twofold.

But to fully understand Luther's theological anthropology, one must appreciate both the uniqueness of human ignorance after the fall, and its inability to self-repair. Humanity retains its mind, memory and will, but these are weakened and depraved, even "leprous," as a contagion within the human subject.[8] Only the bare essence of the knowledge of one's lost image may be inferred, albeit negatively, from the utter deprivation of the fallen intellect.[9] In short, the human subject recognizes that something is amiss. Yet it is somehow aware that all of this pretention, envy and hard-heartedness is a disordering yet oddly alien presence that coexists alongside aspirations for good, the selfless love of another, and the stirrings of faithfulness that seek no heraldry. In Luther's thought, one sees not a classical or Medieval theological anthropology of sin as the passive privation of God's original justice. Instead, any comprehension of a former image in positive detail is irrevocably lost to the human being in the past and remains a corrosive dynamic feature of life in the present.[10]

The loss of God's image, and the consequent *via negativa* acquisition of ignorance, enables the human subject, for whom sin "flatters and delights," to blame God for his or her state: "God is the author of his flight."[11] "This is the last step of sin, to insult God and to charge Him with being the originator of sin."[12] In his much later theological thinking, Luther portrays the human subject within this sheen of hubris, with an emphasis upon existential self-distrust and a commensurate, menacing psychological brittleness. Human subjectivity is like a failing structure: "When they hear the creaking of a beam, they are afraid that the entire house may collapse."[13]

Luther provides a comprehensive and pastoral view of the ontology of human brokenness, always with the whiff of the foreboding anxiety that he discovered first in both himself and in the young Augustine. It is fitting that Luther chose to become an Augustinian friar, as Augustine provided Luther with an anthropological lens for interpreting the human propensity for self-idolatry. Luther would agree that the classical warning of runaway self-love in the Greek figure of *Narcissus* was more fact than fable. The fact of our humanity, in Luther's view, is the seemingly limitless power of self-adoration evident in human beings, be they great or low.

In effect, for Luther, the corrosive psycho-social implications of human brokenness do impact every measurable barometer of the human capacity to govern itself, or to be governed in civic affairs.[14] Decades before René Descartes' introduction of the modern *cogito*, or indomitable "I," Luther's theological anthropology is a kaleidoscopic blend of three theological worldviews: Augustinian, Medieval and early Modern. These worldviews meet in a curious confluence within Luther's theological anthropology in this manner: The human subject is incapable of saving itself; *and yet* the vocation of the Self, the elevated liberty of the Family, and the freedom of the Christian within society all find expression in Luther's early Modern period, and more often first by his own hand.

We transition now to our second reformer, even though we must thereby admit that reformers come in many stripes. Certainly, this was true of Niccolò Machiavelli. From his influential 1498 appearance on the scene of Italian politics as second chancellor of the Florentine Republic, Machiavelli was and continues to be popularly conceived of as a person of low moral intent, as a man who infused his political philosophy with a brutal license for human immorality, and even as the smoking gun that first configured the political lie as a princely virtue.[15] We might even track the coercion of the "good lie" from early Modernism to our own post-Modern moment, and up to the coy reemergence in the twenty-first century of the so-called "alternative fact."[16] In large part, however, these are fanciful characterizations of Machiavelli, unaware of historical context and not wholly relevant to a critical appreciation of Machiavelli the reformer. Even as Machiavelli rationalizes the use of deceit in political governance, it is also the case that political coercion did not wait for Machiavelli's permission to justify its *raison* d'*être*; its dark stain was, and is today, evident on the floors of legislative chambers and circles of public governance everywhere.

What is true: Machiavelli was a political philosopher of the early sixteenth century whose pragmatism compelled him to assess the harsh, yet practicable, realities necessary for successful governance, with particular attention paid to his native Florence. He knew well the works of the Roman historians and moralist philosophers, including Livy's *History* and Cicero's *On Moral Obligation*, as well as *Tusculan Disputations* which offered moral advice to the youth of the Roman Empire.[17] His aim was to elevate Florence to a respectable stature within sixteenth century European politics; and in this quest, he thought he perceived the necessary corollaries for greatness to lie between the Roman Republic and his sixteenth century home. Of particular interest is how Machiavelli's philosophical anthropology—his interpretation of the human subject in the world—informed his stance on the human capacity for governance in society.[18]

In his short treatise, *Exhortation to Penitence*, Machiavelli writes that the created order was instituted for the sole benefit of humankind, and yet humans exhibit an existential pattern of ingratitude and envy.[19] Ingratitude and envy make up the two-stroke engine within the prideful human disposition, which is often obstreperous and unpleasant. Through pride, the human subject overreaches its own best interests in actions that uplift self-interest at the expense of the regulating sovereignties of the subject and the state. In humanity's overreach, Machiavelli is (unlike Luther) not principally concerned with the psychological deterioration of sin from assent to act; rather, he tracks the degenerative agency of ingratitude and envy both in terms of the human subject's interior vision and in its external loyalties as a citizen.[20]

For Machiavelli, interior ingratitude and envy are at their worst in the sunlight of daily life. But in what manner? Consider the human subject, who can conceal ingratitude and envy, and indeed may have no conscious awareness of either. Left untamed these vices will grow into more public displays of avarice and ambition within society.[21] Machiavelli is resolute on this fact: The unchecked combination of ambition and avarice within a citizenry retains enough fissional potential to lay to ruin an entire republic, a lesson Machiavelli believes he witnesses in his beloved classical Rome.[22] Machiavelli sees a peculiar alchemy of societal forces in sixteenth century Florence like that we identify after the French Revolution, and in particular within the modern and post-modern critique, as *ideology*.

By ideologies we mean those webbed and enclosed matrixes of belief that are imposed on daily life, and that often excite the powerful against perceived enemies within society. This alchemy is as evident within sixteenth century Florence as it is in within the twenty-first century, in the following way: Ambition will convince avarice that its cause is rational and must be defended, and avarice will compel ambition that it is just to defend its cause. This simplified, enclosed binary of a justice-minded yet vengeful rationale is capable of defending the presumed good—no matter *how* diabolical—even if it means attacking every perceived enemy with impunity. This is the pattern Machiavelli sees in societal life, and it poses dangers to effective governance.

In Machiavelli's philosophical anthropology, his two-stroke prideful engine of ingratitude and envy operates as the ontological site or condition of the human subject.[23] Daily wickedness of the spirit is due principally to these two vices. Machiavelli and Luther would agree with the Apostle Paul's glimpse into the window of his own soul: Paul rebukes himself for doing the things he does not desire to do, and in an equally telling fashion is astonished for not doing what is clearly within his reach and which he desired all along.[24]

If we accept the views of two reformers, what must we conclude about humanity in general terms? Contrary forces are at work in the interiority of the human subject, and these forces greatly impact both self-governance and the governance of society writ large. For both thinkers, effective laws will thus always be a necessity, even as the lawful constraint of human conceit will never be equivalent to healing what ails humanity. In this analysis, both Luther and Machiavelli are learned pragmatists; one would endure attempted assassinations and the other would endure torture, and in life both also knew enough of history to commend to the world a proper, functional and lasting reliance on jurisprudence and the juridical mandates of the state.[25] And yet, each reformer considered the regulatory power and mutual proximity of religion to the state in different ways, which is our next consideration.

Religion and the state

Machiavelli and Luther are both early modern challengers of the political supremacy of the papacy through independent critiques of the abuse of the power and influence of the Catholic Church. These challenges continued through the Enlightenment and became enshrined in modern constitutions via the separation and protection of religion from government (and vice-versa). In fact, given the culture wars in the United States of the last two decades, and considering the heightened degree of sectarian-influenced conflict all over the world, the perspectives of Machiavelli and Luther upon the relationship between religion and government, are important to understand.

Martin Luther did not formulate a systematic political ethic in his lifetime, even as he was not naïve about the consequential art of political coercion. He was a pastoral theologian above all else, and in this capacity advised numerous constituencies: his congregation, pupils, local princes, town leaders, the broader church and the wider magistrates of the state. At the axis of religion-state relations, much of Luther's professional attention is dedicated to the aims of civil obedience, the limitations of secular force and the vocation of the Christian in civic affairs. At the crescent of early Modernity, he was a pioneer figure in configuring the gospel and the church as divinely instituted and autonomous realms under God's sovereign power. The state thus retains its authority; but in Luther's age, it also acquires an emerging early Modern accessibility by which Christians may, in good conscience, heed their divinely ordained vocation within the secular realm. This has meant that Lutheran-Christians have had little license to be political quietists, unlike Anabaptist separatists of the time. Luther saw no evidence of quietism in Jesus of Nazareth.[26] As such, a Christian is always a servant in both realms of God's ultimate authority.

Under the canopy of this divine authority, the conventional relationship between Luther's popularly named "two governments" or "two kingdoms" drew first upon the long shadow of Augustine's argument with the Donatists, and Augustine's theological differentiation between God's society and the society of the World, crystalized within Augustine's *City of God* a thousand years prior to Luther.[27] For Augustine, there are two societies and two citizenships. One society is ordered by the love of God and neighbor, whereas the other society is disordered and fragmented, due principally to the loss of God's original image (*Imago Dei*) through sin.[28] Augustine never fully reconciled the Manichaean divide that cleaved his theology, evident in his description of the society of God and the society of the World, one often characterized as a higher realm of spirit and light, the other a mundane domain of flesh and darkness.

Although Luther accepted an initial Augustinian dichotomy between religion and state, as noted, his theological project was focused on how the Christian subject participates in both realms. In *On Secular Authority*, Luther sees a scriptural optic for Christian service in the Sermon on the Mount: God is sovereign over all the earth and thus over both governments (i.e., church and kingdom, or church and secular government). Those who endeavor within these two governments seek a shared goal, which is the common good of humankind in the divine order. Even so, both governments are distinguished by their divinely instituted, autonomous laws and duties, and therefore have their own separate means of attaining this common goal. If the means or laws of one government encroach upon the authority of the other in the attainment of this good, chaos ensues.[29] For instance, if a prince rules the secular realm with the gospel, Luther writes that he will have loosed "the bands and chains of the wild and savage beasts and [let] them tear and mangle everyone, and at the same time say they were tame and gentle creatures; but I would have the proof in my wounds."[30] For Luther, in short, state-sponsored theocratic rule based on the gospel must never be permitted to rule the secular realm, where "the wicked always outnumber the good." No!—for the purpose of maintaining order, "it is out of the question that there should be a common Christian government over the whole world, nay even over one land or company of people."[31] In this aspect of his thought, we see Luther as the theological and pastoral pragmatist; his theological anthropology even here informs the essential corrective nature of the law and the state.

But then, in a global context of two governments, and indeed in light of two distinct realms of authority, how shall the Christian-citizen live? For Luther, a close dialectical relationship exists between religion and the state: Even as the gospel never supersedes the rule of secular government, it does preserve a chief function of procuring a "good conscience" within the Christian.[32] It is through a good conscience that the Christian acts in all ways in service to the neighbor within both governments. And, in essence, every good work performed in service to the state is a work on behalf of the neighbor.[33] Insofar as the two governments are separate realms and jurisdictions, temporal power is necessary *not* as a means of protecting my needs first, but primarily and certainly as a vehicle for the protection and advancement of my neighbors.[34] Put another way, the secular law is an instrument of divine capacity in the world and a secular means of achieving the gospel dictum of loving the neighbor. What should not be lost in this discussion is Luther's early Modern emphasis upon the liberty of the other *as distinct from* the later Enlightenment abstracted emphasis upon the right of the state. Luther's view is likewise not identical with any contemporary exercise of the law in defense of abstract, individual rights. His interpretation of the law is almost always connected to the defense of neighbors in proximity to one another. Every public and private act is in service to the neighbor.

In his career, Luther's views of justice for the neighbor are always placed in relation to what he sees as the immutable justice of God. For instance, in *Bondage of the Will* (1525), Luther describes God's immutable justice and kindness as aimed at persuasion and correction of the religious enthusiasts and rebellious peasants.[35] After the disastrous Peasants' Revolt, however, Luther's position matures with the experience: the canons of the law do favor one party over another and, in the execution of swift justice, the law will appear inequitable and oppressive. Luther makes a distinction between the mandates of the law and the advancement of justice in this way: The aspirations of justice are never identical with the severity of the law. "The strictest law is the greatest wrong, and therefore equity is necessary. This is not a rash relaxation of laws and discipline ... but the weighing [for equity] must be of such kind that the law isn't undermined."[36] For the later Luther, law and equity are both essential for justice. Luther's later ruminations on justice square with the early Luther's core pastoral approach in the theology of the cross: Even as the cross of Christ provides redemption in one kingdom, perfect justice is never achieved in the other kingdom. Nevertheless, the struggle for justice continues because the neighbor lives in both kingdoms.

Luther's theology encourages Christian values as a *means* of service in both kingdoms, where both are essential as a means of serving the neighbor. Machiavelli's political philosophy, however, is a partial reaction to what he sees as the weakness of Christian virtues already far too ensconced in the business of the state.[37] His sense of the usefulness of religion pertains to its proper *end* for maintaining the obedience and civility of its citizenry.[38] Machiavelli's ends-based approach to religion is what he found admirable within the Roman Republic: Roman paganism created vigorous citizens bound together through a sacred oath. Their allegiance to the gods and the state was unambiguous, earnest and a catalyst for corporate strength.[39]

Machiavelli's unfavorable view of Christian virtue as soft on moral strength, and his idealized view of the Roman pagan virtue of fortitude, is an early Modern critique that reaches its apex in the nineteenth century and principally within Friedrich Nietzsche's superlative creation of the superman (*übermensch*).[40] In the sixteenth century, Machiavelli writes, "our religion [Christianity] has glorified humble and contemplative men rather than active ones," and in so doing has prized humility above the Roman grandeur of mind; Christianity has chosen weakness over "all other things apt to make men exceedingly vigorous."[41] And, when one is vigorous—or has the true *vir* within his character—then the citizen will exude a moral constitution that, first, never conceives of suffering as an elevated virtue akin to faithfulness; and second, is able to exhibit all of the necessary fortitude required for a noble life.[42] "Though our religion asks that you have fortitude within you, it prefers that you be adapted to suffering rather than to do something vigorous."[43] The problem with Christian morality is its misalignment of fortitude with a life of suffering, rather than as a personal virtue of strength within and for the public good.

As noted above, Machiavelli is sometimes misconstrued as a twenty-first century Bannon-*esque* populist ideologue; he is instead a sixteenth century political philosopher who is focused on advising his native Florence. Machiavelli witnessed in his own lifetime how quickly the structures of society can come unfastened through revolt; as a consequence, he trusted education to both inspire the citizen, and constrain his or her more ignoble and savage features.[44] Note here Machiavelli's ultimate emphasis on the 'we' (*citizenry*) over the 'I' (*citizen*). Machiavelli's social and political philosophy is reliant upon, and trusts, a strong collective citizenry. This is not true for Luther, whose pastoral focus is chiefly on the liberty of the individual conscience before God. Luther's prevailing and pastoral desire to address the individual often conceals his mistrust for collective human action and his skepticism as to whether human beings will act in concert for the benefit of all. Luther learned a lesson through the Peasants' Revolt; all in all, human subjects act differently in groups; riots are always activities in the plural, and a lynching is very seldom a private affair. For both Luther and Machiavelli, education in the proper virtues is an essential and perhaps only ultimately enduring corrective, to the mob.[45] But these reformers will differ on which virtues are a means toward that educational corrective.

Finally, according to Machiavelli, religion has a few discernable functions.[46] It is the best public instrument for inspiring fear and awe, and for persuading a public toward obedience. In fact, Machiavelli regularly commends the rituals of religion, which must be preserved from corruption insofar as their symbolic power is always *both* signaling a citizenry to endeavor beyond the imposition of its own limitations *and* correcting aberrant moral and public dissonance within its ranks.[47] Religious rituals also foster the best of public memory, ascertain a citizenry's present identity, and signal its future promise. This is the nature of a ritual—to repeat the story of the public, to avail that public with the deeds of its native heroes, and to encourage the citizenry to go and do likewise. Religious ritual is central to Machiavelli's assessment of religion as a public good.

In end effect, Machiavelli is very clear about the relationship between religion and the state: The aspiration of religious activity is about curating allegiance to the singular vision of the state. One can thus read in Machiavelli both late Feudalism and early Modernism. Machiavelli desires subjects of the state to be obedient above all else for the unity of the state, which is not to be mistaken as an appeal to Enlightenment egalitarianism. Consider this clarification: *Unicity* is a term that underscores allegiance to oneness, whereas *unity* implies the collective achievement of many parts toward a whole or consensus. For Machiavelli, *unicity*, or allegiance to unmitigated oneness, (and *not* unity as described above) is the highest achievement of the citizenry within the state.[48]

Machiavelli's emphasis on unicity over unity, or singular oneness over collective wholeness, is especially evident in our final assessment of the relationship between religion and government. In a phrase, for Machiavelli, religion will always be the handmaiden of the state. Religion will be exercised through political control and, where necessary, through political coercion, whenever and wherever the state requires the support of religion to buttress its authority. Where unicity is the highest achievement of the state, then the state will necessarily foster the allegiance of a well-ordered citizenry and military alike.[49] The religious stories of heroes, shared virtues, the morals of public life, the obedience of the citizen, and even singular ambition are all within the proper gaze of the state and the needs of its administrators, the princes and magistrates. Finally, we might ask whether Machiavelli believes that religion is true or needs to be true. We might conclude that for him, religious truths are always *true* insofar as they are useful to the public.

Conclusion

Martin Luther and Niccolò Machiavelli are two reformers and contemporaries, whose histories positioned them at the confluence of shifting societal forces. These forces range from Feudalism and late Scholasticism to the Reformation and late-Humanist reconsideration of the human subject and emerging interpretations of the relationship between religion and the state. It is possible to read these thinkers and their times as a final product, as a complete and static history of ideas, but this is not advisable. Rather, both emerged within their historical locus and responded to serious societal questions that are still unresolved today, including: What is the mystery of the human subject? How does it govern itself in community and the world? And, what are the realms of collective governance that are necessary for societal well-being in this age?

Both Machiavelli and Luther share a pre-Enlightenment view of the human subject untainted by the ideology of evolutionary progressivism, abstract rights, and the nation state as a hegemonic power. Even so, matters of effective governance, the specter of theocratic rule, the equitable pendulum between law and justice, and in particular the relationship between religion and government, are as complex now as they have ever been. Amid these complexities, Luther's emphasis upon the law as protective of the neighbor rather than established in the pursuit of abstract right, and Machiavelli's invocation of fortitude when the public conversation in our age is alight with notions of "resilience" are ideas worthy of our continued attention.

For all their exploration of the human subject, both of these thinkers are more romanticist than either would have imagined possible in his own self-assessment. They both provide distinct yet mutual admiration for a former time of human excellence, untarnished by the present; and, in so doing, they teach humanity something about itself. Namely, humans are often haunted by nostalgic yearning, then as now; in our poetry, prose, music, film and more, we often attempt to reclaim a narrative of our former innocence that is always only part truth, and always ever part fable. And yet, even here on the matter of the human subject, Luther and Machiavelli delight us with insights: Both understand the ravages of narcissism on the interior subject and the public good; both recognize a human capacity for loss of memory (amnesia) or a lack of desire (ambivalence); both distrust the individual or collective citizenry in navigating a future external to the constraints of the law; and both struggle to interpret how to understand the facets and features of a citizen's vocation and obedience in the world.

In the last analysis, these reformers inspire the reader with a confidence for meeting the challenges of their historical moments. They applied themselves amid division, and with no small amount of danger to themselves, in order to make sense of their worlds. Their convictions, however different from each other, assisted their age, and ours also, with an influence that has traversed a half a millennium to our day.

Notes

1 Martin Luther, *Lectures on Genesis*, trans. George V. Schick, American edition of *Luther's Works* (hereafter *LW*), eds. Jaroslav Pelikan, and Helmut T. Lehmann, 55 vols. (Philadelphia, PA: Fortress Press and St. Louis, MO: Concordia Publishing House, 1955–1986), 1, 141–144.
2 Ibid., 6–7, 82–84. Luther's analogy of humanity as the potter's clay is worthy of a read. "Until our death and in the grave, we remain the clay of this potter."
3 Ibid., 62–63. See also *Sermon at Leipzig & Erfurt* (1519), *LW* 51, 62.
4 Luther, *Lectures on Genesis*, *LW* 1, 141; Martin Luther, "Bondage of the Will," in John Dillenberger, ed., *Martin Luther: Selections from His Writings* (New York: Anchor Books, 1962), 192.
5 *Lectures on Genesis*, *LW* 1, 147, 155, and 159. See also Martin Luther, "Preface to Romans," in John Dillenberger, ed., *Martin Luther: Selections from His Writings* (New York: Anchor Books, 1962), 22. Luther describes sin as the disobedient impulse operating in the depths of human hearts.
6 *LW* 54, 426; see also *LW* 51, 245, *Two Funeral Sermons* (1532).
7 *Lectures on Genesis*, *LW* 1, 120. A parallel is found in *LW* 51, 39, *Two Lenten Sermons* (1518).
8 *Lectures on Genesis*, *LW* 1, 61; see also *LW* 51,114.
9 *Lectures on Genesis*, *LW* 1, 113; see also *Two Sermons at Weimar* (1522) where Luther describes human fallenness as a "blind nature."

10 *Lectures on Genesis, LW* 1, 35; nuances on these themes of forgetfulness and lack of personal insight are evident in *Ten Sermons on the Catechism* (1528), *LW* 51, 164.
11 *Lectures on Genesis, LW* 1, 163, and 266–267.
12 Ibid., 179; see also Martin Luther, "Preface to the Psalms," in John Dillenberger, ed., *Martin Luther: Selections from His Writings* (New York: Anchor Books, 1962), 39.
13 *Lectures on Genesis, LW* 1, 170; similar themes are resonant in Martin Luther "Freedom of a Christian," in John Dillenberger, ed., *Martin Luther: Selections from His Writings* (New York: Anchor Books, 1962), 57.
14 *Lectures on Genesis, LW* 1, 170.
15 See Leo Strauss, *Thoughts on Machiavelli* (Glencoe, IL: The Free Press, 1958), 9.
16 Ibid., 9–10.
17 Quentin Skinner, *Great Political Thinkers: Machiavelli, Hobbes, Mill, Marx* (Oxford: Oxford University Press, 1992), 11–12.
18 Principal texts of Niccolò Machiavelli are from Allan Gilbert, trans., *Machiavelli: The Chief Works and Others.* 3 vols. (Durham, NC: Duke University, 1965).
19 *Exhortation to Penitence*, in Gilbert 1, 170. In 1495 Machiavelli became a member of a Florentine religious company called the Company of Piety. This particular oration, although of indeterminate date, originated between 1495 and 1500.
20 Niccolò Machiavelli, *Tercets on Ingratitude*, in Gilbert 2, 740, 744. Machiavelli writes: "When the stars, when the heavens were indignant at human pride, for man's abasement Ingratitude was born into the world."
21 Machiavelli, *Tercets on Ambition*, 10, 735; 67, 736.
22 *Discourses*, Bk. 1: 46–47, 290–291, in Gilbert 1; see also *Tercets on Ambition*, 88, 737. Ambition and avarice welcome disorder. Machiavelli laments this in France's occupation of Italy. "And why upon these lands has come the affliction of that wicked seed which Ambition and Avarice bring to fruit."
23 Niccolò Machiavelli, *Discourses*, Bk. 3.9, 452.
24 Romans 7:15–19.
25 This was Cicero's conviction as well. A solid moral education may mend the loose threads in a person's moral character; see also *Tercets on Ambition*, 112, 737, "... for disciplines can make up where Nature is lacking."
26 The vocation of Jesus Christ is defined by a lack of quietism, which informs Luther's Christology, ecclesiology and Christian ministry of vocation. From the mediating presence of Christ in *Freedom of a Christian*, to the vocational office exercised in *On Secular Authority*, Luther assumes the redemptive power of Jesus Christ to cross every viable frontier of human life, just as the human response to the activity of redemption is never a passive state in relation to God, neighbor, or indeed the whole world.
27 Augustine, *On Baptism against the Donatists, Nicene and Post-Nicene Fathers*, ed. P. Schaff, vol. 4 (Grand Rapids, MI: Eerdmans, 1929), 421, 424.
28 Augustine, *The City of God*, ed. V. Bourke (New York: Image Books, 1953), 14.1.
29 Walter Altmann, "Interpreting the Doctrine of the Two Kingdoms: God's Kingship in the Church and in Politics," *Word & World* 7: No. 1 (1987): 47.
30 Martin Luther, "On Secular Authority," in John Dillenberger, ed., *Martin Luther: Selections from His Writings* (New York: Anchor Books, 1962), 371.
31 Luther, *Freedom of a Christian*, *LW* 31, 349, 371, and 372–373.
32 Luther, *LW* 14, 179.
33 Luther, *On Secular Authority*, 374–376.
34 Ibid., 373–375.
35 Luther, *Bondage of the Will*, 371.
36 Martin Luther, "Laws Must Be Interpreted with Equity," Table Talk, No. 4178, *LW* 54, 325.
37 Machiavelli, *Discourses* Bk. 2.2, 331 and *Tercets on Ambition*, 118–121, 737.
38 Maurizio Viroli, "Machiavelli and the Republican Idea of Politics," in Gisella Bock, Quentin Skinner, and Maurizio Viroli, eds., *Machiavelli and Republicanism* (Cambridge: Cambridge University Press, 1993), 57.
39 Quentin Skinner, "The Republican Ideal of Political Liberty," in Gisella Bock, Quentin Skinner, and Maurizio Viroli, eds., *Machiavelli and Republicanism* (Cambridge: Cambridge University Press, 1993), 306.
40 Machiavelli, *Discourses*, Bk. 1.12, 227.

41 Ibid., Bk. 3.27, 328–337.
42 Machiavelli, *Tercets on Ambition*, 118–121, 737.
43 Machiavelli, *Discourses*, Bk. 3.27, 328–337.
44 Niccolò Machiavelli, *Familiar Letters* 10, August 25, 1513. 920; see also Cicero, *Tusculan Disputations*, 5.21–24, 449.
45 Machiavelli, *Tercets on Ambition*, 112, 737. "... for disciplines can make up where nature is lacking."
46 See Machiavelli, *Discourses*, Bk. 1.12, 227 and 3.9, 452.
47 Ibid., Bk. 1.12, 227.
48 Ibid., Bk. 1.12, 227.
49 Ibid., 1. 11, 225; see also Bk. 3.2–4, 421–426.

6 Luther's two strategies and political advocacy

Law, righteousness, reason, will, and works in their civil use

Craig L. Nessan

How might a Christian think theologically and ethically about participation in political advocacy for legislation or public policy? This question is particularly urgent given the persistent—yet mistaken!—notion that separation of church and state would preclude Christian involvement in the work of political advocacy. Political advocacy refers to efforts by the church to change society's structures, promote economic policies, and enact legislation that is consistent with God's purpose of bringing forth the kingdom/shalom of God. Employing Luther's two kingdoms as a constructive paradigm for interpreting his theology proves fruitful as a framework for understanding the dynamics of Christian political advocacy. In order to appropriate Luther's teaching, we first need to reinterpret Luther's two kingdoms teaching constructively as God's two strategies for ruling the world. Next we clarify several misinterpretations of and apparent contradictions in his thought. Just as it has proven customary and insightful to distinguish between two uses of the law in Luther's writings, so we also gain clarity about his understanding of righteousness, reason, will, and works by recognizing both a civil and a theological use of these key concepts. Finally, this chapter draws conclusions for the work of political advocacy by contrasting religious identity politics with neighbor politics as alternative approaches by Christians.

Luther's two kingdoms as two strategies

Although the usefulness of Luther's two kingdoms teaching has been severely challenged due to its tragic misinterpretations in the late nineteenth and twentieth centuries, especially in the Nazi period, it remains a constructive paradigm for understanding the dialectical character of Luther's thought.[1] One fundamental mistake involves interpreting the "two" kingdoms as two separated realms of activity, often identified as the division between church and state.[2] Whereas separation of church and state refers constitutionally to the limitation placed upon government to impose religious beliefs on citizens, many Christians persist in thinking that the Establishment Clause of the First Amendment to the U.S. Constitution means that the church as church (and thereby Christians as Christians) should have nothing to do with politics. This leaves many church members questioning the legitimacy of the church's social teaching as a guide to political advocacy, particularly as it comes to expression in social statements.[3] By contrast, a dialectical interpretation of Luther's two kingdoms, understood as God's two strategies for ruling the world, distinguishes between the two kingdoms but does not separate the interconnections between them. Whereas it is confusing to employ the spatial metaphor of "kingdom" to conceptualize Luther's proposal without thinking in terms of a separation of realms, the use of the term "strategies" is conducive to understanding that God can work in two distinguishable but interrelated ways.[4]

Luther had a vivid imagination about how God was engaged in a battle with Satan for the control of this world.[5] This is another challenging aspect of Luther's two-strategies approach in a world where many no longer understand Satan as a personal figure against whom God contends for human allegiance. The reinterpretation of the principalities and powers in the New Testament as "structural evil" can be of assistance in reclaiming the dynamism of Luther's theology in opposition to the influence of evil.[6]

According to Luther, God employs two distinct but interrelated strategies for extending God's kingdom. Each of these strategies employs particular means to accomplish God's purposes. According to the right-hand strategy, God accomplished salvation by the work of Jesus Christ. Central to Luther's concept is that this occurs according to justification by grace through faith. This gift is mediated through Word and Sacrament as the means of grace. Proclamation of the Word includes preaching and teaching but also encompasses verbal communication of the Christian faith by church members in all their roles and relationships in life.[7] Holy Baptism and Holy Communion are sacraments by which Jesus Christ incorporates members into the body of Christ and nourishes them with his body and blood.

For Luther, a central gift of the Gospel of Jesus Christ is Christian freedom. Jesus Christ grants believers *freedom from* everything that holds them in bondage. This means, according to the Small Catechism, that Jesus Christ sets people free from all sins, from death, and from the power of the devil. It is equally vital to understand that Jesus Christ also grants believers *freedom for!* Although Christian existence always remains under the proviso of *simul justus et peccator* (simultaneously saint and sinner), Christian freedom also really means freedom for service to the neighbors God gives us in this world. By the power of the Holy Spirit working through the Gospel as mediated by the means of grace, Christians are sent into the world to embody the neighborliness (*diakonia*) of all believers.[8] This sending propels the baptized to participate in God's left-hand strategy for ruling the public world as described in this chapter.

Justice is the public form of love.[9] God's left-hand strategy involves God's governing the public world through structures that serve to protect from harm and to approximate justice. In the sixteenth century, Luther named three institutions established by God to order the world: family, government, and church. At that time family encompassed not only familial relations but the economic livelihood of the family. Given the demarcation between family and work after the Enlightenment, it is more useful today to think about four interrelated arenas of public responsibility for Christians: family, work, government, and church as religious institution (commensurate with synagogue, mosque, temple, etc., in their respective religious contributions to the public good).

Christians are formed by worship and the narrative of Scripture to render service to neighbors in God's left hand strategy.[10] These neighbors include members of one's own family, persons served through relationships in the workplace and through the work itself, those whose lives are affected by involvements in one's local community, those served by political advocacy for just legislation and policies, and people impacted by the contributions of religious institutions to civil society. It is important to stress that it is not only Christians who serve neighbors through these arenas but, according to Lutheran theology, God also seeks to engage all people, whether religious or not, to serve neighbors through these arenas in the left-hand strategy. While Christians may be aware that it is for Christ's sake that they are serving neighbors in these arenas, for Luther, all people are serving neighbors in these capacities whether they know it or not, thereby doing God's will.

God's left-hand strategy aims at an ever greater approximation of justice for the common good, evaluated by how the most vulnerable (for example, the poor; ethnic, racial, and religious minorities; victims of violence; and endangered creation) are faring. This norm for evaluating political advocacy sets priorities in each of four arenas. First, family politics involves guaranteeing nutrition (food security) and nurture (strong public education) for the next generation. Food security and public education are foundational for the stability of the social order and for the informed participation of citizens needed in civil society. Second, central priorities in advocating for economic justice involve securing sufficient livelihood for those engaged in employment and taking into consideration the intrinsic significance of work, so that people's abilities and talents are put to use in meaningful ways. Not only are adequate wages and benefits needed for just work, but also affirmation of the dignity and gifts of those doing the labor.

Third, participatory democracy entails advocacy before government officials—at local, state, and federal levels—toward serving the common good through laws that provide equity among all members of civil society with particular attention to the well-being of the most endangered ("the least"). People of religious faith have responsibility not only to advocate for laws that serve the well-being of the entire society but to privilege the needs of the poor and marginalized in their political advocacy. Good government must always be measured by how those most vulnerable and marginalized, including creation itself, are treated. The contribution of religious institutions to the public good involves instilling a sense of gratitude among religious people that leads to generosity on behalf of neighbors. Regardless of the faith tradition, religious beliefs can foster a basic sense of thankfulness for life that leads to a generous response to the needs of others.

Christians are called to work together and build coalitions with all those who share their commitments to the common good, whether or not those allies are Christian or religious. In order to clarify the dialectical relationship between God's right-hand theological and left-hand civil strategies, it is useful to contrast and distinguish how we understand several human capacities in relation to each of these strategies. In every case the theological use correlates with Christian *freedom from* what holds humans in bondage according to the right-hand strategy, while the civil (and proper!) use corresponds to *freedom for* according to the left-hand strategy.[11] In this regard, it is useful to distinguish not only between two uses of the law from a Lutheran perspective, but also two uses of righteousness, reason, will, and works. Precision about these categories from a Lutheran perspective can assist in elucidating the particular responsibilities of Christian engagement in political advocacy.

Two uses of the law

As evidenced by classical interpreters, it is conventional in Lutheran theology to distinguish between a first civil use of the law and a second theological use. Bernard Lohse makes the bold claim that "Luther is clearly the first in all of the history of dogma and theology to view the law from the viewpoint of its *usus*, thus in its concrete function."[12] Lohse concisely analyzes Luther's twofold use of the law:

> The two functions of the law are the "political" or "civic" and the "theological." Here too there is a profusion of formulas and terms. By means of the political use, external order on earth is to be maintained, and peace and the securing of justice preserved. The law has also the task of inculcating the divine commandments and of instructing the consciences. It also furnishes the needed means by which to punish evildoers. The

> order established by the political use of the law is effected through the offices of the temporal authorities, of parents, of teachers, and of judges, instituted by God for this purpose. If the law in its political use is obeyed, then an "external," "civic" righteousness is achieved, to which Luther assigned the highest value ... The "theological" use comprises the authentic task of the law. It is, so to speak, the law in its spiritual sense. This use serves to show persons their sin, to "convict" them of sin.[13]

The distinction between the two uses of the law by Luther is grounded directly on his theological paradigm of the two strategies.[14] Due to the prevalent misinterpretation of the two kingdoms as realms separating church from public life, leading to political quietism (for example, under fascism in Nazi Germany), a more dynamic approach views the two kingdoms as distinct but complementary forms of divine activity. God engages ambidextrously to rule the world with the Gospel of Jesus Christ according to the right hand theological strategy and by means of the structures and institutions of public life according to the left hand civil strategy.

Two uses of righteousness: civil and alien

It is equally compelling to parse other central categories of Luther's thought according to their contrasting uses and functions in relation to the two strategies. Thus Luther also distinguishes two contrasting forms of righteousness. In God's right hand theological strategy, the only righteousness that matters is the alien righteousness that belongs to the sinner through justification by grace alone through faith alone in Christ Jesus:

> The righteousness of Christ is imputed to the sinner. God sees the sinner as one with Christ. He forgives his sin and considers the sinner to be righteous for Christ's sake. Thus the righteousness granted to the sinner is not his own produced by himself but an "alien" righteousness belonging to Jesus Christ.[15]

By the work of Christ, the sinner receives the alien righteousness of Jesus Christ as pure gift (*extra nos*) and becomes for Christ's sake, through faith, truly righteous before God.

Civil righteousness, by contrast, is that form of righteousness that all persons perform in doing justice through the right functioning of institutions, offices, relationships, and roles in service to neighbors in God's left hand civil strategy. God structures daily life and provides order through those who live out their roles with responsibility for the care of others as neighbors.

> Thus this outward righteousness is indeed considered less valuable than the true righteousness of the Christian. However, it does have positive value, for it says "that in his station everyone should do his duty." If people were seriously concerned about this secular righteousness, "there would be no rascality or injustice, but sheer righteousness and blessedness on earth."[16]

Human ethical capacity, even under the condition of sin, can and does contribute a measure of civil righteousness to the created world according to the left hand civil strategy. This civil righteousness remains at best an approximation of God's created purposes, however, due to the pervasiveness of human waywardness, which becomes manifest in not only personal but also structural sinfulness.

The distinction between the first and second uses of righteousness is fruitful for elucidating not only the centrality of the work of Christ in imputing alien righteousness according to God's theological strategy but especially for promoting the ethical responsibility of human beings in contributing to public righteousness for their neighbors according to God's civil strategy. Both forms of righteousness have their proper location and uses within Luther's theology.

Two uses of reason: gift and "harlot"

Luther famously asserted against reason, "And what I say about the sin of lust, which everybody understands, applies also to reason; for reason mocks and affronts God in spiritual things and has in it more hideous harlotry than any harlot."[17] The standard view regarding Luther's understanding of human reason is largely informed by his polemic in The Bondage of the Will. Here Luther, in defense of the doctrine of justification by pure grace through faith in Jesus Christ, takes an aggressive stance against the synergism of late medieval scholastic theology, even as represented by a moderate figure like Erasmus. Reason confronts its absolute limit in relation to what God has revealed in Jesus Christ for accomplishing salvation. God's right hand theological strategy has been fulfilled neither through human reasoning nor by the cooperation of the human will, but solely by God's inscrutable action in the death and resurrection of Jesus Christ:

> Ask reason herself whether she is not convinced and compelled to confess that she is foolish and rash in not allowing the judgment of God to be incomprehensible, when she admits that everything else divine is incomprehensible ... We cannot for a while believe that he is righteous, even though he has promised us that when he reveals his glory we shall all both see and feel that he has been and is righteous.[18]

Human beings do not cooperate with God in the attainment of eternal salvation. To claim a human role, even a minor one, would be an affront to the majesty and glory of God, who has taken sole responsibility for all matters pertaining to human redemption.

Whereas Luther takes a decidedly negative stance against the use of reason in the right-hand theological strategy, his writings demonstrate the positive and valued use of reason through human engagement with creation according to the left-hand civil strategy:

> [I]t is certainly true that reason is the most important and the highest in rank among all things and, in comparison with other things of this life, the best and something divine ... It is the inventor and mentor of all the arts, medicines, laws, and of whatever wisdom, power, virtue, and glory men possess in this life ... By virtue of this fact it ought to be named the essential difference by which man is distinguished from the animals and other things ... Holy Scripture also makes it lord over the earth.[19]

Luther himself was an educator, providing materials for the instruction of the church at every level, including especially the Small and Large Catechisms. Consequently, Lutheran theology always has placed a high value on the contributions of human reason for understanding the nature of the world.[20] Moreover, the Lutheran churches have dedicated themselves to institutions of higher learning, understanding education as a great contribution to civil society.[21]

Perhaps the most compelling reference by Luther to the gift of reason in the left-hand civil strategy was his testimony before the Emperor at the Diet of Worms on April 18, 1521:

> Since then your serene majesty and your lordships seek a simple answer, I will give it in this manner, neither horned nor toothed: Unless I am convinced by the testimony of Scriptures or by clear reason (for I do not trust either in the pope or in councils alone, since it is well known that they have often erred and contradicted themselves), I am bound by the Scriptures I have quoted and my conscience is captive to the Word of God. I cannot and I will not retract anything, since it is neither safe nor right to go against conscience.[22]

Here Luther not only demonstrates the practice of sound reasoning through the logic of his statement, but he grounds his reasoning on the two sources of authority most befitting each of the two strategies: Scriptural authority in the right-hand theological strategy and reason as authority in the left-hand civil strategy. Not only Scripture but also reason has its proper use, for example, when standing before the tribunal of an emperor.

Two uses of the will: limited within creation and in bondage regarding salvation

Not only through the exercise of reason, but also in the exercise of the will is it fruitful to distinguish between two uses. Regarding the saving work of God in Jesus Christ according to the right-hand theological strategy, the will is totally and completely in bondage and of no use:

> For my own part, I frankly confess that even if it were possible, I should not wish to have free choice given to me, or to have anything left in my own hands by which I might strive toward salvation ... But now, since God has taken my salvation out of my hands into his, making it depend on his choice and not mine, and has promised to save me, not by my own work or exertion but by his grace and mercy, I am assured and certain both that he is faithful and will not lie to me, and also that he is too great and powerful for any demons or any adversities to be able to break him or to snatch me from him.[23]

Again, Luther clearly demonstrates that neither human righteousness nor reason nor will have anything constructive to contribute to the winning of salvation according to the right-hand theological strategy.

Though Luther is consistently skeptical about the human exercise of the will, affected as it always is by the power of sin, when arguing against Erasmus in *The Bondage of the Will* he does allow for circumscribed exercise of free choice in relation to human involvements in the left-hand civil strategy:

> But if we are unwilling to let this term go altogether—though that would be the safest and most God-fearing thing to do—let us at least teach men to use it honestly, so that free choice is allowed to man only with respect to what is beneath him and not what is above him. That is to say, a man should know that with regard to his faculties and possessions he has the right to use, to do, or to leave undone, according to his own free choice, though even this is controlled by the free choice of God alone, who acts in

> whatever way he pleases. On the other hand in relation to God, or in matters pertaining to salvation or damnation, a man has no free choice, but is a captive, subject and slave either of the will of God or the will of Satan.[24]

In relation to the created order, the human will can play a useful role "with respect to what is beneath him." Only by distinguishing between two contrasting uses of the will can we interpret accurately Luther's theology.

Two uses of works: for the neighbor and works righteousness

Finally, with regard to Luther's interpretation of human works, again there is a clear distinction between works righteousness in the right-hand theological strategy and the performance of works for the sake of the neighbor in the left-hand civil strategy. The Reformation was launched in protest against the late medieval theological program that promoted the performance of religious rituals as the way to earn status before God.[25] Luther roared against the "claim to be justified by works, whatever their character:"

> Wherefore it ought to be the first concern of every Christian to lay aside all confidence in works and increasingly to strengthen faith alone and through faith to grow in the knowledge, not of works, but of Christ Jesus. No other work makes a Christian.[26]

This quote elucidates Luther's thesis that "A Christian is a perfectly free lord of all, subject to none."[27] In the right-hand theological strategy, faith, trusting in the saving work of Christ, is the only good work.[28]

Luther, however, does preserve an essential place for the performance of good works—not for earning merit from God towards salvation, but as a service to the well-being of the neighbor. This is the meaning of Luther's second thesis in his treatise on Christian freedom: "A Christian is a perfectly dutiful servant of all, subject to all."[29]

> Lastly, we shall also speak of the things which he does toward his neighbor. A man does not live for himself alone in this mortal body to work for it alone, but he lives also for all men on earth; rather, he lives only for others and not for himself ... Therefore he should be guided in all his works by this thought and contemplate this one thing alone, that he may serve and benefit others in all that he does, considering nothing except the need and advantage of the neighbor.[30]

Luther's theology retains a prominent place for the performance of good works, not in relation to God's saving work in Christ but as an indispensable aspect of God's left-hand civil strategy through service to our neighbor. Good works proper, as described in the *Treatise on Good Works*, are those due others according to the Ten Commandments, particularly in the Second Table of the Law.[31] Luther's distinction between two uses of works elucidates his theology in compelling ways.

Luther's two strategies and political advocacy

Like other Christians, Lutherans have had to chart a precise course for involvement in political advocacy to influence law and public policy for the benefit of neighbors and the common good, given the theological distinctions taught by Luther. Reinhold Niebuhr famously wrote, “Man’s capacity for justice makes democracy possible; but man’s inclination to injustice makes democracy necessary.”[32] Sin is not only a personal reality but becomes embedded as structural sin in legal systems, which can advantage the few at the expense of the many, always tending to harm the most vulnerable.[33] The distortions caused by structural sin, especially through imperfect legislation, make the work of political advocacy indispensable for Christians. Political involvement can take many forms, such as partisan grassroots organizing for political candidates during elections, building relationships with and meeting with elected officials to make the case for particular political concerns, engaging in demonstrations of public support for specific issues, or involved citizenship through political advocacy in relation to particular legislation and policies.

The charters of organizations like the Fellowship of Reconciliation, Bread for the World, 350.org, and Amnesty International provide reference points for this distinctive type of political advocacy. Denominational advocacy efforts with regard to racism, sexism, heterosexism, poverty, hunger, homelessness, refugees, violence, war, arms proliferation, prisons, capital punishment, environmental concern, and other causes belong to Christian participation in God’s left-hand strategy. Likewise, congregations and their members are called to raise their voices in political advocacy to achieve laws and policies that serve the common good and protect those disadvantaged by injustice.

The social teachings of the church give guidance for Christian involvement in political advocacy regarding the most urgent issues of our times. Civil protections of the rights of all people regardless of race, gender, and sexual orientation belong to the church’s theological and ethical commitments. In an era when discrimination against LGBTQ+ persons remains prevalent, it is urgent that the church advocate for equality and civil rights for this threatened population. Wage inequality between men and women calls for political and economic advocacy to attain parity. Caring for the poor, feeding the hungry, providing shelter for the homeless, and welcoming the stranger remain central commitments throughout church history. Today the challenges of mass forced migration demand equitable legal provisions and processes for dealing with the influx of refugees for not only political but also economic reasons.

The proliferation of violence in American society, exacerbated through the lack of adequate regulation of guns domestically and by international arms sales, contradicts commitment to reconciliation through peaceful means as well as traditional just war criteria (as inadequate as the latter may be). The mass incarceration of young black men due to inequitable arrest rates, charges, legal defense, and sentencing demands political advocacy.[34] Inequitable application of the death penalty in the United States based on race and class requires reasoned political arguments to advocate changes in the enforcement of the death penalty, if not its abolition. As a final example, the destruction of the environment through exploitation of natural resources, chemical pollutants, and carbon emissions threatens the ecosystems upon which all life depends. Because the harmful effects of the degradation of earth, air, and water are suffered disproportionately by poor people of color, particular legal protections are necessary to address environmental racism.

One fundamental reason for controversy about the place of political advocacy in the church and by Christians involves conflicting views about the proper relationship of church and state. There is deep division over whether churches should seek to influence their members by advocating not only for certain political issues, but even for particular candidates and parties. A *first* temptation facing the church involves *political quietism* in relation to political advocacy. Large numbers of Christians interpret separation of church and state to entail *privatizing* the role of the church, limiting ministry to meeting the theological needs of people through worship and pastoral care, perhaps with a secondary role for the church in offering charitable assistance to people in need. For many mainline Christians, the church's ministry belongs to the private realm of individuals and families who choose to participate. Here the church's ministry becomes highly individualized, based on concern for the spiritual welfare of persons and helping with individual needs. In this view the ministry of the church is relegated to the private sphere. It remains separated from matters debated in the public square, except perhaps when those debates explicitly threaten the legal rights of the church to function in the circumscribed realm assigned to it.[35] Beginning with the nineteenth century, the church has been increasingly subject to the privatization of religion, with its relegation to an isolated sphere or compartment, leading to the quietism of the church in public affairs.[36]

A *second* and dramatically contrasting approach for relating church and state has been developed and implemented, for example, by the so-called Christian right.[37] According to this approach, which can be characterized as *religious identity politics*, the church is called to be vigilant in ordering society according to Christian principles. In this view, the biblical God has revealed the truth about key social issues (for example, regarding abortion, marriage, homosexuality, or the teaching of evolution) and it is a Christian's responsibility to become involved in the political process to ensure that the "Christian" position on each of these issues prevails. Churches operating according to a religious identity politics often issue directives to their membership about how to vote, not only on particular issues but sometimes also for particular political parties and candidates, who they reckon will offer the best support for their agenda. These churches also may actively advocate with legislators according to their established agenda. For example, Christian religious identity politics has attempted to influence school districts to prevent the teaching of evolution in the curriculum of public schools and to restrict the legalization of gay marriage. The arguments for these positions are derived primarily from biblical warrants not accessible to public reasoning.

Many Christians in American society understand the relationship of church and state according to the paradigm of religious identity politics, and its significant influence on the outcome of key elections may lead politicians to calculate how they can best appeal to the power of this voting bloc.[38] At the same time, the assertiveness of the Christian right has led to a significant backlash by those who reason differently about particular issues, not only among Christians but especially among those not affiliated with the church. Many secular citizens and those from other faith traditions wrongly assume that all Christians share the Christian right's approach to politics, which complicates the challenge not only for Lutherans who recognize God's "two strategies," but also for those Christians who operate according to other paradigms for relating church and state.

According to God's left-hand strategy, a *third* approach to political advocacy sees the responsibility as belonging to the baptized, both through the personal initiatives of Christians as citizens and through the collective efforts of the institutional church as a public actor. In contrast both to political quietism and to the approach of the Christian right and the practice of religious identity politics, Christians are called to engage in *neighbor politics.* Neighbor politics recognizes Luther's first political use of the law, acknowledging that civil righteousness, reason, will, and good works are God's gifts to humans for analyzing and understanding the world.

Neighbor politics rejects the claim that political judgments must be based on explicit biblical warrants or conformed to biblical commands. Instead, effective Christian participation in politics requires that Christians employ language and reasoning that are accessible, intelligible, and coherent to all citizens, not just to those who share their Christian theological commitments. They are to direct their attention primarily to the well-being of the neighbor in their advocacy, reasoning according to what contributes most to the common good of society, and with particular concern for those who are suffering disproportionately under current laws, policies, and programs. While this approach does not preclude references to biblical or theological authority, such appeals are most appropriate when they strengthen arguments and rhetoric that are otherwise publicly accessible. For example, Martin Luther King Jr. appealed powerfully to biblical passages in making public arguments for civil rights legislation, as with his "I Have a Dream" speech. The biblical warrants were not ends in themselves, however, but provided a measure of persuasive religious rhetoric to advocate for laws and policies that were arguable entirely through public reasoning apart from references to biblical authority.

Neighbor politics differs dramatically from the religious identity politics of the Christian right, which is heavily laden with explicitly biblical and religious arguments and whose goal is to impose its particular viewpoint on the whole society. In neighbor politics, Christians—freed by the Gospel of Jesus Christ for neighbor love—are motivated to participate in God's left-hand strategy by speaking out and engaging in the political process as citizens who advocate for the well-being of the neighbor, using reasonable arguments that appeal to the consciences and common sense of others, building coalitions wherever possible with those who share a common vision, and avoiding special pleading based on a "Christian" agenda narrowly understood. Christians engaging in neighbor politics favor reasoning and explanations accessible to all, for example, in advocating for environmental protections or food assistance for the poor.

While informed by Christian motives and values, the left-hand strategy translates these into political reasoning that appeals not only to Christians but also to non-Christians, both to people of faith and to those who claim no faith at all. It is an approach that honors the authentic spirit of the separation of church and state as Christians intentionally avoid trying to convince the state to impose legislation and policies upon citizens that are fundamentally based on appeals to religious authority. This is dramatically different from the religious identity politics of the Christian right, which on almost every key issue has as its agenda the theocratic imposition of its religious agenda on society.

Conclusion

This chapter demonstrates that it is constructive for Christians, especially in the United States, to reclaim Luther's understanding of the two strategies as a comprehensive paradigm for interpreting the work of political advocacy. Moreover, it is fruitful to distinguish not only between the first and second uses of the law, but also between the first and second uses of righteousness, reason, will, and works in Luther's theology. These categories find their coherence by consistent reference to the paradigm of God's two complementary and dialectically related strategies for ruling the world. According to their second use in relation to the right-hand theological strategy, these are rejected by Luther as threatening divine sovereignty in securing salvation through Jesus Christ by grace alone. However, according to their first use in the left-hand civil strategy, these categories describe human capacities that contribute indispensably to the work of political advocacy, whose aim is the approximation of the common good and preservation of God's creation. Because of Luther's affirmation of the uses of law, righteousness, reason, will, and works in the left hand civil strategy, this paradigm offers a distinctive and constructive foundation for Christian engagement in the work of political advocacy, an approach that contrasts dramatically with the religious identity politics manifest in many other prominent forms of political engagement by Christians.[39]

Notes

1 See Johannes Heckel, *Lex Charitatis: A Juristic Disquisition on Law in the Theology of Martin Luther*, trans. and ed. Gottfried G. Krodel (Grand Rapids, MI: Eerdmans, 2010).
2 For a discussion of this controversy in German theology, see "Germany in the Twentieth Century" in Karl H. Hertz, ed., *Two Kingdoms and One World: A Sourcebook in Christian Social Ethics* (Minneapolis, MN: Augsburg Publishing House, 1976), Chapter 10.
3 See, for an example of Lutheran social teaching on political advocacy the explanation of social responsibility by the Evangelical Lutheran Church in America, "The Church in Society: A Lutheran Perspective," (1991). Accessed November 6, 2017. http://download.elca.org/ELCA%20Resource%20Repository/Church_SocietySS.pdf?_ga=2.155438712.2121097623.1503888636-889091389.1502033567.
4 Craig L. Nessan, "Reappropriating Luther's Two Kingdoms," *Lutheran Quarterly* 19, no. 3 (2005): 302–311.
5 For a compelling portrait of Luther's worldview, see Heiko Obermann, *Luther: Man between God and Devil*, trans. Eileen Walliser-Schwarzbart (New Haven, CT: Yale University, 1989).
6 Cf. Walter Wink, *The Powers that Be: Theology for a New Millennium* (New York: Doubleday, 1999).
7 Richard H. Bliese and Craig Van Gelder, eds., *The Evangelizing Church: A Lutheran Contribution* (Minneapolis, MN: Augsburg Fortress, 2005), 128–130.
8 Craig L. Nessan, "The Neighborliness (*Diakonia*) of All Believers," in Kathryn A. Kleinhans, ed., *Together by Grace: Introducing the Lutherans* (Minneapolis, MN: Augsburg Fortress, 2016), 143–146.
9 Cf. Paul Tillich, *Love, Power, and Justice: Ontological Analyses and Ethical Applications* (London: Oxford University Press, 1954), 71.
10 Craig L. Nessan, *Shalom Church: The Body of Christ as Ministering Community* (Minneapolis, MN: Fortress, 2010), Chapter 3.
11 Martin Luther, *Treatise on Christian Liberty (Freedom of a Christian)*, trans. George v. Schick, American edition of *Luther's Works* (hereafter *LW*), eds. Jaroslav Pelikan and Helmut T. Lehmann, 55 vols. (Philadelphia, PA: Fortress Press and St. Louis, MO: Concordia Publishing House, 1955–1986), *LW* 31, 343–377, particularly the formula on 344: "A Christian is a perfectly free lord of all, subject to none. A Christian is perfectly dutiful servant of all, subject to all." The former corresponds to *freedom from* in the right-hand strategy, the latter to *freedom for* in the left-hand strategy.
12 Bernard Lohse, *Martin Luther's Theology: Its Historical and Systematic Development*, trans. and ed. Roy A. Harrisville (Minneapolis, MN: Fortress Press, 1999), 184, 270.
13 Bernard Lohse, *Martin Luther's Theology*, 271. Both Althaus and Bayer interpret the two uses of the law in a corresponding manner. See Paul Althaus, *The Theology of Martin Luther*, trans. Robert C. Schutz (1966; Philadelphia, PA: Fortress Press, 1970), 253–255, and Oswald Bayer, "What Does 'Evangelical' Mean? The Reformational Turning Point in Luther's Theology," trans. Thomas H. Trapp, in Bayer, *Martin Luther's Theology: A Contemporary Interpretation* (Grand Rapids, MI: Wm. B. Eerdmans Publishing Co., 2008), 61 n. 27.
14 For a fuller exposition of the two kingdoms as two strategies, see Craig Nessan, "Reappropriating Luther's Two Kingdoms," 304–11.
15 Paul Althaus, *The Theology of Martin Luther*, 227.
16 Paul Althaus, *The Ethics of Martin Luther*, trans. Robert C. Schultz (Philadelphia, PA: Fortress Press, 1978), 49–50 (citing Luther at *LW* 46, 99–100; *LW* 21, 26.
17 Martin Luther, *Sermons I*, and trans. ed. John W. Doverstein, *LW* 51, 374.
18 Martin Luther, *The Bondage of the Will*, *LW* 33, 290.
19 Martin Luther, *The Disputation Concerning Man* (1536), *LW* 34, 137.
20 See the several essays underscoring the value of reason in the Lutheran tradition in Jennifer Hockenbery Dragseth, ed., *The Devil's Whore: Reason and Philosophy in the Lutheran Tradition* (Minneapolis, MN: Fortress Press, 2011).
21 See Richard W. Solberg, *Lutheran Higher Education in North America* (Minneapolis, MN: Augsburg Publishing House, 1985).
22 *Luther at the Diet of Worms: The Account and Actions of Doctor Martin Luther the Augustinian at the Diet of Worms*, *LW* 32, 112.

23 Martin Luther, *Bondage of the Will*, *LW* 33, 288–289. For further commentary, see Bayer, *Martin Luther's Theology*, 185–192.
24 Ibid., 70.
25 Martin Luther, *Ninety-Five Theses, or Disputation on the Power and Efficacy of Indulgences*, *LW* 31, 25–33.
Other forms of pious works earning merit included venerating saints, pilgrimages to shrines, private masses without communicants, and venerating relics.
26 Martin Luther, *Treatise on Christian Liberty*, *LW* 31, 347.
27 Ibid., 344.
28 Cf. Martin Luther, *Treatise on Good Works*, *LW* 44, 23–39.
29 Martin Luther, *Treatise on Christian Liberty*, *LW* 31, 344.
30 Ibid., 364–365.
31 Martin Luther, *Treatise on Good Works*, *LW* 44, 80–114.
32 Reinhold Niebuhr, foreword to the first edition of *The Children of Light and the Children of Darkness: A Vindication of Democracy and a Critique of Its Traditional Defense* (Chicago, IL: University of Chicago Press, 2011), xiii.
33 See Cynthia D, Moe-Lobeda, *Resisting Structural Evil: Love as Ecological-Economic Vocation* (Minneapolis, MN: Fortress Press, 2013).
34 See, for example, Michelle Alexander, *The New Jim Crow: Mass Incarceration in the Age of Colorblindness* (New York: New Press, 2012), 83–117.
35 Cf. Robert Benne, "How Should Modern Lutherans Try to Shape Secular Law?" in Ronald W. Duty and Marie A. Failinger, eds., *On Secular Governance: Lutheran Perspectives on Contemporary Legal Issues* (Grand Rapids, MI: Wm. B. Eerdmans, 2016), 328–340.
36 Sydney E. Mead, *The Lively Experiment: The Shaping of Christianity in America* (Eugene, OR: Wipf & Stock, 2007), 140–143.
37 Other church bodies in particular contexts also may operate in this fashion, for example, when the Roman Catholic Church engages in advocacy according to the logic of Christendom.
38 William E. Connolly, "The Evangelical-Capitalist Resonance Machine," Chapter 2 in *Capitalism and Christianity, American Style* (Durham, NC: Duke University Press, 2008).
39 Portions of this essay are adapted from work previously published and are used by permission of *Currents in Theology and Mission* and Fortress Press. See Craig L. Nessan, "Law, Righteousness, Reason, Will, and Works: Civil and Theological Uses," *Currents in Theology and Mission* 41, no. 1 (2014): 51–56 and Craig L. Nessan, *Shalom Church: The Body of Christ as Ministering Community* (Minneapolis, MN: Fortress Press, 2010), 19–22.

7 A case for toleration

Religious exemptions, conscientious objection, and the public good

H. David Baer

Disagreements concerning the nature and extent of religious freedom have suddenly assumed a neuralgic place in American politics. The debate focuses largely on the issue of religious exemptions, that is, situations in which an individual demands to be excused from obedience to certain laws for reasons of religious conscience. The classic case of such an exemption is the conscientious objector status granted historically to members of Christian peace churches. Today, however, the issue of exemption appears most frequently in other contexts. Should pharmacists be exempted from requirements to distribute contraception to which they religiously object? Should landlords with religious objections to homosexuality be exempted from a legal requirement to rent their property to homosexual couples? Should employers with religious scruples be exempted from government regulations requiring them to provide health insurance coverage for contraception methods they consider abortifacient?

Those who advocate for such accommodations usually appeal to the right of religious freedom. The question they force us to consider, therefore, is whether the right of religious freedom includes an entitlement to exemption from generally applicable laws, or whether such exemptions are a discretionary matter to be adjudicated through regular political processes. Insofar as exemptions are rights, the state must recognize them regardless of prevailing political tastes. If exemptions are only privileges, however, then advocates cannot demand them, although they might urge them on the state.

My answer to the above question will, unfortunately, not be clean cut. Religious freedom is a universal human right, a fact attested by international treaties and covenants, such as the *Universal Declaration of Human Rights*, the *International Covenant on Civil and Political Rights*, the *European Convention on Human Rights*, and so on. As a universal human right, the right of religious freedom envelops certain core practices with absolute immunities. Even so, the full scope of those immunities is a matter for political deliberation. Concrete rights are always articulated within the context of a given society. Religious freedom flourishes most fully within societies committed to a regimen of toleration built on respect for individual conscience and a commitment to societal pluralism. This means, however, that the scope any given society grants to religious freedom will depend upon the depth of its respect for the individual and the integrity of conscience. A society that grants religious exemptions evinces deeper respect for the individual than societies that do not, and in this respect is superior to less tolerant societies even if those less tolerant societies have not violated a universal right.

Another way to get at what I am trying to suggest is to consider the distinction between human rights and civil rights. Human rights are universal and admit of few, if any, derogations. Civil rights, by contrast, are societally specific. If not completely relative, they nevertheless reflect a "margin of appreciation." Their exact content and scope are the outcome of social and political negotiation. Liberal societies will be more disposed to carve out exemptions for religiously based practices because they are more appreciative of the crucial role conscience plays in sustaining democratic polity. Insofar as possible, liberal societies will want to carve out social space for acts of conscience; and hence, insofar as possible, they will make provisions for conscientious objectors by granting religious exemptions.

In certain respects, I am suggesting, the right of religious freedom moves along a continuum. It begins as a human right, rooted in an absolute, universal core, but pushes outward toward increasing civil recognition of rights of conscience. Although the precise point of crossover from human right to civil right is not clearly demarcated, that lack of clarity does not always matter. A society committed to liberal values will be open to acknowledging rights of conscience. Insofar as it succeeds in recognizing those rights, it secures an achievement which illiberal societies do not. I thus hope to make a case for religious exemptions, first by locating the right of religious freedom within the context of the good of pluralism, and second by suggesting a pluralist conception of the common good that pushes us from a narrow construction of the right of religious freedom toward a more expansive recognition of the right of conscientious objection.

The limited state and a pluralist common good

Pluralism is a central value for liberal democracies. Although one can make the case for a pluralism in a variety of ways, Christians have their own reasons to advocate and defend it. A pluralist conception of the common good follows from the Christian commitment to a limited state. For Lutherans, the necessity of limiting the state is entailed by Luther's teaching on the two kingdoms. This point was made forcefully in the mid-twentieth century by Helmut Thielicke and Eivind Berggrav, two Lutherans who personally confronted the evils of totalitarianism.

Luther understood the two kingdoms as two communities existing simultaneously under two lordships.[1] The kingdom of heaven was ruled by Christ while the kingdom of earth fell under the dominion of the devil. Overlapping both kingdoms were three hierarchies *(ecclesiastica, politica, oeconomica)*, or estates, or what later Lutherans often referred to as orders. The orders were sometimes understood to operate in the kingdom of earth autonomously from Christ's rule, but Helmut Thielicke argued they should be understood within an eschatological framework. According to Thielicke, the two kingdoms were actually two aeons. The kingdom of earth referred to the old aeon, which is in rebellion against God and passing away, while the kingdom of heaven referred to the new aeon of Christ, which is breaking into the kingdom of the world and changing it. The law of love, which Luther identified as proper to the kingdom of heaven, was also present in the kingdom of earth through the orders, although imperfectly. God, Thielicke said, had established the orders as "emergency measures" to preserve the world from the destruction of sin until the new aeon arrived in fullness. The orders were thus both constrained and transformed by the kingdom of God as it impinges on the present aeon, or the kingdom of earth.[2]

As an "order of preservation," Thielicke said, the state rightfully claims obedience from Christians, but the shape of that obedience is affected by knowledge of the new aeon. Knowledge of the kingdom of heaven relativizes the state and places limits on it. Thielicke illustrates the character of this eschatological relativization with an interesting discussion of Paul's injunction against taking disputes to court; "When one of you has a grievance against a brother, does he dare go to law before the unrighteous instead of the saints? Do you not know that the saints will judge the world?" (1 Cor. 6:13 RSV). Thielicke calls attention to the fact that although rendering legal judgment is one of the state's primary functions, Paul still admonishes Christians to avoid turning to the state even in matters pertaining to its primary purpose. This is because the state has been relativized by the kingdom of God. Christians are to remain aloof from the state, which means they will seek to constrain the state's activities as much as possible.[3] "Whenever the Christian can dispense with the state without threatening its existence, he should do so," says Thielicke, quoting the biblical scholar Oscar Cullman.[4]

Knowledge of the two kingdoms thus leads Christians, in Thielicke's words, to "postulate a minimal state." The postulate is a guiding principle rather than a strict directive. As a general orientation, Christians will seek to limit the influence and scope of the state, so that it does not encroach upon Christ's dominion and usurp the place of the Kingdom of God. "Social responsibilities which can be handled apart from the state (by families, neighbors, business enterprises, etc.)," Thielicke says, "should not be sloughed off onto the state."[5]

The possibility that the modern state, even in its benign forms, might evolve in ways hostile to the two kingdoms was a grave concern for Bishop Eivind Berggrav, the famous leader of Norway's resistance against Hitler. Berggrav argued that the inherent tendency of the modern welfare state was to regulate and supervise. By expanding its control over more and more aspects of life, the welfare state squeezes out independent spheres of life and threatens to usurp the place of God's kingdom. In his address to the 1952 assembly of the Lutheran World Federation, Berggrav warned:

> The specific characteristic of the welfare state is this: on the one hand, it is totally secular, and does not in any way whatever acknowledge God as the Lord of life; on the other hand, it acts as though it were Providence itself and assumes the right of entering into all the spheres of human life. The problem arises whether the Lutheran doctrine of the two regimes may be maintained under these changed conditions or whether the new state enters so deeply into the spiritual regime that there is no longer any room for the church. The welfare state does not shrink from violating the secrecy of the individual's conscience; it seeks to exercise total rule.[6]

Although Berggrav recognized that the growth of the modern welfare state was to some extent inevitable, it was not something to which Christians should simply acquiesce. By usurping formerly independent spheres of life, the modern state threatens to homogenize society and level away valuable differences. If left to its own devices, the modern state will even pose a threat to conscience, because it encroaches on the freedom and responsibility each individual has to discern and commit to God and the good.

A limited state, however, leaves individuals free to pursue the true and the good according to the judgments of their own conscience. A society of conscientiously committed individuals will also be pluralistic. Individuals perceive the good differently and come together to form different sorts of associations, committed to different, and sometimes competing, conceptions of the good. Insofar as the state seeks to supervise and regulate voluntary associations and individual conscience, it works to undermine the social conditions that sustain pluralism. An overly regulated, excessively supervised society will cease to be pluralistic.

The commitments to the limited state and to political pluralism are also necessary conditions for recognizing the right of religious freedom. Historically, arguments for religious freedom have always been linked to questions about the character of the common good.

Things not lawful in the ordinary course of life are not lawful in the worship of God. For example, says Locke, if a religious society should desire to sacrifice a calf in the course of its worship, that cannot be prohibited *as a religious practice*. If, however, a law prohibits the killing of animals in general, the case is different. In that case, the law would be directed against the killing of animals in general, and thus the killing of animals in religious worship would also be prohibited. The prohibition is justified because the law is not directed against a religious practice as such. In other words, Locke draws a distinction between laws of general applicability and laws directed specifically against a religious practice. Laws expressly intended to prohibit or regulate religious practice are illegitimate. Laws of general applicability, however, are written for the public good. Their restriction of religious practice is indirect and unintended, and hence legitimate. To put it simply, Locke did not allow for religious exemptions.

Part of the reason for this may have been that Locke believed the occasion for exemptions would be rare if the laws were well formulated. He was optimistic about the ease with which religious toleration could be reconciled with reasonable laws. Considering the issue today, from within deeply pluralist societies, we are perhaps less optimistic and more sensitive to the possibility of intractable conflicts of conscience. Sensitivity to the possibility of conflicts may also lead us to pause over a puzzling moment in Locke's argument.

Although Locke believed conflicts between religious conscience and well formulated laws would be rare, he still considered the problem explicitly and proposed a certain solution. In situations where the magistrate commands something "unlawful to the Conscience of a private Person," then, according to Locke:

> Such a private Person is to abstain from the Action that he judges unlawful; and he is to undergo the Punishment, which is not unlawful for him to bear. For the private judgment of any Person concerning a Law enacted in Political Matters, for the publick Good, does not take away the Obligation of that Law, nor deserve a Dispensation.[21]

Locke appears to recognize a moral, but not a legal right to adhere to conscience. A person bound in conscience must break the law, but he must also pay the penalty for doing so.

One wonders though, why, if there is a moral duty to obey conscience, that duty is not recognized by the law. A law which refuses to accommodate the rights of conscience places citizens in a moral crisis, and a society that consistently refused to accommodate rights of conscience would undermine the moral sensibility of its citizenry. To recognize this is to begin to think about the possibility of religious exemptions grounded in a right of conscientious objection. In fact, the case for conscientious objection parallels the case for religious toleration; both depend upon arguments about the character of the common good.

The case for conscientious objection

The case for accommodating conscientious objectors is closely linked to the case for liberal democracy itself. Democracies depend upon the engagement of their citizens to perdure, and the wellspring of political engagement is committed conscience. Thus, democratic regimes are constitutionally disposed toward accommodating conscientious objectors, even if those accommodations are not always possible.

Respect for the rights of conscience has been present in American history from the earliest days. The most striking example of this has been a willingness to grant exemption from military service to persons with religious scruples against killing. Even in the midst of the

War of Independence, a moment when one might think military exemptions would hurt the nation, the Continental Congress urged the accommodation of religious pacifists.[22] In the First Session of Congress, representatives from a number of states proposed amendments to the Federal Constitution which would have protected individuals with religious scruples from compulsory military service.[23] Although those federal amendments were never ratified, 22 states had clauses protecting conscientious objectors in their state constitutions.[24] Later, when the United States established a national army, conscientious objector status for the members of peace churches was protected by legal statutes.

This early solicitousness for conscientious objectors was no doubt made easier by the fact that pacifist religious groups were a definite minority. Accommodating them did not call into question the country's capacity for self-defense. Even so, one ought not underrate the extent to which those accommodations were rooted in respect for conscience and a commitment to tolerance. Earlier generations of Americans, understanding that the success of their experiment in self-government depended upon citizens who were conscientiously engaged, may have recognized that refusing to tolerate dissenting consciences would work to undermine the democratic habits needed to sustain a republic.

The important role played by conscience in sustaining democracy was keenly explored by Michael Walzer in a collection of essays dating back to 1970 titled *Obligations.* Walzer notes, as have others, that etymologically the word conscience refers to shared knowledge. Although religious believers have understood that to be knowledge shared with God, one can also construe the shared knowledge in a more sociological way. Knowledge held in conscience is shared with other men and women, and with communities.[25] Conscience, as we encounter it in civil society, is knowledge shared with what Walzer calls secondary associations.

When individuals choose to disobey the state for reasons of conscience, Walzer says, their acts usually have a collective dimension. Civil dissenters explain and justify their conscientious objection by referring to the values of a secondary group to which they have made a commitment. Their act of disobedience is thus simultaneously an act of obligation. Bound by his commitment to other members of secondary group, the civil dissenter is caught up in a conflict between his obligation to the group and his obligation to the state. The secondary groups make primary claims about ultimate matters, like justice, truth, or God. These groups, or more precisely their members, demand that society recognize the primacy of their claims in some area of their life. They demand to be exempted from obedience to the law.[26]

Many political regimes do not tolerate dissent. They view primary claims advanced by secondary associations as threats to their authority. A liberal democratic regime, however, can never do this. The ideal of liberal democracy includes an active and independent civil sphere. It envisions precisely the sort of society where individuals freely enter into, and form, secondary associations. A civil society without civil associations would be one where citizens are unengaged and indifferent, and a society comprised of indifferent citizens will not long remain democratic. It will slide into either mild or harsh forms of despotism.

At the same time, any state which allows for the type of society in which secondary groups freely work out their moral principles is bound to find itself challenged by conscientious individuals.[27] More often than not, those conscientious individuals will ground their objections not in a subjective personal code, but in a shared set of principles held in common with other members of a group. Secondary memberships give rise to commitments which compete, and sometimes conflict, with larger societal judgments and norms. Although a tyrannical state can enforce conformity by isolating individuals from the kinds of social groups that sustain personal moral commitment, a liberal state will be loath to do this.[28] The liberal state seeks to protect secondary associations, yet in doing so it inevitably encounters groups who demand exemption from some of its laws.[29] Thus the liberal state perpetually encounters questions about, and challenges to, its regimen of toleration. While not every claim of conscience needs to be accommodated, a state which consistently refuses to accommodate such claims would cease to be liberal.

Liberal regimes, as Walzer points out, claim to derive their authority from the consent of the governed. To account for that consent, liberal political theory often invokes the myth of the social contract, an imaginary point in time at which individuals voluntarily compacted to form a political union. This mythical act of consent, even within the terms of the theory, is construed quite narrowly; it occurs at a single moment in time but has permanent significance. Genuine consent, however, is an ongoing affair. It is given over time and offered in the present by actual, living members of society.[30]

The conscientious objector dissents from the law, which is to say, he withholds his consent. Understandably, the regimes from which that consent is withheld, even the liberal ones, see that dissent as a threat. Their fears, however, are often exaggerated. According to Walzer, "There is considerable evidence to suggest that the state can live with, even if it chooses not to accommodate, groups with partial claims against itself."[31] Walzer distinguishes between total and partial claims against the state. Total claims are advanced by revolutionaries, and they do represent a threat to the established political order. Partial claims, however, are the more common sort. Groups advancing partial claims are engaged not in revolution, but civil disobedience. They do not deny the sovereignty of the state, but they refuse to acknowledge that sovereignty without qualifying it with primary claims that transcend the state. Rather than seeking to overturn the political order, those engaged in civil disobedience are demanding that society recognize their primary claims in a particular area of life.[32]

A limited state, the kind implied by a Christian vision of the two kingdoms, has an obligation to recognize the existence of primacy claims beyond the order of politics. The claims of the conscientious objector, therefore, rightly demand a degree of political solicitation. The liberal state, because it is limited and recognizes the value of conscience, should also be disposed to accommodate the claims of conscience. This does not mean every accommodation is guaranteed. Certain practices may be so subversive of the common good that even the most open society ought not to tolerate them. At the same time, a state which consistently refused to accommodate claims of conscience would force questions about the extent to which its laws rest on popular consent. The challenge posed by conscientious objection, therefore, is to identify the outer limits of social toleration.

The work of identifying those outer limits lies beyond the scope of this chapter. In the past, they have been identified by courts through the application of various scrutiny standards. Although the exact nature of those standards is open to debate, a scrutiny standard of some sort would seem implied by a liberal conception of government as resting on consent. Compelling minorities to comply with laws to which they do not consent shifts the foundation of the law, even if slightly, toward force. Laws resting on force, if they grow in number, undermine the integrity of conscience by demanding unthinking obedience, and a society whose laws rest on obedience rather than consent has ceased to be liberal. A commitment to evaluate seriously the claims of the conscientious objector is a necessary mark of liberal democracy.

Conclusion

In laying out a case for conscientious objection, I have not gone so far as to identify a basic right to conscientious exemptions. I have, however, identified those exemptions as highly desirable political goods. While the concrete shape that exemptions will take in any society is a matter for deliberation and negotiation, provision for conscientious objection in some form seems a necessary requirement for liberal democracies. A liberal society appreciative of the central role played by conscience in democratic polity will seek to provide protections for conscience in its laws.

Nor in discussing religious exemptions did I take up the controversial cases of recent years; e.g. the contraceptive mandate associated with the Affordable Care Act, the Christian bakers who refused to bake a wedding cake for a same-sex marriage, etc. However, if the approach to justifying religious exemptions suggested in this paper is sound, then the initial presumption must favor protecting the right of conscientious objection even in these cases. One irony of current debates is that the strongest advocates for conscientious exemptions are now located on the political right, when in the past those proponents were on the left. However, to approach the question of religious exemptions through a lens of partisan politics is a big mistake. Neither religious freedom nor the dignity of conscience is an inherently partisan issue. They are core democratic value inseparably linked to judgments about the healthy shape of civil society. To think through these questions seriously requires stepping back from the partisan context. Today, as in the past, arguments about the rights of conscience concern the character of civil society, the breadth and depth of social toleration, and the future of liberal democracy.

Notes

1 To provide an exposition of Luther's concept of the two kingdoms about which everyone can agree is notoriously difficult. My exposition follows that offered in my book *Recovering Christian Realism: Just War Theory as a Political Ethic* (Lanham, MD: Lexington Books, 2015): 26–33. Two good English language discussions of Luther's two kingdoms doctrine are Per Frostin, *Luther's Two Kingdoms Doctrine: A Critical Study* (Lund: Lund University Press, 1994) and John Witte, *Law and Protestantism: The Legal Teachings of the Lutheran Reformation* (Cambridge: Cambridge University Press, 2002): 87–117.

2 For Thielicke's revisionist account of the two kingdoms, see Helmut Thielicke, "Foundations," in William H. Lazareth, ed., *Theological Ethics* (Grand Rapids, MI: William B. Eerdmans Publishing Co.), vol. 1 (1966/1979), 359–382.

3 Helmut Thielicke, "Politics," in William H. Lazareth, ed., *Theological Ethics* (Grand Rapids, MI: William B. Eerdmans Publishing Co, 1969/1979), vol. 2, 248–250.

4 Ibid., 250 (footnote omitted).

5 Ibid.

6 Eivind Berggrav, "State and Church Today: The Lutheran View," in Carl Lundquist, ed., *Proceedings of the Second Assembly of the Lutheran World Federation* (Gunzenhausen, Bavaria: Buchdruckerei, Reidel, 1952): 81 (lecture in proceedings that occurred in Hannover, Germany, July 25—August 3, 1952).

7 On this general point, see Kenneth L. Grasso, "John Courtney Murray, the 'Juridical State,' and the Catholic Theory of Religious Freedom" *Political Science Review* 33 (2004): 16; see also David Baer, "Four Theses about Religious Freedom" in *A vallásszabadság védelmében/Essays in Defense of Religious Freedom* (Budapest: Wesley János Kiadó, 2014), 136–137.

8 A good overview of Aquinas' understanding of conscience is available from Douglas Langston, "Medieval Theories of Conscience," *The Stanford Encyclopedia of Philosophy* (rev. fall 2015), ed. Edward N. Zalta. Accessed November 5, 2017. http://plato.stanford.edu/archives/fall2015/entries/conscience-medieval/

9 Thomas Aquinas, *Summa Theologica* I-II, Q. 19, a5. Accessed November 5, 2017. www3.nd.edu/~afreddos/papers/st1-2-q19-aa5-6.pdf.

10 Ibid., II-II, Q. 10, a8, reply obj. 3.

11 Ibid., II-II, Q. 10, a11.

12 Martin Luther, *Temporal Authority: To What Extent It Should Be Obeyed*, in *Luther's Works* (hereafter *LW*), eds. Jaroslav Pelikan and Helmut T. Lehmann, 55 vols. (Philadelphia, PA: Fortress Press and St. Louis, MO: Concordia Publishing House, 1955–1986), *LW* 45, 105.

13 See ibid., 106–114.
14 Edmund S. Morgan, *Roger Williams: The Church and The State* (New York: Harcourt, Brace & World, Inc., 1967), 5.
15 Roger Williams, *The Bloudy Tenent of Persecution for Cause of Conscience Discussed; and Mr. Cotton's Examined and Answered*, ed. Edward Bean Underhill (London: J. Haddon, Castle Street, Finsbury, 1848): 172. Accessed November 5, 2017. https://archive.org/details/cu31924029333014.
16 Roger Williams, "The Bloody Tenent yet More Bloody" in James Calvin Davis, ed., *On Religious Liberty: Selections from the Works of Roger Williams* (Cambridge, MA: The Belknap Press of Harvard University Press, 2008), Kindle edition, loc. 2366.
17 Roger Williams, *The Bloudy Tenent of Persecution*, ed. Edward Bean Underhill, 141.
18 Michael W. McConnell argues that Roger Williams supported religious exemptions in "The Origins and Historical Understanding of Free Exercise of Religion," *Harvard Law Review* 103 (1990): 1410–1517. McConnell is followed by Martha Nussbaum, *Liberty of Conscience: In Defense of America's Tradition of Religious Equality* (New York: Basic Books, 2008), 48–50, 120–126. However, McConnell's argument rests on inferences about how Williams would have answered the question of exemption were it posed to him explicitly. I am not aware that the question was ever addressed by Williams explicitly (although the volume of his work is enormous). Much of what Williams did say as well as the policy toward Quakers in Rhode Island suggest that McConnell and Nussbaum's reading of Williams is strained. For a view contra McConnell, see Philip Hamburger, "A Constitutional Right of Religious Exemption: An Historical Perspective," *George Washington Law Review* 60 (1992): 915–948. Exemptions were made in the colonial period, however, and at the beginning of the republic for conscientious objectors and those with religious scruples against swearing oaths.
19 See, John M. Barry, *Roger Williams and the Creation of the American Soul: Church, State, and the Birth of Liberty* (New York: Penguin Group, 2012), 371–375.
20 John Locke, *A Letter Concerning Toleration*, ed. James H. Tully (Indianapolis, IN: Hackett Publishing Company, 1983), 39.
21 Ibid., 48.
22 John Witte, Jr. and Joel A. Nichols, *Religion and the American Constitutional Experiment*, 4th edition (New York: Oxford University Press, 2016), 66.
23 Ibid., 73.
24 Ibid., 100.
25 Michael Walzer, *Obligations: Essays on Disobedience, War, and Citizenship* (New York: Simon and Schuster, 1970), 121ff.
26 Ibid., 3–11.
27 Ibid., 132.
28 Cf. ibid., 140–142.
29 Cf. ibid., 131–132.
30 Cf. Walzer's essay, "The Obligation to Die for the State" in *Obligations*, esp. 97–98.
31 Ibid., 11.
32 Ibid., 11–12.

Part IV

International law and human rights

8 Liberation, law and proleptic dignity

Ted Peters

I want to protect dignity. More precisely, I want to confer dignity when it is not recognized. I believe it is my mission as a Christian and as a citizen of the modern world to confer dignity whenever and wherever it is unrecognized, denied, or violated. I believe that conferring dignity is the heart of liberation.

My impetus to protect dignity and confer dignity exhibits a theoretical tension, however. To protect dignity assumes that dignity is already present, that it is threatened and that it needs protection. To confer dignity, in contrast, implies that it is absent; my conferral actually constructs a dignity which was missing. Is inherent dignity, then, a social construction? The theoretical tension between these two is exposed in the question: is dignity immanent or is dignity constructed?

The tension can be resolved by trusting in God, by relying upon retroactive ontology. What does this mean? First, to trust God is to have faith in what is unseen. If dignity is not seen, we must place our trust in God that dignity is present, valid, and real. Second, ontologically, it is God's eschatological future which determines retroactively what is real in the present. Dignity for each of God's beloved creatures is eschatologically real; and our task today is to believe it, trust it, and to confer dignity upon those without dignity. For us to confer dignity today is to act proleptically by borrowing dignity's immanent reality from God's imminent future.

Where do we find dignity denied? Cursing followed by murder, war, or genocide denies dignity to victims. When about to commit first degree murder, the killer curses the victim by declaring him or her to be excrement, immoral, and worthless. When U.S. presidents prepare their people to go to war, they describe the targeted enemy as evil or even Hitler-like. When genocidists prepare to wipe out a segment of the human population, they justify it by declaring the victims to be less than human: Nazis curse Jews as a cancer; Hutus curse Tutsis as vermin; ISIS curses Syriac Christians as infidels. Such cursing denies dignity. The mission of the church and the state is to bless instead of curse; to bless is to confer dignity in the face of its denial. Such conferral relies upon a future reality in which that dignity will be immanent even though today it is still imminent.

Roman Catholics, along with the United Nations and the ambient *Zeitgeist*, already take as a matter of faith that each human person possesses dignity and, further, the public denial of this dignity warrants legal action to restore it. The law both protects existing dignity and seeks to restore it when it is violated. Is our faith combined with this legal practice well placed? Yes, indeed. But, we might ask: on what grounds? Despite the observation that both religious and non-religious sectors of modern culture take dignity for granted, its theoretical justification as a basis for secular law, both domestic and international, is about as stable as a skate board on an ice rink.

If one would scratch a Roman Catholic or a Reformation Protestant and ask where dignity comes from, the most likely answer would be this: we human beings are created in God's image. It is the presence of the divine image that warrants treatment of each human person with dignity. This makes dignity immanent, archonic, and inviolable.

In this chapter, I will offer a brief phenomenology of dignity, showing that in our common experience, dignity is first conferred and then claimed as immanent. I want to affirm the Enlightenment definition of dignity–dignity means a person must be treated as a moral end and never merely as a means to a further end—a definition which rose to global recognition in the 1948 United Nations *Universal Declaration of Human Rights*. Then I will briefly evaluate the Vatican understanding of the church as the pastor to the larger culture through its commitment to dignity, then showing how Roman Catholic theology and Lutheran theology rely on both the *imago Dei* and natural law to justify this public ministry. I will conclude that proleptic eschatology provides the theologian with an ontological justification for conferring dignity, which takes the form of an ethics of liberation.

The phenomenology of dignity

Dignity is first conferred, then claimed.[1] A child who comes into the world and begins to gain an understanding of his or her relationship with the world does not presuppose self-worth. Rather, it is the relationship with doting parents who treat the child with attention, love, care, concern, devotion, and encouragement that prompts the inchoate realization, "I am valuable." While the baby is still limp and expressionless, the mother and father look the infant in the eye, smile, speak in a high pitch, and engage the tiny face. In time, that tiny face reacts, responds, and engages in return. This is the process by which mother and father confer dignity which, in time, the child claims for himself or herself. Personhood is relational before it becomes individual.

Jesus conferred dignity in similar fashion. Jesus described his own ministry: Matthew 11:5: "the blind receive their sight, the lame walk, the lepers are cleansed, the deaf hear, the dead are raised, and the poor have good news brought to them."[2] Those on the margins without social status or wealth or any reason to brag about themselves experience Jesus coming into their lives and treating them as persons of worth. This is the heart of the mission of liberation. Jesus' historical demonstration of the worth of marginalized persons testifies to the theological affirmation that, in the incarnation, God confers dignity on the human race and even on the entire creation. Dignity is now for the Christian to claim, recognize, realize, and re-confer.

When an oppressed class in modern society cries out for dignity, marginalized people want conferred what they already sense belongs to them. Here is one of my former doctoral students, Tshenuwani Simon Farisani, crying out for dignity before the apartheid laws of South Africa were overturned.

> We do not have, as a people, an intrinsic, nonnegotiable value. We are always migrating between existence and nonexistence, floating between earth and heaven, rejected by God and unacceptable to the devil. We are in South Africa but not of South Africa, every square inch human but not members of the human race.[3]

On the one hand, the apartheid government failed to confer dignity to persons or tribes of color within their land. On the other hand, those who were denied dignity were fully aware that such conferral was warranted; they sensed the innateness of their dignity.

Phenomenologically, dignity is first conferred and then claimed. Yet, it can work in reverse: dignity can be intuited and then conferral demanded. Perhaps dignity can be thought of as a circular interaction between conferral, claiming, and conferral again. Conferral of dignity is the core of the liberation dynamic.

Theologically, conferring dignity is one way to describe *agape* love, the love that treats the beloved as a moral end. According to Martin Luther, faith "does not seek its own good, but that of another ... Because it seeks the good of another, it works love."[4] We love by conferring dignity on the beloved.[5] Love almost by definition requires that the lover seek the good of the beloved solely for the beloved's benefit. *Agape* is the New Testament word for this. *Agape* becomes effective in liberation when one loved stands up to claim and own that dignity.

Dignity in the Enlightenment and the United Nations

The central role of dignity in Western culture arose during the Enlightenment, both in concert with theological commitments and in defiance of ecclesiastical authority.[6] Immanuel Kant provides the definition of dignity which has become the tacit if not the articulated essence of modern human personhood: each human person possesses dignity when we treat him or her as an end, and never as merely a means to a further end. "Act in such a way that you always treat humanity, whether in your own person or in the person of any other, never simply as a means, but always at the same time as an end."[7] Kant's formulation presupposes a moral relationship: one person treats another person as valuable. This is the case even though dignity appears to be individually claimed and owned. This relational formulation has sustained our Enlightenment belief in the immanent and unalienable worth of the individual person.

We remember the 1776 U.S. *Declaration of Independence* for putting into words the eighteenth century commitment to dignity. Relying on a rationalist version of Christian natural law, the immanence of dignity became justified because it is self-evident. Modernity relies on "self-evident" endowments by our "Creator" which become "rights" to be guaranteed by governments.

> We hold these truths to be self-evident, that all men are created equal, that they are endowed by their Creator with certain unalienable rights, that among these are Life, Liberty and the pursuit of Happiness.[8]

Even though the term *dignity* is not employed here, a phrase such as "endowed by their Creator" designates traits which are assumed to be inherent, innate, undeniable. The only warrant for writing such a declaration is the historical experience of the denial of dignity by England, a wrong to be righted. Subsequent American history records the ongoing process of dignity conferral to slaves, women, immigrants, and LGBTQ persons. Dignity must be conferred before it can be claimed, and then it requires protection by legislated and enforced law. The allegedly self-evident quality of dignity provides moral and legal justification for revolutionary strategies to recognize dignity where it is not publicly recognized.

Following the genocides of the Second World War, the United Nations elected a Committee on Human Rights, headed by Eleanor Roosevelt, to articulate for the world the need for protecting human dignity. According to the *Universal Declaration of Human Rights* of the General Assembly of the United Nations (UN) in 1948, "recognition of the inherent dignity and of the equal and inalienable rights of all members of the human family is the foundation of freedom, justice and peace in the world ..." Dignity provides the foundation upon which human rights are constructed.

> Article 1: All human beings are born free and equal in dignity and rights. They are endowed with reason and conscience and should act toward one another in a spirit of brotherhood.[9]

Although dignity is not precisely defined, the drafters of the UN Declaration took it for granted that everyone knows what it means and what it requires by way of political practice. Because the Western democracies and the Soviet Marxists could not agree regarding protection of individual rights, no definition of *dignity* was spelled out. The UN hoped it could rely on common acceptance and overlook any official ambiguity. What was not ambiguous was that the UN drafters presumed as self-evident that dignity is immanent.

In his postmodern treatment of dignity, Gaymon Bennett at Arizona State University says that

> whatever else it may be, human dignity is that which is inherent and it is that which can be, and must be, recognized. Moreover ... it is the source of political goods. The recognition of dignity issues in freedom, justice, and peace, and its violation brings with it outrage and disunity.[10]

The presupposed immanentist ontology provides justification for moral judgment and for restorative if not constructive legal action. Dignity is assumed without argument to be archonic [*archonic*, from the Greek αρχη meaning both "origin" and "governance"]. Dignity is built-in, innate, and universal. By making such an assumption, UN framers could avoid religious preference. "The key framers of the document affirmed an inherent human dignity in order to provide an explanatory basis for the validity of universal human rights while eschewing any religious or metaphysical justification for this affirmation."[11]

A theoretical tension remains buried here.[12] On the one hand, many persons and peoples in our world today do not experience or exhibit dignity, yet we can affirm theologically that they have dignity despite their apparent lack of dignity. On the other hand, non-religious entities such as the UN rely upon such a universal claim despite the fact that such a universal claim must itself rely upon a transcendental grounding. Roman Catholic thinkers claim to know where that dignity is grounded, namely, it is grounded in natural law and the *imago Dei*.

Dignity as the Vatican's pastoral ministry to the world

From the Second Vatican Council (1962–1965) to the present, the Roman Catholic Church has come to see itself as the world's shepherd, guiding the world's peoples toward a realization of their inherent dignity. For the church, this dignity is, first of all, immanent because it is written in the natural law readable by every rational soul. This mandate to recognize human dignity is articulated in *Gaudium et Spes*. "In the depths of his conscience, man detects a law which he does not impose upon himself, but which holds him to obedience ... For man has in his heart a law written by God; to obey it is the very dignity of man; according to it he will be judged."[13] God's law is written on the heart of natural humankind. So also is dignity. This has become the tacit political theology of the Roman Catholic Church in our generation. "At the Second Vatican Council in the 1960s," writes Bennett,

> dignity was put forward as an answer to the problem of how the church should relate pastorally to the secular world ... [I]t also raised the question of whether human dignity, framed as intrinsic and universal, could be recognized and understood apart from the church's theological vernacular and doctrinal commitments.[14]

The church sought "to figure dignity in such a way that it could be discursively taken for granted."[15] The post-Vatican II church rode the UN horse. "Humanity, in its essence and need for actualization, is a common object of responsibility for the church and the United Nations."[16]

This appeal to natural law in the created order presumes as self-evident that dignity is immanent, inherent, innate, archonic. Yet, dignity is also eschatological.

> §39. For after we have obeyed the Lord, and in His Spirit nurtured on earth the values of human dignity, brotherhood and freedom, and indeed all the good fruits of our nature and enterprise, we will find them again, but freed of stain, burnished and transfigured, when Christ hands over to the Father: 'a kingdom eternal and universal, a kingdom of truth and life, of holiness and grace, of justice, love and peace.' On this earth that Kingdom is already present in mystery. When the Lord returns it will be brought into full flower.[17]

Now, which is it: immanent or imminent? Is dignity archonic? Or, is it conferred by God eschatologically? Or, might it be a synthesis?

> They are synthetic in that destiny and origin are folded into each other; the one indicates and is constituted by the other. Their relation is nonlinear in that destiny is not a state subsequent to origins but rather is the actualization and completion of the rule anticipated and prescribed in the origin.[18]

Or, to say it my way, the eschatological kingdom will retroactively determine what has been archonic all along. Dignity is first imminent, then immanent. When we confer dignity where it is denied today, we are proleptically affirming what will be eschatologically true. To confer dignity on a person who is denied dignity is to act out of faith, to act implicitly out of trust in God's future.

The first use of God's law in Lutheran political theology

How might Reformation Lutherans cultivate this farmyard of theological contentions? Lutherans plow the same natural law field even if they reap fewer bushels per acre than the Vatican does. Lutherans along with their Reformed neighbors split God's law into three parcels:

1 the political (*usus politicus*) or civil use (*usus civilis*) which sustains political community;
2 the theological or prophetic use (*usus theologicus, usus spiritualis, usus paedogogicus*) which renders judgment against injustice and sin, and which relates to the gospel of divine forgiveness dialectically;[19]
3 the guidebook use which, in response to the gospel, channels the energy of love into productive effort. Law, all by itself, is only a cookie cutter, a frame, a shape, a template. For law to accomplish its mission, the form must be filled by love in the pursuit of justice.

When plowing the field of God's law, Lutherans spend most of their hours planting and harvesting the law in its second use. It is this use that stands in dialectical relationship with the gospel of grace.

> The law commands and demands of us what we are to do … The gospel, however, does not preach what we are to do or to avoid. It demands nothing of us, but instead reverses the matter, does the opposite, and says, 'This is what God has done for you.'[20]

The law in its second use provides the prophetic leverage the social critic needs to render judgment against political structures which foster injustice and deny dignity.[21] There is only one divine law, to be sure; but we creatures experience the law in three uses.

God's law in the first use (let alone the third use) lies almost like a fallow field. But, it is fertile. Perhaps we should plant the seed of dignity and see if it grows.

For Martin Luther, as for the Vatican, legislated laws drink from a well of justice springing up from God's reservoir of natural reason. "We should keep written laws subject to reason, from which they originally welled forth as from the spring of justice."[22] The gospel may inspire love, but it is the law which provides guidance on how to love, especially how to love through practicing justice.

Article XVI of the Augsburg Confession attests that "lawful civil ordinances are good works of God and that Christians are permitted to hold office …"[23] Although sixteenth century Lutherans frequently spoke of civil law with a negative slant—civil law protects us from crime and punishes criminals—one could easily reinterpret the civil use positively as a means for enhancing safe community. This is what Bernard Lohse does. "By means of the political use, external order on earth is to be maintained, and peace and the securing of justice preserved."[24] Positive or legislated law should reflect natural law in constructive fashion.

This law structuring our political order comes from God, even if formulated in the words of secular legislators. Justice transcends those who are responsible for establishing and protecting the social order.[25] The laws we live by, whether the Ten Commandments of Moses or the legislation of a secular government, are positive expressions of a more fundamental natural law.[26] At least, this is what Luther thought.

> It is natural to honor God, not steal, not commit adultery, nor bear false witness, not kill. What Moses commands is not new … they [just moral codes] have been implanted in me by nature, and Moses agrees exactly with nature.[27]

Luther got this reliance on natural law from St. Paul (Romans 2:15), about whom post-modern theologian John Milbank remarks, "human positive law, while it had a relative, circumstantial aspect, had both to retain an equitable unity with natural law and to seek ultimately to promote the reign of charity."[28]

Although dimly lit in human consciousness, God has buried the light of natural law within the human conscience, according to the Reformation mind. Taking an admittedly minimalist approach, Philip Melanchthon identifies four components to the law of God inborn in us. Intuitively, first, we hear from within us a voice commanding us to "worship God!" Second, "since we are born into a life that is social, a shared life," we are prompted to "harm no one but help everyone in kindness." Third, "if it is impossible that absolutely no one be harmed," then we set up a government with police and courts to keep "the number of harmed … to a minimum." Fourth, "property shall be divided for the sake of public peace ... to alleviate the wants of others through contracts."[29] This law is natural, built-in, innate, and universal, according to Melanchthon. It is archonic.

The light of natural law shines too dimly, however, leaving much of our civil life in the shadows. Some civic leaders strive for genuine justice, and we should be grateful to them. Yet, not all social arrangements conform to what is natural. Slavery, for instance. "What is more foreign to nature than slavery?" asks Melanchthon rhetorically.[30] Although natural law may enlighten the civic mind, any society can elect to live in the shadows rather than the light. Melanchthon in the sixteenth century does not yet construct a doctrine of dignity, but he certainly recognizes that slavery is incompatible with God's law. Modernity has seen the wisdom of Melanchthon's insight. What we need from Lutherans now in the twenty-first century are middle axioms—bridge axioms—which connect God's law in the first use with the ministry of conferring dignity in a world where liberating vigilance can never rest.

Can disciples of Luther think of the law proleptically? Wolfhart Pannenberg contends that the actualization of God's law is eschatologically dependent. "Thus the eschatological expectation of a better community of law in the future constitutes the condition for justice in the future ... only the future realization of justice under law will correspond completely to the will of God."[31]

Grounding human dignity in the eschatological Christ

Such reliance on natural law must avoid the archonic fallacy, the fallacy that finds essence and salvation in a past point of origin. Our essence is found in our redeemed future, not our past. This applies even to human nature, to humanity's status before the God of grace. Human nature is defined largely by the *imago Dei,* and the *imago Dei* is defined proleptically by Jesus' Easter resurrection.

Humanity's "essential and original nature is to be found, therefore, not in Adam but in Christ," argues Karl Barth forcefully. "In Adam we can only find it prefigured. Adam can therefore be interpreted only in light of Christ and not the other way around."[32] True humanity has yet to become true humanity; it will become true only in God's promised resurrection when each of us becomes fully Christlike. Just as Jesus Christ rose from the dead on the first Easter to embody both the image of God and the image of the true human being, so also will we rise into Christ's double image.

This requires a proleptic anthropology. Proleptically, the person of faith today is *simul justus et peccator.* Yet, as justified by faith, he or she anticipates full godlikeness in God's future. If human dignity is based on human godlikeness, then it must be based on a prolepsis of a godlikeness which will attain its fullness only in the eschatological consummation. When we confer godlikeness on sinful persons today, we are borrowing redeemed reality from God's tomorrow. In short, immanent dignity derives from imminent dignity.

This proleptic approach to anthropology seeks the *imago Dei* not in the old *Adam* but in the new *Adam,* not in the old creation but in the new one, not archonically but eschatologically. With obvious excitement Paul proclaims, "the gospel of the glory of Christ, who is the image of God" (εἰκών τὸ θεοῦ; 2 Cor. 4:4b). The term εἰκών (icon) is used both of Christ and of the person who has faith in Christ, and Paul describes us as "being transformed into the same image" (2 Cor. 3:18; see Rom. 8:29). The Christ of whom he speaks is the Easter Christ, the risen Christ, the first fruits of those having fallen asleep (1 Cor. 15:20, 48), the advent of the new creation. Christ as the divine image is our prototype. We live now as the *imago Dei* insofar as we live in him, insofar as we participate in the reality of the resurrection.

This leads UCC theologian Brent Waters to define dignity as something conferred before it becomes immanent. "Human dignity is not an inherent quality, but is derived from the gift of grace given by God in Christ."[33] Conferring dignity as a gift of grace upon those in our world today who are not treated with inherent worth is the moral mission of Christ's disciples and of the citizens of each modern nation as well. The biblical command to love God and love one's neighbor takes the form of dignity conferral. It is both a religious and a political mission to confer dignity on the poor, the marginalized, and all victims of injustice. When this mission is accomplished, those upon whom dignity was conferred can then enjoy it, claim it, and demand justice under the law. Today's theologians rightly refer to this *dignity conferral* as *liberation*.[34]

Conclusion: liberation as the conferral of dignity

My understanding of liberation as dignity conferral is eschatologically dependent. The eschatology required here dares not be of the escapist type, but rather of the transformational type. "Liberation theology emerges in Latin America claiming that there is no pie in the sky without pie on earth," Filipe Maia reminds us.[35] What happens in Latin America provides inspiration for the work of the church in the remainder of the world.

"Members of the body of Christ are called to embody the hope in the promised future of God, where suffering and death shall be no more," says feminist theologian Deanna Thompson, drawing on the eschatological promise. "This is the eschatological horizon opened up by God's gift of justification and the resurrection promise of new life given in the midst of our current sinful existence."[36]

I recommend that we piece together a liberation ethic with dignity conferral to construct a political theology conditioned by the eschatological proviso, the proviso that the ground of being grants us existence retroactively from God's consummate future. The theologian of hope who most directly connects Christian hope with the liberation mission is Jesuit Johannes Metz. "When the Church is faced with modern political systems, she must emphasize her critical, liberating function again and again, to make it clear that [human] history as a whole stands under God's eschatological proviso."[37] A political theology which focuses on liberation will hold up a vision of global community inspired by God's law in the first use and also rely on the second use to judge the social order when it denies dignity in any quarter.[38]

In sum, the *mission of the church today is to provide religious substance to political forms so that the body politic orients itself toward the protection and conferral of dignity on behalf of all of its citizens. Law is the means by which the state accomplishes this mission.*

Notes

1 For the further implications of this argument, see Ted Peters, "Dignity," in *Encyclopedia of Science, Technology, and Ethics*, ed. Carl Mitcham 2 (New York: Macmillan, Thomson, Gale, 2005), 528–530; Ted Peters, "Cells, Souls, and Dignity: A Theological Assessment," Boston College Law School Law and Religion Program Matters of Life and Death: Selected Publications (2006–2007): 15–36.

2 2 Matthew 11:4–6 (New Revised Standard Version, Anglicised (NRSVA).

3 Tshenuwani Simon Farisani, "South Africa: Unasked Questions and Unquestionable Answers," *Journal of Law & Religion* 2 (1987): 265.

4 Martin Luther, *The Annotated Luther*, eds., Hans J. Hillerbrand, Kirsi I. Stjerna, and Timothy J. Wengert, 5 vols. (Minneapolis, MN: Fortress Press, 2015), 2, 17.

5 Is it reasonable to think of immanent dignity as relational? According to philosopher Jürgen Habermas, "human dignity ... is, in a strict moral and legal sense, connected with this relational symmetry. It is not a property like intelligence or blue eyes, that one might 'possess' by nature; it rather indicates the kind of 'inviolability' which comes to have a significance only in interpersonal relations of mutual respect, in the egalitarian dealings among persons." Jürgen Habermas, *The Future of Human Nature* (Cambridge, UK and Malden, MA: Blackwell Polity, 2003), 33.

6 In 1486, Giovani Pico della Mirandola delivered his address, "Oration on the Dignity of Man," which kicked off Renaissance Humanism in Western Europe. "Man is, with complete justice, considered and called a great miracle and a being worthy of all admiration." Giovani Pico della Mirandola. "Oration on the Dignity of Man," (1486). Accessed November 6, 2017. http://bactra.org/Mirandola/. The dignity lauded by Mirandola referenced the human race in distinction from brutes below and angels above; dignity did not refer to the incalculable worth of the individual human person. That development would come later.

7 Immanuel Kant, *Groundwork of the Metaphysic of Morals*, trans. H. J. Paton (New York: Harper, 1948), 96. The concept of dignity stands within a larger framework of ethical reflection that theologians would refer to as *agape*, as disinterested love—that is, love for the sake of the other rather than for the sake of furthering one's own interests. For philosopher Kant, what we now know as the principle of dignity is embedded within a set of categorical imperatives. These moral imperatives are called "categorical" because they transcend the self-interests of the one who answers their call. First, Kant enjoins us to act only according to a maxim which we can also wish to be a universal law—that is, a law that would apply to ourselves and others equally. "*Handle nur nach derjenigen Maxime, durch die du zugleich wollen kanst, dass sie ein allgemeines Gesetz werde.*" Immanuel Kant, *Grundlegung zur Metaphysik der Sitten, Immanuel Kant Werke in Sechs Banden*, ed. Wilhelm Weischedel IV (Darmstadt: Wissenschaftliche Buchgesellschaft, 1998), 51. Second, he enjoins us to act so that we treat humanity, not only in our own person but also in the person of all others, never as a mere means but always as an end. "*Handle so, dass du die Menschheit, sowohl in deiner Person, als in der Person eines jeden andern, jederzeit zugleich als Zweck, niemals bloss als Mittel brauchest.*" Ibid., 61. Third, Kant enjoins us to act so that all maxims we establish for ourselves as law will cohere with a possible kingdom of goals like a law of nature. "*Alle Maximen aus eigener Gesetzgebung zu einem moglichen Reiche der Zwecke, als einem Reiche der natur, zusammenstimmen sollen.*" Ibid, 61. My appropriation of Kant here has to do solely with the moral relationship that produces dignity. Kant's model of the individual moral agent as autonomous or sovereign apart from such a relationship, however, is problematic for feminist theorists. Kantian moralism is so principled and austere that the idea that the philosopher Kant could be "wedded to 'the moral law' and nothing else, neither family, nor faith, nor nation—is entirely unreal," according to Jean Bethke Elshtain. Jean Bethke Elshtain, *Sovereignty, God, State, and Self* (New York: Basic Books, 2008), 176.

8 The Declaration of Independence (1776). Accessed November 6, 2017. www.ushistory.org/Declaration/document/.

9 G.A. Res. 217 (III) A, Universal Declaration of Human Rights, art. 2 (Dec. 10, 1948). The *Universal Declaration of Human Rights* was actually about rights; dignity was assumed and implied. See the interesting account of Eleanor Roosevelt's work in Gary M. Simpson, "Innovating National Sovereignty and the Just War Tradition: The Responsibility to Protect, the Universal Declaration of Human Rights, and the Anticipatory, Interruptive, and Resiliently Empathetic Eleanor Roosevelt," *Word and World* 34, no. 4 (Fall 2014): 349–57.

Dignity has become an international criterion by which the behavior of nation states is measured. For example, note how a prosecutor of the International Criminal Court words his complaint: "Members of US armed forces appear to have subjected at least 61 detained persons to torture, cruel treatment, outrages upon personal dignity on the territory of Afghanistan between 1 May 2003 and 31 December 2014." An outrage against personal dignity is deemed a crime. Mike Corder, "ICC Prosecutors: US Forces May Have Committed War Crimes," *The Associated Press*, November 15, 2016. Accessed November 6, 2017. https://apnews.com/7ebe643c029d4e01b4a2e794118b3b1e/icc-prosecutors-us-forces-may-have-committed-war-crimes.

10 Gaymon Bennett, *Technicians of Human Dignity: Bodies, Souls, and the Making of Intrinsic Worth* (New York: Fordham University Press, 2016), 42.

11 See generally Glenn Hughes, "The Concept of Dignity in the Universal Declaration of Human Rights," *Journal of Religious Ethics* 39 (March 2011): 1.

12 See generally Peters, "Dignity."
13 Pope Paul VI, *Gaudium et Spes: Pastoral Constitution on the Church In the Modern World*, The Vatican (1965) §16. Accessed November 6, 2017. www.vatican.va/archive/hist_councils/ii_vatican_council/documents/vat-ii_cons_19651207_gaudium-et-spes_en.html.
14 Bennett, *Technicians of Human Dignity*, 4.
15 Ibid., 8.
16 Ibid., 30.
17 *Gaudium et Spes* §39.
18 Bennett, *Technicians of Human Dignity*, 71.
19 For Luther, God is double handed. God's left hand presents to us the law; the right hand extends to us grace. Craig Nessan sees a continuity between the law in its first two uses and other polar doublets in Luther's thinking: two kinds of righteousness, reason, will, and works. "The first use of the law functions as God's way of ordering and structuring the world in the left hand strategy, while the second use of the law functions to expose and condemn sin in preparation for proclamation of the gospel in the right hand strategy." Craig L. Nessan, "Law, Righteousness, Reason, Will, and Works: Civil and Theological Uses," *Currents in Theology and Mission* 41, no. 1 (February 2014): 52. Nessan comes close to saying that the second use of the law represents God's right hand, whereas it seems to me that Luther intends to put the gospel of grace in the right hand. Nessan comes close to confusing law and gospel. Ibid.
20 *The Annotated Luther*, vol. 2: 133–134.
21 Robert Benne, "How Should Modern Lutherans Try to Shape Secular Law?" in Ronald W. Duty, and Marie A. Failinger, eds., *On Secular Governance: Lutheran Perspectives on Contemporary Legal Issues* (Grand Rapids, MI: Wm. B. Eerdmans, 2016), 328–340. Robert Benne ascribes prophetic judgment to the gospel rather than the law. Ibid., 335. I believe this is a mistake, because it is the law which judges and the gospel which forgives. Benne risks turning the gospel into law and dissolving the dialectic of law and gospel. Bradley Wendel gets it right. "The law stands against the gospel as something that accuses us, against which we cannot stand, but the gospel frees us from this condemnation." W. Bradley Wendel, "*Nomos* and Narrative in Civil Law and Theological Ethics," in Ronald W. Duty, and Marie A. Failinger, eds., *On Secular Governance: Lutheran Perspectives on Contemporary Legal Issues* (Grand Rapids, MI: Wm. B. Eerdmans, 2016), 13.
22 Martin Luther, *Word and Sacrament*, George V. Schick, trans., American Edition of *Luther's Works* (hereafter *LW*), eds. Jaroslav Pelikan, and Helmut T. Lehmann, 55 vols. (Minneapolis, MN: Fortress Press and St. Louis, MO: Concordia Publishing Company, 1955–1986). *LW* 45, 130.
23 Robert Kolb and Timothy J. Wengert eds., *The Book of Concord: The Confessions of the Evangelical Lutheran Church* (Minneapolis, MN: Fortress Press, 2000), 49.
24 Bernard Lohse, *Martin Luther's Theology: Its Historical and Systematic Development* (Minneapolis, MN: Fortress Press, 1999), 271.
25 Intuitively, we human beings feel a sense of duty, an attraction to justice accompanied by an obligation to uphold justice. This sense of duty rises to articulation as law, as both an invitation to pursue justice and a judgment when we fall short. "This sense of obligation is, in fact, the claim which the essential nature of man makes upon him in his present sinful state. The virtue which corresponds to the true nature of man therefore appears to sinful man in the form of law." Reinhold Niebuhr, *The Nature and Destiny of Man* (London, Westminster John Knox Press, 1996) vol. 1: 272. Our conscience becomes the voice of the law within the soul. "Man's uneasy conscience is, in other words, and expression of the law written in his own heart." Ibid., vol. 1:274.
26 "*Natural* law refers to what reason can discover about rectitude in human choosing; these discoveries are not the product of revelation or the decrees of authority ... Natural law is antecedent to all human choosing." Gerard W. Bradley, "Natural Law," in Michael W. McConnell, Robert F. Cochran, Jr., and Angela C. Carmella, eds., *Christian Perspectives on Legal Thought* (New Haven, CT: Yale University Press, 2001), 277.
27 Luther, *Word and Sacrament*, *LW* 35, 168.
28 John Millbank, *Beyond the Secular Order* (Oxford: Wiley Blackwell, 2013), 119. As Carl-Henric Grenholm points out in Chapter 2 of this volume, pp. 21–22, the Lutheran Reformers viewed positive law as responsible to a higher morality embedded in natural law; they would not approve of cutting the tie between positive law and morality.

29 Philip Melanchthon, *Loci Communes* in *Library of Christian Classics*, XIX, ed. Wilhelm Pauck (Louisville, KY: Westminster/John Knox Press, 1969), 52–53.

30 Ibid., 53.

31 Wolfhart Pannenberg, *Ethics*, trans. Keith Crim (Philadelphia, PA: Westminster, 1981), 50. Few say it more beautifully than John Witte. "The Bible teaches that time is linear, not cyclical. Biblical history moves forward from a sin-trampled garden to a golden city, from a fallen world to a perfect end-time." John Witte, "God's Joust, God's Justice: An Illustration from the History of Marriage Law," in Michael W. McConnell, Robert F. Cochran, Jr., and Angela C. Carmella, eds., *Christian Perspectives on Legal Thought* (New Haven, CT: Yale University Press, 2001), 407.

32 Karl Barth, *Christ and Adam: Man and Humanity in Romans 5*, trans. T.A. Smail (New York: Collier Books, 1956), 39–40. The human race finds its unity—including the dignity of women—in the one Christ. "A feminist theologian of the cross works to deter theologies of glory that suppress and oppress women," contends Mary Streufert, "for the promise that we are all justified by grace through faith means that all humanity is found in Christ Jesus." Mary J. Streufert, "The Person of Christ from a Feminist Perspective of Human and Divine, Male and Female" in Mary J. Streufert, eds., *Transformative Lutheran Theologies: Feminist, Womanist, and Mujerista Perspectives* (Minneapolis, MN: Fortress Press, 2010), 148.

33 Brent Waters, "Saving Us from Ourselves: Christology, Anthropology and the Seduction of Posthuman Medicine," in Celia Deane-Drummond, and Peter Manley Scott, eds., *Future Perfect? God, Medicine and Human Identity* (London: T. & T. Clark International, 2006), 190. Waters grounds dignity in the incarnation, in redemption. It is much more common in Christian theology to ground dignity in creation. One way is to appeal to *creatio ex nihilo*, wherein the very creation of the world is a gift of divine grace. "In short, creation from nothing dictates that *everything* is of immediate (i.e., noninstrumental) concern to God insofar as it exists at all, and what is of concern to God cannot be a matter of indifference to us who are called to life in communion with God." Ian McFarland, *From Nothing: A Theology of Creation* (Louisville, KY: Westminster John Knox Press, 2014), 185.

34 Dignity conferral is the essence of liberation, I contend, without oversimplifying the complexities. Sometimes the claim must trump the lack of conferral. "Human dignity cannot be conferred from one human to another, and it cannot be engendered through development," contends South African theologian Retief Müller. Retief Müller, "Historiography and Cross-cultural Research into African Indigenous Christianity (AIC): A Challenge to Human Dignity," *Studies in World Christianity* 19, no. 1 (2014): 5–24. During the period when white religion dominated, black South Africans lacked dignity due to a false consciousness that reinforced racial stratification. The implication is this: white society is not in a position to confer dignity; black people will have to claim it on their own. Ibid.

35 Maia, Filipe Maia, "With What Can We Compare the Kingdom of God? Latin American Liberation Theology and the Challenge of Political Projects," *Union Seminary Quarterly Review* 64, nos. 2–3 (2013): 124–137.

36 Deanna A. Thompson, "Hoping for More: How Eschatology Matters for Lutheran Feminist Theologies," in Mary J. Streufert, ed., *Transformative Lutheran Theologies* (Minneapolis, MN: Fortress Press, 2010), 232.

37 See generally Johannes B. Metz, *Theology of the World*, trans. William Glen-Doepel (New York: Herder and Herder, 1969), 118. Political theology in our postcolonial period must employ the first use of the law to promote a single global community, and it must employ the second use in the form of prophetic judgment against institutions and cultural habits which deny human dignity. According to Paul Chung, "postcolonial public theology assuming transformative ethical activity is future-oriented, sharpening its ethical direction in the spirit of *metanoia* from the wrongdoing in the past toward God's promised new activity in our midst. Paul S. Chung, *Postcolonial Public Theology* (Eugene, OR: Cascade Books, 2016), 7. Tillich, among others, retrieved the Protestant Principle from the Reformation to render political critique. "Theology—both Reformation theology and prophetic theology—is also the description of *the new reality*. But this description always has an element of expectation, or eschatology, or looking at that which is not yet and will come." Paul Tillich, "The Recovery of the Prophetic Tradition in the Reformation" in Carl Heinz Ratschow, ed., *Main Works/Hauptwerke* (Berlin and New York: De Gruyter, 1989) vol. 6, 338.

38 According to William T. Cavanaugh, "the dominant mode of political theology in the West since World War I has been critical. Christian political theology since Barth has generally taken for granted and even celebrated the fact that the church no longer occupies a position of privilege and coercive power in most places. Liberation theology and the other influential movements it has inspired have not ceased to call upon the church to abandon its last vestiges of privilege and take its position firmly among the marginalized. It is not, for all that, any less a political theology." William T. Cavanaugh, "Am I Impossible? A Political Theologian's Response to Kahn's *Political Theology*," *Political Theology* 13, no. 6 (December, 2012): 739.

9 U.S. war-culture, the post-9/11 "unlawful alien combatant," and "Peace in God's World"

Kelly Denton-Borhaug

Introduction

The 1995 Lutheran Social Statement "For Peace in God's World" declares that Lutherans draw from the principles of just war in order to evaluate national decisions about "permitting recourse toward war in exceptional circumstances."[1] In this chapter, I explore post-9/11 developments in U.S. policy regarding covert operations connected to the rhetoric of "the illegal/unlawful alien enemy combatant" employed by the George W. Bush administration. This rhetoric played an important role in justifying the isolation of detainees from the human rights protections of longstanding treaties such as the Geneva Conventions and the Convention against Torture. It served as a lynchpin to rationalize serious deviations from mainstream national and international law interpreting these treaties. Most importantly, such language empowered morally problematical mis-description of torture, justification of extraordinary rendition and dismissal of detainees' right to legal recourse. After this history, I place these developments within the wider frame of U.S. war-culture and ask how the 1995 ELCA statement may assist Lutherans (with other citizens) in the important work of ethical deliberation regarding these events. Striving for honesty and awareness regarding our own reality in the United States, how should citizens and people of faith respond?

It is telling that on his second day of office, January 22, 2009, President Barack Obama signed "Executive Order 13491: Ensuring Lawful Interrogations," which summarily revoked a number of legal interpretations and decisions made during the previous presidential administration. As one key section of 13491 reads:

> Section 1. All executive directives, orders, and regulations inconsistent with this order, including but not limited to those issued to or by the Central Intelligence Agency (CIA) from September 11, 2001, to January 20, 2009, concerning detention or the interrogation of detained individuals, are revoked to the extent of their inconsistency with this order.[2]

Coming extraordinarily early in President Obama's term in office, this was an unambiguous rejection of President Bush's Executive Order 13440. In order to better understand the significance of these presidential actions, this narrative turns to the period just after September 11, 2001. For it was in these early days, after those traumatic national events, that the process began in the Bush administration to systematically reframe legal rhetoric to justify "enhanced interrogation," "extraordinary rendition" and the undermining of *habeas corpus* rights. Though by 2006, the Supreme Court decision in *Hamdan v Rumsfeld*[3] invalidated some of these legal practices concerning combatant detainee treatment, the Bush administration pushed back. In Order 13440 (July 20, 2007), President Bush restated the thrust of his administration's legal philosophy: accused "unlawful combatants" such as Salim Ahmed Hamdan, a Yemeni national who was Osama Bin Laden's driver and guard, could not claim the right to *habeas corpus* guaranteed to prisoners of war by the Common Article III of the Geneva Conventions. As 13440 stated,

> On February 7, 2002, I [President Bush] determined for the United States that members of al Qaeda, the Taliban, and associated forces are *unlawful enemy combatants* who are not entitled to the protections that the Third Geneva Convention provides to prisoners of war. I hereby reaffirm that determination.[4] (italics mine)

How did the occupant of the highest office of the United States arrive at such a place? One important thrust of Executive Order 13440 regarded its affirmation of presidential power to wield constitutional authority and interpret the meaning and measure of the Geneva Conventions and the Convention on Torture for the United States. This interpretation was not new; in fact, Vice President Cheney especially prized the philosophy of "the supreme executive" in the decades preceding the George W. Bush administration.[5] In 1987, during the Iran-Contra affair, Congress had admonished President Reagan for abuse of authority and secrecy regarding the NSA and financial support of Contra rebels in Nicaragua. However, Cheney, a congressperson at the time, signed a minority report that disagreed with these legal proceedings. Together with his legal counsel, David Addington, he defended the philosophy of the "supreme" executive power in government. Legal scholars Gershon Shafir and Cynthia E. Shairer write, "Cheney and Addington's living memory of [this earlier] era... infused the new [Bush] administration with their own single-minded focus."[6] As Human Rights Watch later reported, following 9/11, Cheney "was the principal political force pressing OLC [Office of Legal Counsel] lawyers to justify the use of coercive interrogation methods. As Cheney notably said during a media interview in which he defended the actions of [John] Yoo and other OLC lawyers, the lawyers did 'what we asked them to do.'"[7]

But enormous changes to established human rights norms and laws would not remain unchallenged. In 2009, the Senate Select Committee on Intelligence mounted an investigation upon learning that the CIA had destroyed videotapes of their detainee interrogations.[8] According to the "Committee Study of the Central Intelligence Agency's Detention and Interrogation Program," popularly known as the "Senate Torture Report" and partly declassified in 2014, just six days after the 9/11 attacks, President George W. Bush signed a far-reaching "Memorandum of Notification" (MON). This covert order authorized an array of new powers in the CIA "to undertake operations designed to capture and detain persons who pose a continuing, serious threat of violence or death to U.S. persons and interests or who are planning terrorist activities."[9]

The significance of this MON cannot be overstated; according to the Intelligence Committee, it provided "unprecedented authorities, granting the CIA significant discretion in determining whom to detain, the factual basis for the detention, and the length of detention."[10] By November of 2001, merely weeks after the MON, Guantánamo Bay had been identified as a likely facility for the incarceration of detainees, and additional covert "black sites" were in the process of being developed. By December 2001, further "blanket approval" had been granted to CIA officers to determine who posed the requisite "continuing serious threat of violence or death to US persons and interests or who are planning terrorist activities,'" and how and where to detain them.[11] The consolidation of power and secrecy was well underway.

Nevertheless, according to investigative journalist Jane Mayer, the MON of September 17 did not emerge out of a vacuum, but was reprised from an "amalgamation of years' worth of thinking about all the powers the [Central Intelligence] Agency might like to exercise in its fondest dreams."[12] It was based on an earlier set of proposals, the "Blue Sky Memo," drawn up by Cofer Black, the CIA senior counterterrorism agent, at the end of the Clinton era.[13] Just two days after the 9/11 attacks, on September 13, 2001, using the "Blue Sky Memo" as a template, Tenet proposed to President Bush that the U.S. not only militarily support the Northern Alliance of Afghanistan, but also create "covert on-the-ground support from CIA paramilitary teams and Special Forces from the U.S. military."[14]

Labeled "The New Paradigm," this authorization inaugurated what Bush would call "an invisible war." Massive covert actions would be reported to only four congressional elected representatives, who then would be prohibited from discussing what they learned with anyone else in the government. Most important, the plan had distinct implications for the rule of law in the United States. "Don't ever let this happen again," Bush reportedly ordered his attorney general, John Ashcroft. Mayer comments, "The top lawyer in the country was being told to do anything and everything to stop the terrorists—whatever it took."[15] Meanwhile, CIA Director Tenet proposed the assumption of CIA "blanket authority" to decide whom to kill, kidnap and interrogate, and how to provide the president plausible deniability for any legal wrongdoings. The CIA would also be authorized to monitor communications, break into private property, and follow financial transactions of those suspected of terrorism, both inside and outside the United States.[16]

These were the early steps of a presidential administration that eventually would set aside obligations to enforce international treaties, redefine torture, justify extraordinary rendition, and rationalize indeterminate detention without access to legal recourse, among other acts. Michael Rolince, the head of the International Terrorism Operations Sections at the FBI, described the new approach as "rule-of-law be damned." One year into the new "program," Cofer Black explained to the House and Senate Intelligence Committee: "[a]ll I want to say is that there was a 'before 9/11' an 'after 9/11.' After 9/11, the gloves come off."[17]

Digging deeper into the legal arguments: the "unlawful combatant"

By February 7, 2002, President Bush had signed a memorandum to Vice President Cheney summarizing "extensive discussions" regarding the status of al Qaeda and Taliban detainees.[18] This memo, with the uniquely Orwellian title, "Humane Treatment of al Qaeda and Taliban Detainees," was shared with the Secretaries of State and Defense, the Attorney General, the Chief of Staff, the Director of the CIA, the NSA Assistant to the President, and the Chair of the Joint Chiefs of Staff. Declaring that "a new paradigm" and "new thinking about the law of war" are essential in the "war against terrorism," Bush outlined new positions that were key departures from previous legal interpretations. First, as the memo boldly stated, "none of the provisions of Geneva apply to our conflict with al Qaeda in Afghanistan or elsewhere throughout the world."[19]

Second, the memo affirmed Bush's own authority as president "to suspend Geneva as between the United States and Afghanistan." Third, al Qaeda and Taliban detainees were newly defined as "unlawful combatants," who did not qualify as prisoners of war under Article IV of The Geneva Conventions. Additionally, as the memo stated, "Article 3 of Geneva does not apply" either to al Qaeda or Taliban detainees. In the end, the memo concluded with a vague promise "to be a strong supporter of Geneva and its principles," and to "treat detainees humanely, and to the extent appropriate and consistent with military necessity, in a manner consistent with the principles of Geneva." How are we to understand such enormous changes?

The significance and danger of these legal departures from longstanding American understandings are evidenced by the speed with which they were revoked in the succeeding presidential administration: by the second day in office, the Obama administration was scrubbing executive orders clean of perceived human rights violations as much as possible. Yet, legal scholars today argue that systemic changes wrought by the Bush-Cheney administration continued into the Obama administration in significant ways, and in some cases, morphed and expanded.[20] I return to this troubling reality later in this chapter. At this point, what is paramount are the consequences of Bush administration changes in terminology and philosophy: a group of human beings now were assigned to the category of "unlawful/illegal alien enemy combatants," redefining their status in essence as less than human, and thus not deserving of the protections that human rights law provides.

The Bybee/Yoo memos

Over a dozen executive memoranda in this period addressed the treatment of detainees, with the "most controversial" memos coming from the OLC (Office of Legal Counsel) and written by Professor John Yoo.[21] On January 22, 2002, Alberto Gonzales, Counsel to the President, forwarded a legal memo drafted by Yoo and signed by Assistant Attorney General Jay S. Bybee, titled "Application of Treaties and Laws to al Qaeda and Taliban Detainees." This memo argued that neither the federal War Crimes Act nor the Geneva Conventions applied to the detention conditions of al Qaeda prisoners.[22] Why? First, the memo argued, because al Qaeda is not "a high governing state," the U.S. military is not bound to govern its treatment of these captives according to Geneva's stipulations regarding prisoners of war. Second, the memo writers underscored, if al Qaeda is not a sovereign state, neither does it belong within other non-state categories spelled out by the treaty, "other militia or volunteer forces" (described in Geneva as being commanded by responsible individuals, wearing insignia, openly carrying arms and obeying the laws of war). According to Bybee/Yoo, these two points supported the claim that al Qaeda fighters "do not qualify for POW treatment under Article 4" of Geneva.

Drawing on Defense Secretary Donald Rumsfeld's earlier description of the Taliban as "an illegitimate, un-elected group of terrorists," the memo described both al Qaeda and the Taliban as "armed violent militants," or "non-governmental terrorist organizations."[23] This early rhetoric would morph into President Bush's subsequent February 7, 2002 Memorandum term: "unlawful combatants,"[24] which continued to develop in later legal documents into the descriptor: "unlawful/illegal alien enemy combatants."[25]

The impact of this rhetoric for those detained in the new CIA program was far-reaching indeed. The Bush-Cheney administration not only was keen on maintaining the category of "unlawful combatant," but pushed it to limits that now seem hard to believe. Legal counsel for the United States went so far as to argue that the Executive authority could detain even such individuals as:

> "'[a] little old lady in Switzerland who writes checks to what she thinks is a charity that helps orphans in Afghanistan but [what] really is a front to finance al-Qaeda activities',

> a person who teaches English to the son of an al Qaeda member, and a journalist who knows the location of Osama Bin Laden but refuses to disclose it to protect her source."[26]

Moreover, the justification included additional arguments. As Bybee and Yoo concluded in the January 22, 2002 memo, the President *also* was not obligated to fulfill the Geneva Conventions with regard to Afghanistan, because Afghanistan is a "failed state."[27] In such a case, the President could "decide that no treaty obligations are owed." In essence, this argument reduced Taliban and al Qaeda combatants to "statelessness." Interestingly, Bybee and Yoo did not mention that many of the al Qaeda combatants hailed from sovereign states that the U.S. considers to be strong allies and friends, such as Saudi Arabia. Most importantly, the argument did not address the reality of a non-state actor involving citizens from diverse sovereign states. Further stipulating that the President could ignore Geneva based on "military necessity" or "self-defense," they concluded, "neither the detention nor trial of al Qaeda fighters is subject to Geneva or the War Crimes Act."[28]

However, according to Jane Mayer, Secretary of State Colin L. Powell and his legal adviser, William Howard Taft IV, wasted little time in responding. Just three days later, on January 25, 2002, Powell weighed in with grave reservations. Acknowledging that the Bybee/Yoo argument "on its face provides maximum flexibility," they followed this short statement with a long list of "cons" in which they noted,

> It will reverse over a century of U.S. policy and practice in supporting the Geneva Conventions and undermine the protections of the law of war for our troops ... [W]hile no one anticipated the precise situation that we face, the GPW (Geneva Article III on the Prisoners of War) was intended to cover all types of armed conflict and did not by its terms limit its application.[29]

Taft put it even more bluntly, "There is no such thing as a non-covered person under the Geneva Conventions. It's nonsense. The protocols cover fighters in everything from world wars to local rebellions."[30] Mayer's investigation reveals, however, that Powell's and Taft's access to the President was no match for Vice President Cheney's. She writes, "It remains unclear, in fact, whether anyone ever fully explained the countervailing arguments to President Bush before he signed off on the plan." Powell and Taft had made an attempt, but "fought a rear-guard action against Bush's lawyers and lost."[31]

But Powell and Taft proved prescient in their objections and fears. As Humans Rights Watch's 2015 report, "No More Excuses: A Roadmap to Justice for CIA Torture," later determined that arguments like military necessity and self-defense

> Ignore[] well-established US Supreme Court precedent making clear that the executive branch *does not have unbridled authority* in the conduct of foreign affairs—it is bound by congressional statutes and judicial decisions. *Torture is prohibited* by US and international human rights and humanitarian law *at all times and for all reasons.* There is no exception for war or public emergencies.[32] (italics mine)

Meanwhile, the "increasing breadth and malleability" of the term "illegal enemy combatant" represents human rights dangers that have not been resolved. As legal scholar Allison Danner writes, this term continues "to catch many in its sweep that would not be considered combatants under the law of war."[33] The policies and practices aimed at terrorist groups from the post-9/11 era have leaked beyond the fields of war. For instance, rhetoric of the "alien unlawful combatant" slips into accusations against undocumented immigrants in the United States who then are stereotyped as "terrorists."[34] In the post-9/11 era, immigration policy was subordinated to counterterrorist policy, as evidenced by the fact that the INS (Immigration and Naturalization Service) was transferred to DHS [the Department of Homeland Security].[35] One hears in the rhetoric of "the illegal alien unlawful combatant" similarities to the label "illegal alien," used to describe undocumented immigrants in the United States. If the institutional restructuring of the INS "communicates the view that immigrants, including refugees and asylum seekers, are potential terror threats," as Karen C. Tumlin claims, the shift in rhetoric only undergirds the cognitive justification for the same.[36]

Moreover, the human rights abuses that this rhetoric enabled are by no means new in the history of the United States. For as international scholar Darius Rejali reminds us, practices of torture *persist* within democracies, including the United States. Vice President Cheney was "a big fan" of the CIA's Vietnam-era Phoenix Program: this covert program made extensive use of torture techniques on both combatants and non-combatants and resulted in many more deaths among civilians than combatants.[37] The "Senate Torture Report" of 2014 duly lists many of the Vietnam era forms of torture that sprang back into service following the events of 9/11. It also highlights some newer methods, such as "rectal hydration," "forced grooming," the use of insects in confined spaces, the combination of stress positions with diapering detainees, and more.[38] But many citizens of the United States remain enthusiastic about so-called "enhanced interrogation," and some approve torture outright, up to and including candidates for the highest office. During his first week in office, President Donald Trump emphatically declared in a national television interview, "torture works!"[39] And it was President Obama who signed an executive order on March 7, 2011, for "a review process … to hold detainees indefinitely and without trial," and approved the decision to kill a U.S. citizen, Anwar al Awlaki, on October 2011 by way of a drone assassination without consulting Congress or the judicial branch.[40] In addition, though many of its prisoners have been sent to other sites, as of this writing, Guantánamo Bay remains an open sore on the nation, despite President Obama's promises to shut it down once and for all.

All of this history points to the heightened urgency of tracing the genealogy of dominant rhetorical patterns that supported the philosophy and specific acts that resurged during the Bush-Cheney era, so that we may better understand not only how and why this took place, but also the longstanding and enduring problems that define and maintain war-culture in the United States.[41] I return to this point later in this chapter.

Redefining torture

Legal philosopher David Luban argues that the post-World War II thrust to emphasize human rights internationally "drove underground whatever torture persists in many states."[42] Common Article 3 of Geneva (appearing in all four of the Geneva Conventions) prohibits mistreatment of captives within sovereign states' territories. Before it was "decriminalized" in 2006, U.S. law categorized torture and cruel treatment (as outlined in Article 3) as "war crimes" deserving of a sentence of death. However, Luban emphasizes that "the most decisive step" to undergird human rights was the international Convention against Torture (CAT) in 1984. Its preamble appeals to the basic principles in the Charter of the United

Nations, declaring that "the equal and inalienable rights of all members of the human family" are "the foundation of freedom, justice and peace in the world." These Convention rights are not conditional but "derive from the inherent dignity of the human person."[43] Front and center is the following statement in the CAT: "no one shall be subjected to torture or to cruel, inhuman or degrading treatment or punishment."[44] The treaty then goes on to define "torture:"

> the term "torture" means any act by which severe pain or suffering, whether physical or mental, is intentionally inflicted on a person for such purposes as obtaining from him or a third person information or a confession, punishing him for an act he or a third person has committed or is suspected of having committed, or intimidating or coercing him or a third person, or for any reason based on discrimination of any kind, when such pain and suffering is inflicted by or at the instigation of or with the consent or acquiescence of a public official or other person acting in an official capacity.[45]

Luban emphasizes that the only way for the Bush administration to bypass such strong policy was to "loophole its way around" the clear Convention mandates that (a) require states to ensure that torture does not take place within their territories; (b) prohibit extraditing of accused to places where they may be tortured; (c) insist on the criminalization of torture; and (d) create and protect the procedures for victims of torture to demand and receive compensation.[46] In contrast, while Cheney, Addington, Bybee, Yoo, Gonzalez and others minimized and dismissed Geneva and the Torture Convention, they did so through a kind of "linguistic subterfuge"[47] which confused and muddled public dialogue, and provided legal excuses for acts and policies the CAT prohibits. As Mayer describes it, "[t]he Bush Administration's corruption of language had a curiously corrupting impact on the public debate as well. It was all but impossible to have a national conversation about torture if top administration officials denied they were engaged in it."[48] In addition to the linguistic subterfuge involved in the rhetoric of "unlawful alien enemy combatants," an additional example regards the attempts to redefine "torture" altogether; in contrast to the definition from the CAT, Yoo would flagrantly propose that now only those acts leading to "... injury such as death, organ failure or serious impairment of body functions," would rise to the level of "torture."[49]

Steps towards a vigilant ethics in U.S. war-culture

This narrative of the United States response to 9/11 calls out for ethical analysis and redress; here I draw on liberation theologian Jon Sobrino's methodology stressing the importance of "honesty toward reality," and the 1995 Evangelical Lutheran Church in America Social Statement, "For Peace in God's World," intended to provide guidance to the church on matters of war and peace.[50] As followers of Jesus of Nazareth and members of the institution of the ELCA, Lutherans have a prophetic role to play, grounded in their religious heritage, vision and understanding, and in common cause with other citizens of diverse backgrounds, to name and denounce the ethical deformations and death-dealing propensities of the nation. "Peace in God's World" articulates a vision of hope for a way of life that shapes individuals and communities for heightened awareness and ethical vigilance to *see and resist* the institutional and systemic nature of violence and injustice that remains all too concealed from our vision. Lutherans are committed to joining with citizens of diverse loyalties who share similar values, if through different theological routes. Lutherans strive for peace, "relationships between and among nations that are just, harmonious, and free from war."[51]

The place to begin is with theologian Jon Sobrino's stress on the first step in any theology: we must strive for "honesty toward reality."[52] What does this mean? Writing from his lived experience working with the people of El Salvador, Sobrino declares that honesty toward reality necessitates the analysis of three intertwining dynamics that characterize our world*: institutionalized violence, systemic injustice, and institutionalized concealment of both injustice and violence.* Sobrino's striking insight about "concealment" is critical, for injustice and violence tend to be concealed, normalized, legitimated, and excused within different kinds of social constructs and practices. Thus, Lutherans must join with other citizens *to increase honest awareness* regarding the truth of the systems and structures of our social reality. Ethical vigilance is not possible without this essential practice; events are hidden and misunderstood, and reporting of them is distorted and confused.

Moreover, followers of Jesus of Nazareth root their own efforts at "honesty toward reality" in the doctrine of the incarnation: these efforts are directed at discerning how God is present with and embodies the material reality of human lives, and all life, including the treatment of those who are labeled "illegal alien non-combatants." The dynamics of disposability and instrumentalization of human persons that are explored in this chapter are not new in human history. Jesus' own seeing, ministry and embodiment in the historical reality of the 1st century *also* pulled back the cover of concealment from similar distortions in his time. Post-9/11 rhetoric of the "illegal alien enemy combatant," developed intentionally and used by the highest officials of the nation as a mechanism to provide cover, promote confusion about human rights, and legitimate injustice and violence, led to the treatment of certain human beings as not only "stateless," but something less than human. In contrast, not only the CAT, but also Lutherans stress the "dignity of the human person." And "Peace in God's World" takes this even further; the explicit materiality of God in this world is expressed through the "unity and goodness of reality, and oneness of humanity." Moreover, these values form the very ground for the right to "security from violence and aggression."[53]

So how did we stray so far? Only by doing the hard work of analyzing the structural and systemic nature of our own reality do we really have any chance of addressing it ethically, to work toward substantive change. I suggest that the legal rhetoric of the post-9/11 period only makes sense if we examine it through the lens of "war culture" in the United States.[54] The ethos, institutions and practices of war and militarization seep into and impact vast other areas of culture at large in our nation. War-culture perpetuates the normalization and legitimation of violence, and all too easily conceals injustice at the heart of many of our institutions and our everyday life. As I have written elsewhere, if already in the 1960s President Eisenhower's awareness led him to communicate his concern about a growing "military industrial complex," today sociological scholars such as Nick Turse understand that the interpenetrations of war-culture in the United States have multiplied and deepened in ways that Eisenhower never could have imagined. As Turse puts in, at the beginning of the twenty-first century, we in the United States live in a "military-industrial-technological-entertainment-academic-scientific-media-intelligence-homeland-security-surveillance-national-security-corporate complex."[55]

The *ease* with which misrepresentation of torture, dismissal of treaty obligations, erasure of legal rights and more took hold in the post-9/11 period is *related to* the centrality of war and militarism in our culture and nation. Consider the CIA's conditioned response to reach back and resurrect Cofer Black's plan once the crisis of the 9/11 attacks had occurred.

Remember Cheney's fondness for the Phoenix Program. Recall Addington's dismay about the legal ruling against President Reagan's Iran-Contra scheme; and ponder President Bush's Memorandum of Notification, coming just six days after the 9/11 attacks. Given the acculturation and institutionalization of war-culture in the United States, we should not be surprised that these were the dominant reactions and frames of response. Moreover, without honesty about the reality of U.S. war culture, and serious efforts to reform it, the kinds of horrific lapses that characterize the post-9/11 period are likely to continue to take place.

Thus, speaking truth to our war culture will require a structural analysis of just how the corporate structures of weaponization/militarization, political structures, institutions of surveillance and the military, and vast reaches of supposedly "civilian culture" (including religion) are all intertwined in the ethos of war and militarism in the United States, promoting concealment of the reality of our war-culture from alert awareness. Even our imaginations are sequestered; we are locked into "habits of speech that make war a normalizing discourse."[56] We tend *not* to "mourn" war in the United States, as the Lutheran social statement advocates; no, we celebrate war, and confirm its central place in our national identity in countless ways. Think, for instance, of the propensity of "fly-overs" at sporting events such as National Football League games; or the compulsory speeches in civil religious discourse that unquestioningly emphasize "the necessity-of-war-as-sacrifice" as central to the meaning of citizenship. In one of countless examples, in a recent Memorial Day speech, Vice President Biden proclaimed, "You are the veterans of America, the most trusted among us, and the most tested of all Americans ... who have served and sacrificed for all of us. You are not only the heart and soul, but you are the very spine of this nation."[57]

"Law" is but one example of many civic institutions that are profoundly porous and vulnerable to the shaping deformations of war-culture. Good, just, life-giving law is incredibly important; but in the end, law remains in the hands of human beings whose worldviews and ethics are profoundly shaped by their context. Philosopher Martha Nussbaum writes, "A constitutional tradition ... is only as robust as are the judges and legislators who interpret and implement it. Our own has known many back-slidings ..."[58] Law may be twisted, distorted, mis-described, mis-remembered, and misrepresented. Democracy and law indeed are traditions that require attention, awareness, and ongoing vigilant ethical analysis; we especially experience fear and vulnerability in times of crisis and perceived and actual danger and conflict. David Luban, for instance, emphasizes how easy it is for the government to "maintain the legal guidelines with a straight face and still assert the state-secrets privilege to avoid revealing the tangled network of secret agreements and contracts that undergirded the torture program ..."[59]

Along just these lines, Lutherans recognize the "entanglement of social structures" with sins that "generate killing and war."[60] "For Peace in God's World" includes a warning about the ways human beings blind themselves: "... elevat[ing] our nation or any nation or people to the role of God; find[ing] ultimate security in weapons and warfare; ordain[ing] the inherent right of one people, race or civilization to rule over others;. . . despair[ing] of any possibility for peace."[61] Tasks that face the church include countering "attitudes that encourage violence," supporting economic conversion to reduce military investment, reducing arms exports and supporting international methods of cooperation and address, such as the International Criminal Court.[62]

I have often returned to the truth and power of one particularly strong statement in the document: "war is a horrendous failure of politics."[63] Those who are the fodder for war understand this statement best, perhaps especially military service members and their families who are too well acquainted with early death, life-destroying physical injury, moral injury and so many other losses. Combatants and civilians on the receiving end of U.S. legal policies explored here, who were labeled as "illegal alien enemy combatants," and subjected to torture and extraordinary rendition, and some of whom remain imprisoned in legal limbo, surely also share visceral awareness of this truth.

However, if we truly internalized this ethical claim, that "war is a horrendous failure of politics," what would we make of the interpenetrations of war that dominate our institutions, culture, politics, and everyday life, even our own imaginations, in the United States? The overriding intent of "Peace in God's World" is to make room for people of opposing perspectives to remain under one tent—the military service member, the "defense industry employee," "people who refuse to participate in wars." But honest analysis of U.S. war-culture does not permit us to view any of these roles as innocent. Moreover, while the statement acknowledges that just war tradition and theory "have been used in self-serving ways," nevertheless it fails to ask whether or how just war theory can be accommodated within the perspective of war as failure, or how understanding war as a failure of politics makes any sense within a national structural and cultural framework geared for war in countless ways.[64]

While I find much to appreciate in "Peace in God's World," I want to push its scope and analysis further, especially with regard to the urgent need for deeper awareness about our reality as citizens in the United States. As a thought experiment, I tried to imagine how, in the Lutheran Church, we might address our reality differently if we truly believed that war is a horrendous failure of politics. Here I am imagining "politics" as Hannah Arendt describes the term, that generative, imaginative process through which people come together to build a collective reality that enables agency, judgment and action.[65] What would we make of the discretionary budget of the United States that dedicates over half our resources to militarism and war? What about the interpenetrations between the fields of our recent wars and entertainment platforms of all types? What about the recent decisions to upgrade and renovate U.S. nuclear weapons at the end of Obama's presidency? What should we make of the enormous numbers of our citizens (and church members) whose livelihoods are directly and indirectly connected to industries of militarism, surveillance, weapons, etc.? What would we make of the fact that five of the six largest weapons-producing corporations are based in the United States?[66] While we euphemistically label this entire enterprise as "defense," these industries dominate more and more of our economy. We spend more than the total of the next *seven* highest military state spenders *altogether; we* are responsible for over half of the total weapons sales world-wide; and our military bases and "lily pads" across the globe number well over 1,000.[67] Finally, what about repetitive political/cultural rhetoric that describes the activities of war as the center of what it means to be an American? A better understanding of U.S. war-culture will require insistent systemic and structural analysis of injustice, violence and concealment in all institutions and facets of culture, including our very language.

All in all, attempts toward a greater honesty reveal the reality of a vast majority of citizens (likely including most Lutherans) whose lives are intricately tied to vast reaches of war-culture in the United States. As Stanley Hauerwas' diagnosis emphasizes, not only are we easy with war "… [but] war sustains American political life." Robert Meagher also puts his finger on the national pulse: "War is our national posture, and we are more or less comfortable with it."[68] Is it naïve to imagine that the Lutheran church, living in the middle of U.S. war-culture, really might embody the prophetic role imagined by this social statement? How excruciatingly difficult it is in our context to live the role ELCA leaders hope for—the Church as a "disturbing presence … that names and resists idols that lead to false security, injustice and war."[69]

Of course, there are some courageous voices. But as I strive for honesty, it seems to me that as a church body, Lutherans have a long way to go toward adequate awareness of our deep rootedness in U.S. war-culture, and its impact on us. Institutionalized injustice, and systemic violence are *concealed* from us; we are both victims of that concealment, and perpetrators of it.

In the end, it simply will not do merely to address the most heinous and inhumane practices of the post-9/11 period of U.S. history described in this chapter. A more profound structural and systemic analysis of our embedded reality in U.S. war-culture inevitably leads to the realization that a much deeper reform of our way of living and understanding of ourselves in the United States is the only way forward. Again, being honest with ourselves, we have to acknowledge that we are far away from meaningfully engaging this process of conscientization and action.[70]

At the same time, there are some signals of hope that may suggest a way forward. At the church-wide assembly in the summer of 2016, the ELCA perhaps made some progress toward acknowledging the need for a deeper, wider and more sophisticated analysis of our reality, a more thorough-going honesty. In a resolution that was unanimously passed by the national gathering, "Call to Discernment on U.S. Foreign and Military Policy," Lutherans shared their yearning for a deeper examination of our reality in the United States. Part of the resolution calls on "the synods, congregations, institutions and people of this church *to a time of communal soul-searching* on the moral impact and societal consequences of expanded U.S. war efforts, and reflection on what reacting to violence with more violence has achieved."[71] (italics mine)

Widespread and profound dynamics of institutional concealment of violence and injustice crisscross our reality. If our lives in the U.S. today interconnect with diverse facets of the twenty-first century "complex" 24 hours a day, every day, then there truly is much soul-searching to do. I suggest we start with our own lives, and our own parishes. Bishops might begin with their synods. Other citizens and citizens' groups are waiting, or already are working on this; they will be better equipped and assisted as a result of Lutheran insistence to mount a thorough structural and cultural analysis, to get to the bottom of U.S. war-culture and come to grips with what it means to be honest about our own reality. Yes, sin always will be with us. But here and now, there's a lot of work to do before us in this world.

Notes

1 Evangelical Lutheran Church in America, "A Social Statement ... For Peace in God's World," August 20, 1995. Accessed March 30, 2017. www.elca.org/en/Faith/Faith-and-Society/Social-Statements/Peace.

2 Exec. Order No. 13491, 3 CFR 13491 (Jan. 22, 2009). Accessed November 5, 2017. www.whitehouse.gov/the-press-office/ensuring-lawful-interrogations.

3 *Hamdan v. Rumsfeld*, 548 U.S. 557 (2006).

4 Exec. Order No. 13440, 72 FR 40707 (July 20, 2007). I am grateful to legal expert W. Bradley Wendel of Cornell Law School for critically responding to this chapter. He points out that the terminology of "unlawful enemy combatant" hearkens back to *Ex Parte Quirin*, 317 U.S. 1 (1942). Such cases debated whether "enemy combatants" could be tried in military tribunals as opposed to civilian courts. Wendell comments that Yoo's error was to try "to make that legal category do work that it wasn't intended to do." I argue further that Yoo's use of this terminology significantly redefined it: now those branded with this label were detached altogether from internationally recognized rights accorded to all human beings. *See* Andrew Buttaro, "Ex Parte Quirin: The Nazi Saboteur Case and the Tribunal Precedent," *American University National Security Law Brief* 6,

no. 1 (2016). Accessed November 5, 2017. http://digitalcommons.wcl.american.edu/cgi/view content.cgi?article=1090&context=nslb.

5 David Luban, *Torture, Power and Law* (Cambridge: Cambridge University Press, 2014), 211.

6 Gershon Shafir and Cynthia E. Shairer, "The War on Terror as Political Moral Panic," in Gershon Shafir, Everard Meade, and William J. Aceves, eds., *Lessons and Legacies of the War on Terror: From Moral Panic to Permanent War* (New York: Routledge, 2013), 29.

7 Laura Pitter and Leslie Haskell, "No More Excuses: A Roadmap to Justice for CIA Torture," Human Rights Watch. Accessed March 30, 2017. www.hrw.org/report/2015/12/01/no-more-excuses/roadmap-justice-cia-torture.

8 Senate Select Comm. on Intelligence, Committee Study of the Central Intelligence Agency's Detention and Interrogation Program, S. Rpt. 113–288 (April 3, 2014). Accessed November 5, 2017. www.intelligence.senate.gov/sites/default/files/documents/CRPT-113srpt288.pdf (hereinafter Committee Study.)

9 Committee Study, 11.

10 Ibid.

11 Ibid.

12 Jane Mayer, *The Dark Side: The Inside Story of How the War on Terror Turned into a War on American Ideals* (New York: Doubleday, 2008), 31.

13 Ibid., 19.

14 Ibid., 30–31.

15 Ibid., 28–33.

16 Ibid., 39.

17 Ibid., 34, 43.

18 George W. Bush, "Memorandum for the Vice President: Humane Treatment of al Qaeda and Taliban Detainees," in Karen J. Greenberg, and Joshua L. Dratel, eds., *The Torture Papers: The Road to Abu Ghraib* (Cambridge: Cambridge University Press, 2005), 134–135.

19 Ibid., 135.

20 Gershon Shafir, Evrard Meade, and William J. Aceves, eds., *Lessons and Legacies of the War on Terror: From Moral Panic to Permanent War* (New York: Routledge, 2013), 39.

21 David Luban, *Torture, Power, and Law* (Cambridge: Cambridge University Press, 2014), 67.

22 Jay S. Bybee, "Memorandum for Alberto R. Gonzales, Counsel to the President: Application of Treaties and Laws to al Qaeda and Taliban Detainees," in Karen J. Greenberg, and Joshua L. Dratel, eds., *The Torture Papers: The Road to Abu Ghraib* (Cambridge: Cambridge University Press, 2005), 117.

23 Ibid., 99–101.

24 George W. Bush, "*The Torture Papers*, 134–135.

25 See for instance the "Military Commissions Act of 2006" in which the rhetoric of the "unlawful enemy combatant" is combined with the rhetoric of the "alien," in "§ 948a. Definitions." Pub. L. No. 109-366, subd. 1 § 948a (October 17, 2006.) Accessed November 5, 2017. www.loc.gov/rr/frd/Military_Law/pdf/PL-109-366.pdf.

26 Allison M. Danner, "Defining Unlawful Enemy Combatants: A Centripetal Story," *Texas International Law Journal* 43 (2007): 5.

27 According to the memorandum, a "failed state" is "without a functioning central government … [and is] marked by the inability of central authorities to maintain government institutions, ensure law and order or engage in normal dealings with other governments…" Bybee, *The Torture Papers*, 95.

28 Bybee, *The Torture Papers*, 117.

29 Colin Powell, "Draft Decision Memorandum for the President on the Applicability of the Geneva Convention to the Conflict in Afghanistan," in *The Torture Papers*, 122–125.

30 As quoted in Mayer, *The Dark Side*, 122–123.

31 Ibid., 123.

32 Pitter and Haskell, "No More Excuses."

33 Danner, "Defining Unlawful Enemy Combatants: A Centripetal Story," 14.

34 Gershon Shafir and Cynthia E. Shairer, "The War on Terror as Political Moral Panic," 30.

35 Karen Tumlin, "How Terrorism Policy Is Shaping Immigration Policy, *California Law Review* 92 (2004): 1178.

36 Shafir and Shirer, 30.

37 Darius Rejali, *Torture and Democracy* (Princeton, NJ: Princeton University Press, 2007), 470–471. See also Kelly Denton-Borhaug, "A Theological Reflection on Torture and Democracy," *Dialog: A Journal of Theology* 47 (Fall 2008): 217–227.

38 Committee Study, especially, "Overall History and Operation of the CIA's Detention and Interrogation Program," 11.
39 Reena Flores, "Trump Says Intelligence Officials Tell Him Torture Works," *CBSNews.com*, January 25, 2017. Accessed November 5, 2017. www.cbsnews.com/news/trump-says-intelligence-officials-tell-him-torture-works/. See also David Wright, "Donald Trump Defends Torture: 'Nothing Should Be Taken Off the Table,'" *CNN*, February 16, 2016. Accessed November 5, 2017. www.cnn.com/2016/02/16/politics/donald-trump-waterboarding-op-ed-usa-today-enhanced-interrogation-techniques-torture/; Connor Adams Sheets, "CIA Torture Report Poll: Half of Americans Say Enhanced Interrogation Was 'Justified,'" *International Business Times*, December 15, 2014. Accessed November 5, 2017. www.ibtimes.com/cia-torture-report-poll-half-americans-say-enhanced-interrogation-was-justified-1758576.
40 Gershon Shafir and Cynthia E. Shairer, "The War on Terror," 22.
41 Kelly Denton-Borhaug, *U.S. War-Culture, Sacrifice and Salvation*, 1st ed. (New York: Routledge, 2014).
42 Luban, *Torture, Power, and Law*, 202.
43 United Nations, G.A. Res. 39/46, *Convention against Torture and Other Cruel, Inhuman or Degrading Treatment or Punishment* (December 10, 1984). Accessed November 5, 2017. www.un.org/documents/ga/res/39/a39r046.htm.
44 Ibid.
45 Ibid., Art. I, sec. 1.
46 Luban, *Torture, Power, and Law*, 203.
47 The term, "linguistic subterfuge" comes from West Point Professor of English Elizabeth Samet. See Elizabeth Samet, "Can an American Soldier Ever Die in Vain? What Shakespeare, Lincoln and `Lone Survivor' Teach Us about the Danger of Refusing to Confront Futility in War," *Foreign Policy 9* (May 2014.) Accessed November 5, 2017. http://foreignpolicy.com/2014/05/09/can-an-american-soldier-ever-die-in-vain/.
48 Mayer, *The Dark Side*, 151.
49 Bybee, *The Torture Papers*, 176. According to 18 U.S.C. s 2340-2340A, torture is declared "a criminal offense" in the United States, and is defined as an "act committed by a person acting under the color of law specifically intended to inflict severe physical or mental pain or suffering (other than pain or suffering incidental to lawful sanctions) upon another person within his custody or physical control," *Torture Papers*, 173. Yoo focuses on the words "specifically" and "severe" in his redefinition above to bypass not only this federal law, but also the Geneva and Torture Conventions.
50 For Peace in God's World," Evangelical Lutheran Church in America, 1.
51 Ibid.
52 I draw from the theoretical backbone of Jon Sobrino's theological endeavor for the process I describe above. Sobrino in turn is indebted to philosopher Ignacio Ellacuría for his investigation regarding the liberative process of seeing reality, bearing reality, and taking charge of reality for a more humane and just world. Among other works, see Jon Sobrino, *Where Is God? Earthquake, Terror, Barbarity, and Hope* (Maryknoll, NY: Orbis, 2004).
53 For Peace in God's World," Evangelical Lutheran Church in America, 7.
54 See Kelly Denton-Borhaug, *U.S. War-Culture, Sacrifice and Salvation*.
55 Nick Turse, *The Complex: How the Military Invades Our Everyday Lives* (New York: Metropolitan Books, 2008), 16. See also Kelly Denton-Borhaug, Chapter One, "War-culture and Sacrifice," *U.S. War-Culture, Sacrifice and Salvation*.
56 Stanley Hauerwas, *War and the American Difference: Theological Reflections on Violence and National Identity* (Ada, MI: Baker Academic, 2011), 44.
57 See Laura Barron Lopez, "Pentagon Paid up to $6.8 Million of Taxpayer Money to Pro Sports Teams for Military Tributes," *Huffington Post*, November 4, 2015. Accessed November 5, 2017. www.huffingtonpost.com/entry/defense-military-tributes-professional-sports_us_5639a04ce4b0411d306eda5e. See also Kristen Bakotic, "The Most Tested among Us: Vice President Biden Pays Tribute to Our Nation's Veterans," *The White House Blog*, November 11, 2014, Accessed November 5, 2017. https://obamawhitehouse.archives.gov/blog/2014/11/11/most-tested-among-us-vice-president-biden-pays-tribute-our-nations-veterans.
58 Martha Nussbaum, *Liberty of Conscience: In Defense of America's Tradition of Religious Equality* (New York: Basic Books, 2008), 176.
59 Luban, *Torture, Power, and the Law*, 280.
60 "Peace in God's World," Evangelical Lutheran Church in America, 2.

61 Ibid., 5.
62 Ibid.,14, 16, 17–19.
63 Ibid., 11.
64 Ibid., 12.
65 Hannah Arendt, *The Human Condition*, 2d ed. (Chicago, IL: University of Chicago Press, 1998). According to the Stanford Encyclopedia of Philosophy, for Arendt, "politics finds its authentic expression whenever citizens gather together in a public space to deliberate and decide about matters of collective concern. Political activity is valued not because it may lead to agreement or to a shared conception of the good, but because it enables each citizen to exercise his or her powers of agency, to develop the capacities for judgment and to attain by concerted action some measure of political efficacy." See "Hannah Arendt," Maurizio Passerin d'Entreves, *Stanford Encyclopedia of Philosophy*, last revised April 10, 2014. Accessed November 5, 2017. http://plato.stanford.edu/entries/arendt/.
66 See the "SIPRI Arms Industry Database," *Stockholm International Peace Research Institute*. Accessed June 30, 2017. www.sipri.org/databases/armsindustry.
67 I discuss many of these interpenetrations in *U.S. War-Culture, Sacrifice and Salvation*. Also see William J. Broad and David E. Sanger, "U.S. Ramping Up Major Renewal in Nuclear Arms," *New York Times*, September 21, 2014. Accessed November 5, 2017. www.nytimes.com/2014/09/22/us/us-ramping-up-major-renewal-in-nuclear-arms.html? _r=0; *The National Priorities Project*. Accessed March 30, 2017. www.nationalpriorities.org/; Kelly Martin and David Vine, "Mapping the Growth of Bases Worldwide," *American University School of Education Investigative Reporting Workshop*, August 25, 2015. Accessed November 5, 2017. http://investigativereportingworkshop.org/investigations/lily-pads/htmlmulti/lily-pad-multimedia/.
68 Hauerwas, *War and the American Difference*, 12; Robert E. Meagher, *Killing from the Inside Out: Moral Injury and Just War*, 1st ed. (Eugene, OR: Cascade Books, 2014), 1.
69 "For Peace in God's World," Evangelical Lutheran Church in America, 5.
70 The term "conscientization" was coined by Paolo Freire, and may be traced to the methodology of liberation theologian José Míguez Bonino. People must "be awakened to their condition of oppression," through "an attitude of engaged criticism that helps to overcome passivity and fatalism." Ivan Petrella, *The Future of Liberation Theology* (London: SCM Press, 2006), 12, 59.
71 "Call to Discernment on U.S. Foreign and Military Policy," *Churchwide Assembly, Evangelical Lutheran Church in America*, August, 2016. Accessed November 5, 2017. www.elca.org/ChurchwideAssembly.

Part V

Domestic legal issues

10 Economic justice and the seventh commandment

Reformation-era insights

Mary Jane Haemig

When American Christians engage in political debates about economic justice, they tend to argue at a relatively high level of generality, talking about principles such as the preferential option for the poor, the duty of Christians to serve their neighbors compassionately, the dignity of the person, the stewardship of God's creation or other values that they believe should drive how Christians respond to social arrangements that distribute economic wealth unevenly. Rarely do they see any connection between principles of economic justice and the direct and specific commands of God, such as those embodied in the Ten Commandments.

This reluctance to turn to God's law as a source of expectation about what economic justice requires is not true of those who followed Luther in Germany. When we review the sermons of German Lutheran pastors in the sixteenth century, it is clear that Lutheran preachers saw God's law speaking loudly and clearly to the justice of economic relationships of their time. They did not think that reflecting on what this commandment meant was something only for lawyers and civic officials. More specifically, Lutheran preaching on the Ten Commandments in the period 1530–1580, discoverable in published collections of catechetical sermons, focused on the economic implications of the seventh commandment (according to the Lutheran way of counting the commandments, "You shall not steal"). These sermons influenced not only those who heard them when preached by their authors; they influenced other preachers who bought the volumes and used them as resources for their own sermons. These sermons may also have been read by literate and interested lay-people. Lutheran preachers used their pulpits to broaden their parishioners' understanding of what it means to steal or commit theft against other persons, and to affirm that, among other things, immoral financial activity that many moderns would not categorize as theft should be punished.

The most popular published series of catechetical sermons during the years 1530–1555 were those preached and published by Andreas Osiander (1498–1552)—twenty-eight editions of his catechetical sermons were published in 10 different cities.[1] (In terms of dissemination, Osiander's sermons were exceptions; most collections of catechetical sermons were published in only one city.) Osiander offered a broad definition of stealing, explaining that both holy scripture and imperial law (note the juxtaposition!) defined stealing as not limited to situations when someone secretly steals another's goods:

> But also [it is theft] when one uses force to rob them or draws them to himself by craftiness and fraud and uses them without the neighbor's knowledge or consent, even if the matter has a good appearance.[2]

In working out his argument about the broad scope of the seventh commandment, Osiander attacked a number of professions but he began with the ruling authorities. God has commanded us to pay taxes to the authorities, he noted, in order that they may protect the upright and punish the evildoers. When these authorities burden their subjects too heavily and demand more than they need to do their task, this is not only tyranny but also theft in God's eyes, for they are taking the goods of their subjects unjustly and without their consent.[3] Next, as examples of those who commit similar wrongs, Osiander attacked bishops, pastors, and preachers "who are silent concerning the truth and preach lies,"[4] and then jurists and lawyers who "convince someone he has a good case, even when it is bad, only so that they have something to do and earn money."[5] Only after these considerable attacks on well-placed professions did Osiander go on to attack the thievery practiced by merchants, artisans, workers and peasants. Osiander's critique of ruling authorities and other powerful groups is especially notable because his catechetical sermons were some of the most widely distributed of the sixteenth century and were incorporated into a number of church constitutions (*Kirchenordnungen).*[6]

Some Lutheran preachers of that era offered relatively short, general definitions of stealing. Some listed activities qualifying as theft, and some listed professions and the types of stealing engaged in by each profession. Regardless of the method used, the net was cast wide: the preachers made clear that every person violates the seventh commandment. Nearly every preacher of the twenty-one studied in the period 1530–1580 directed trenchant criticism toward the rich, powerful, and influential in his sermons on this commandment. Some examples follow.

Some of these preachers distinguished between "big" and "little" thieves, others between "secret" and "open" theft. For example, Johann Gigas devoted one sermon to "big" and one to "little" thieves. At the beginning of the sermon on "big thieves," he made the distinction clear, saying that "little thieves" or pickpockets are those whom one hangs on the gallows or on iron chains, whereas "big thieves" wear gold chains and are those for whom one must take off one's hat.[7] Erasmus Sarcerius (1501–1559) drew that distinction in similar language, saying

> [Those who] steal money, goods, and food secretly or openly are common thieves, whom need or laziness drive to steal. It is common practice to hang these on gallows ... Big thieves are the great merchants and usurers and the leading citizens, whom one must call Lord and Juncker. These one does not hang, so they can steal and rob to their heart's content.[8]

Ludwig Rabus (1524–1592) condemned not only "open, outward, and crude" thievery but also the more sophisticated kind, which works through bad business practices such as false weights.[9] Though other preachers were not so explicit in their condemnation of "big thieves" and "hidden theft," they made the same type of critique implicit in their descriptions of types of theft.

Some preachers provided lists of actions which violate the seventh commandment and other actions which fulfill this commandment. These lists provide some of the most informative, not to mention amusing, parts of these sermons. Cyriacus Spangenberg (1528–1604) listed eleven sins against the seventh commandment, and often associated particular professions with the conduct he condemned. He named "public" or "open" thieves first, but second on his list were cheaters and con men, that is, people who are not honorable in dealing with others. He gave as examples of these cheaters not only merchants with false weights but the man who owns an angry dog that causes harm to others and does nothing about it. Spangenberg went on to name undiligent workers, dishonest trustees, and moneylenders at interest and buyers of futures as other violators of the commandment. Children and servants who "nibble in secret" were named in the same breath with embezzling servants and officials. Sloth and begging, gluttony and drunkenness, games such as cards and dice, greed, and not paying one's workers complete the list.[10] Spangenberg then provided a blunt critique of the thefts committed by governing authorities, accusing them of, among other things, gluttony, luxurious living, useless wars, not keeping up the roads and bridges although they collect tolls for them, confiscation of goods, and using false measurements.[11] (Tellingly, Spangenberg went on to say that subjects cannot excuse their own disobedience to the seventh commandment by pointing to that of their rulers. Instead, he claimed, everyone should be responsible for their own sins.[12])

Rather than listing specific actions which generally violated the seventh commandment, some preachers categorized sins by listing professions and then describing the types of theft in which those professions engage. Caspar Adler (1488–1560) devoted most of the space in his explanation of the seventh commandment to a listing of fifteen different types of occupations and the ways in which those who follow them engage in theft. He led off by excoriating lazy servants and bad artisans, reached the ruling authorities as number six on his list of fifteen, and immediately followed with churchmen who preach false teaching, and those who keep stolen or loaned goods. He named jurists as number ten, followed by fathers who do not provide for their families and "field thieves" who steal fruit.[13]

Nicolaus Gallus (1516–1570) made two separate lists of professions and their activities which violate the seventh commandment. In each list, Gallus criticized not only the economic but also the religious and social status quo. The first list consisted of those who refused to work to earn their own living, those who did not work diligently, those such as monks, nuns, and Anabaptists, who could work but chose to live off the alms of others, and finally those such as moneylenders and merchants who were dishonest in their dealings. The second list consisted of those who refused to give of what they have to God and to others or who gave unwillingly. For Gallus, the chief thief and simonist was the pope and his cardinals, bishops, etc. who sold God's grace, righteousness, the Holy Spirit, and heaven for money. He next listed evangelical preachers who did not carry out their office and secular authorities who overtaxed their people and confiscated church property, then unjust judges and lawyers. Then came unfaithful workers, merchants, and salesmen who sold at a price which was never high enough for them and used false measures to gain advantage. Finally, he named such people as moneylenders, agents, monopolists, highwaymen and con men "compared to which simple thieves and street bandits whom one is accustomed to hang and break on the wheel are small, simple, and poor thieves."[14]

Johann Gigas (1514–1581) provided one of the most complete critiques of the various professions and the types of theft in which they engaged. His sermons revealed his own intimate familiarity with the real-life circumstances faced by his listeners. His list of sixteen professions in his sermon on "little thieves" included merchants "who charge double for their goods," metal craftsmen who dilute the metal, women who dilute beer, servants who do not work diligently, masters who do not pay their servants, students who instead of studying dally in bad company, then sell their belongings and complain they were robbed, medical quacks, those who find something and do not return it, soldiers at all levels who are not content with their wages but instead steal, and sellers of stolen goods.[15] Surely, everyone in Gigas' audience must have believed they had been victimized by the people he describes. Those in lower social and economic classes were not only addressed as people who could and did break the commandment but as people who had been harmed by those who broke it. Gigas went on in his next sermon to attack the "big thieves," naming as criminals usurers, those who took church goods, dishonest officials, rulers who took from their subjects, shavers of coins, lazy professors, and dishonest trustees.[16] His critique of rulers was particularly harsh, stating that rulers who tax too much violate this commandment. Rulers should enable their subjects to become wealthy for "when the subjects are rich and well-to-do people, then the ruler is also rich." Gigas noted that God does not let tyrants go unpunished.[17]

Some preachers were less thorough in their lists of sins against this commandment, but still exhibited a sophisticated understanding of the various ways theft can occur—ways that go beyond person A simply taking an item from person B. Sebastian Froeschel (1497–1570) listed only four sins: (1) intentional theft (naming as examples unfair trade and interest-taking); (2) refusing to give to the common good, including churches, schools, and the poor; (3) wasting one's own property with resultant harm to one's children, land, or people; and (4) having a heart which is never content, does not thank God, and constantly seeks other goods.[18] Notice that numbers two and three can only be committed by people with means; the examples given for number one are also aimed at people with property. Overall, the concern here goes far beyond traditional theft and instead addresses the more general issue of how one uses one's goods.

All of these preachers warned their targets of punishment for the violation of the seventh commandment, generally emphasizing temporal punishment more than eternal, though they varied in the extent to which they discussed these two forms of retribution. Osiander emphasized that God would send other thieves or events to punish the thief temporally.[19] Nicolaus Herko (?–1573) presented a God who punishes thieves both temporally and eternally and noted that the gallows are already full of thieves.[20] For Nicholas Gallus, the ruling authorities were God's instruments to punish theft but because they could possibly punish everything, God would also punish.[21] Gigas, in his sermon on "big thieves," devoted five lines to eternal punishment, but a full one page plus five lines to temporal punishments. Gigas even included a consideration of whether it was right to hang thieves, stating that as a fish belongs in the water, so a thief belongs on the gallows, and worldly authorities must punish thieves. He admonished those authorities to punish both the "small" and the "big" thieves, noting that regrettably the latter are often overlooked.[22] Both Eber and Gigas thought that those who steal will be punished by having their own goods stolen.[23] Thus, these preachers clearly did not think that God would wait until the final judgment to inflict punishment. Rather, ruling authorities or unfolding events would be sure to punish the thief.

Conclusion

From this brief consideration of Lutheran sermons on the seventh commandment in the sixteenth century, we can conclude that for them, God's law had real content. It did not simply serve to condemn the sinner (what Lutherans traditionally call the "second use" of the law), it also served to name injustice and implicitly or explicitly advocate for remedying that injustice. Content mattered. We can also note that preachers and their listeners/readers thought seriously about what God's law meant in their time and place. They did not leave this task to lawyers and civic officials. And they saw at least some coherence between God's law and the law of the state. (For them, secular law was not so secular.) Third, the sermons on the seventh commandment reveal a boldness on the part of the catechetical preachers to address every class, group, interest, level and part of society and to name theft wherever they saw it. No one was immune from violating the seventh commandment or from being condemned for it. Though no social group or class escaped criticism, condemnations directed toward the activities of the economically and politically powerful outweighed those directed toward any other group. It is true that preachers continued to criticize lazy workmen, servants who robbed their masters by not being diligent, and other persons in less powerful positions, but the reader cannot help but be struck by the amount of space and the rhetorical vehemence which the preachers devote to the ways the rich and powerful violate this commandment. Finally, preachers were often sophisticated in their understanding and analysis of economic injustice. They recognized that theft occurred not simply in those situations where person A took an item belonging to person B, but rather saw that theft could occur in myriad ways. Christians did not employ flat, simplistic understandings about what the content of God's law proscribed. These preachers confronted their listeners with the reality that stealing is never abstract but rather takes identifiable forms. Notably, these sermons implicitly and explicitly argued that God's law (the Ten Commandments) had contemporary relevance for the economic conditions in which people lived. Lutheran preachers wanted to help their listeners think about this commandment in terms of concrete economic and social relationships. For them, God's law and secular law were intended to create right relationships, not simply to uphold individual rights to property. They asked what proper conduct should be in any economic relationship, and how a Christian builds up or tears down that relationship.

Voices from the past can inform and challenge the present. Lutheran preachers of the sixteenth century challenge us to think concretely about economic and social relationships today as they did in their time. They encourage us toward honest discussion of economic relationships and bold identification of "stealing," whatever form it may take.[24]

Notes

1 Osiander, Andreas. "Katechismuspredigten," in Gerhard Müller, and Gottfried Seebaß, eds., *Andreas Osiander D. Ä Gesamtausgabe Band 5: Schriften und Briefe 1533 bis 1534* (Gütersloh: Gütersloher Verlagshaus Gerd Mohn, 1983), 182–334. The definitive list of books published in sixteenth century Germany is *Verzeichnis der im Deutschen Sprachbereich Erschienenen Drucke des XVI. Jahrhunderts,* Bavarian State Library, Munich and the Herzog-August Library, Wolfenbüttel, Germany (Stuttgart: Anton Hiersemann, 1983–1995). [*VD*16 lists editions in Nuremberg, Wittenberg, Marburg, Frankfurt/M., Berlin, Erfurt, Leipzig, Königsberg, Magdeburg, and Rostock during the years 1533–1554.]

2 Osiander, "Katechismuspredigen," 239, 241.

3 Ibid., 241.

4 Ibid., 241–242.

5 Ibid., 242.

6 Osiander's catechetical sermons were included in the influential 1540 Brandenburg church constitution but were dropped from the revised edition of this constitution issued in 1572.

7 Johann Gigas, *Catechismus Iohannis Gigantis Northusani. Gepredigt zur Schweidnitz Elystorum veterum, Anno Iesu Christi, 1577* (Frankfurt/O.; Johan Eichorn, 1578), O6r].

8 Erasmus Sarcerius, *Catechismus Erasmi Sarcerij/ Durch M. Bartholomeum Wagner/ Diener der Kirchen zu S. Thomas zu Leipzig/ mit vleis aus dem latein in das Deutsch gebracht/ tro(e)stlich und nu(e)tzlich allen Christen* (Leipzig: Wolff Gu(e)nter, 1550), X3r–X4r.

9 Ludwig Rabus, *Ein Kurtze und Christliche Predig/von notwe(n)digem unnd einfaltigem verstand der Sechs Hauptstuck unsers Christlichen Catechismi. Gepredigет zu Ulm/ Durch D. Ludovicum*

Rabus/ auff Sontag den xv. Augusti deß vergangnen/ M.D. LIX. Iars. Jetzun aber aus bitt viler guot hertzigen im truck erstlich außgangen. (Ulm: Hans Varnier, 1560). Bir.

10 Cyriacus Spangenberg, *Catechismus. Die Funff Heuptstu(e)ck der Christlichen Lere/ Sampt der Haußtafel/ und dem Morgen und Abendt Gebet Benedicite und Gratias etc.* ... (Schmalkalden: Michel Schmuck, 1566). F5v–F8r.

11 Spangenberg, *Catechismus,* F8r.

12 Ibid.

13 Caspar Adler, *Ein Christliche erkla(e)rung des kleynen Catechismi/ mit scho(e)nen Exempeln und gewaltigen sprüchen der heyligen Schrifft besta(e)tigt: Gepredigt Durch M. Casparum Aquilam/ Pfarrherr zu Salfa(e)ld.* (Augsburg: Heinrich Steyner, 1538), C1r–C2r.

14 Nicholas Gallus, *Catechismus Predigsweise gestalt/ für die kirche zu Regenspurg/ Zum Methodo/ das ist/ ordentlicher summa Christlicher lere/ wider allerlei newerung und verfelschung* (Regensburg: Hans Khol, 1554). V4r–X3v.

15 Gigas, *Catechismus,* O1r–O5r.

16 Ibid., O6v–O7v.

17 Ibid., O8v–P1r.

18 Sebastian Froeschel, *Catechismus wie der in der Kirchen zu Witteberg nu viel jar/ auch bey leben D. Martini Lutheri ist gepredigt wordn ... Mit erklaerung etlicher woerter jezt verbessert* ... (Wittenberg: Lorenz Schwenck, 1560), D2r–v.

19 Osiander, "Katechismuspredigen," 244.

20 Nicolaus Herko, *Der Kleine Catechismus: Fu(e)r die gemeine Pfarherrn und Prediger/ D.M. Lutheri. Mit etlichen Kurtzen Nu(e)tzlichen Fragen/ den Kinderlein und einfeltigen zu gut/ newlich gestellet* ... (Erfurt: 1553), C5r.

21 Gallus, *Catechismus Predigsweise,* X3v.

22 Gigas, *Catechismus,* P2v–P3v.

23 Paul Eber, *Catechismuspredigten/ Des Ehrwirdigen und Hochgelerten herrn D. Pauli Eberi/ Weyland Pfarrherrn unnd Superintendenten zu Wittenberg/ Sampt seinem newen jars Gebet/ Anno 1562. Nachgeschriben/ und jetzt inn Truck vergertiget/ Durch Theophilum Feurelium/ Kirchendiener in Kitzingen* (Nuremberg: Catharine Gerlach und Johans vom Berg Erben, 1577), 82v.

24 For a discussion of how Luther's commentary on the seventh commandment in his *Small Catechism* and *Large Catechism* can help preachers today, see Mary Jane Haemig, "Preaching the Seventh Commandment: 'You are not to steal,'" *Word & World* 30, no. 2 (2010): 200–207.

11 The Doctrine of Discovery in American Indian law

A Lutheran theological critique[1]

Ronald W. Duty

Introduction

Through its five metamorphoses in its six-century journey, the Doctrine of Discovery, begun as a Christian justification for European colonialism, has emerged as a key feature of American Indian law. Along this journey, it has decisively shaped the lives of American Indian and non-Indian people alike. In the hands of the U.S. Supreme Court, discovery has been a shape-shifting doctrine used to justify the property rights of European Americans when they collide with Indian peoples' historically prior land claims.

The legally distinct but historically related doctrine of occupation has also undergone transformation from its private Roman law use to justify the first taking of land that belonged to no one, to its nineteenth century international law use to control other nations' sovereignty for commercial purposes.[2] Although the doctrine of occupation has not been an explicit factor in Supreme Court decisions, it may have had an indirect influence in how the Court has applied the Doctrine of Discovery.

Though the Doctrine of Discovery was unquestioned in American law and culture for about 150 years, scholars like Vine Deloria Jr., recently began to challenge its moral and legal legitimacy.[3] In this chapter, I continue this critique from a Lutheran theological-ethical perspective, using both narrative and analytical approaches to assess the effects of this doctrine on Indian property rights in land, natural resources, and financial assets. The aim is to critique the doctrine in both its original Christian form and its further development, especially in American Indian law. Despite its Christian origins, there are ample reasons to critique the doctrine *from within the Christian tradition*. This critique is justified not only because of its tragic consequences for justice for American Indian peoples. The doctrine's origins in ecclesial and early international law also call for a critique of the doctrine in American law through the standards of contemporary international law.[4]

Religious repudiation and legal criticism

Recently, the Doctrine of Discovery has received severe and pointed criticism, leading to some moves towards repentance. The Christian origins and original purpose of the doctrine have led some to indict the doctrine in recent years as specifically a Christian one that has been used by Christians to coercively privilege their own interests at the expense of Indians.[5] Recently, various Protestant Churches and church-related groups have repudiated the doctrine, as has the World Council of Churches.[6] The Leadership Conference of Women Religious also called upon Pope Francis in 2014 to acknowledge harm caused by the Doctrine of Discovery and to repudiate any papal bulls from the fifteenth century on that articulated this doctrine.[7] Legal and historical scholars have also criticized the doctrine's influence on federal Indian law.[8]

Genealogy of the doctrine

Under the Doctrine of Discovery, based on fifteenth century church law and later international law, European Christian countries were presumed to be entitled to colonize the Americas and other parts of the world in order to bring them the so-called "benefits of civilization" or the Christian religion.[9] Each country was entitled to an exclusive claim to territories based on their "first discovery" in those parts of the world, and a "discovering nation" also was entitled to establish commercial colonies in these regions and trade with them. Discovering nations also had the right prior to individual European settlers to acquire land from indigenous peoples, who were assumed to have a right to occupy the land where they lived, by either sale, voluntary cession, or "just wars."

The Doctrine of Discovery developed over centuries within the Roman Catholic Church.[10] The Crusades raised for some Christians the question of what rights "infidels" had to dominion and property in the world. The influential twelfth century decretalist Hostiensis argued that infidels had rights to neither after Christ's coming: dominion over property passed to Christ who "delegated them to his successors on earth—first St. Peter and later the popes—so that at any given moment they had the legal right and the power to annul the existing jurisdictions of the infidel."[11]

Following Hostiensis' lead, subsequent popes issued a series of papal bulls that built up this rationale and asserted papal authority in worldly affairs. Pope Boniface VIII issued *Unam Sanctam* (1302), recognizing not only the spiritual but also the temporal "sword," which should be administered for the church "by the hands of kings and soldiers." "However," he continued, "one sword ought to be subordinated to the other and temporal authority" should be subjected to "the will and sufferance of the priest."[12] This papal claim to both the sacred and secular power—or *plentitudo potestatas* as Skinner calls it—soon elicited a long train of criticism.[13] Nevertheless, later popes employed the temporal authority which Boniface claimed, both to demand freedom for, and to justify exploitation of, other peoples. For example, in the papal bull *Sicut Dudum* (1435), Eugene IV rebuked Portugal and others for enslaving residents of the Canary Islands, called for their release and repatriation, and threatened excommunication of Spanish royalty if this was not done.[14] Nicholas V issued the bull *Romanus Pontifex* (1455) which granted the kings of Portugal a monopoly in European trade with Africa.[15] Relying upon such precedents, Alexander VI issued the bull *Inter Caetera* (1493) which explicitly articulated the **first version** of what became known as the Doctrine of Discovery. Alexander gave to King Ferdinand and Queen Isabella of Spain exclusive right "with full and free power, authority, and jurisdiction of every kind" over any lands Spanish explorers might discover in the New World west of a certain longitude in the Atlantic.[16]

Implicitly endorsing colonization beyond Europe, Paul III qualified the developing doctrine in *Sublimus Dei* (1537). He affirmed the full humanity of indigenous peoples and decreed that they were not to be enslaved and that their liberty and property rights should be respected.[17] Paul thereby repudiated Hostiensis' judgment that infidels had neither liberty nor property rights, although neither his nor Alexander VI's decree justified the infidels' lack of dominion over their own occupied territories. Paul III followed very shortly with *Veritas ipsa*, which urgently emphasized the importance of converting indigenous peoples to Christianity, denounced their harsh treatment and enslavement, reiterated their full humanity, and emphasized their rationality and "understanding, will and freedom of choice since all are created in the image of God."[18]

Luther's critique of papal secular power

Paul III's contemporary Luther stood with other critics of papal claims of secular power. He was adamant about not confusing the functions of the Church and of the government, which he saw as two distinct modes through which God rules the world.[19] His political vision was based on his fundamental theological distinction of law and gospel. For Luther, one of God's two uses of the law—the civil use—is to restrain sin in the world by establishing and enforcing secular laws through police and courts, military forces, the use and enforcement of contracts, and the legal ownership of property.[20] The other theological use of the law, employed by the Church, is to accuse people of sin and call for their repentance before God. Luther rejected claims that the Church had any authority to intervene in regulating Christians' daily activities. "The real focus of Luther's attack, however," argues Skinner, "was not so much on the Church's abuses of its powers, but rather on the Church's right to claim any such powers in Christian society at all."[21] The association of government and the church with their respective and distinctive uses of the law ordinarily precluded, for Luther, their functional interaction.[22]

Luther was deeply and consistently critical of the pope's claim to, and exercise of, secular power, although he was not alone in his opposition at the time.[23] He bitterly and sarcastically denounced these papal pretensions: "Why then does the Roman see so furiously desire the whole world?" he asked. "Why did it steal and rob country, city, indeed, principalities and kingdoms, and now dares to produce, ordain, dismiss, and change as it pleases all kings and princes, as if it were the Antichrist?"[24] Luther took direct aim at Pope Nicholas's use of sacred and secular power,[25] criticizing the pope's claims of authority over the law: "The Roman see indeed imparts authority and power to all laws, but it is subject to none of them."[26] Ultimately Luther seriously questioned the basis of both the secular *and* sacred authority of the pope.[27]

Thus, although he was focused on other controversies with the Vatican, Luther would not have had any trouble rejecting either the pope's authority to formulate the Doctrine of Discovery or the doctrine itself and its uses. Neither the lands of, nor the "full and free power, authority, and jurisdiction of every kind" over, indigenous peoples were the pope's to grant to anyone, in his view.

Discovery after Alexander VI's donation

The widely held pre-Reformation presumption that the pope could adjudicate land disputes between Christian sovereigns was fully abandoned in the 1648 Peace of Westphalia following the wars of religion.[28] "Protestant reformists," says Orford, "challenged papal authority with the argument that there was no '*humanly available presence of the authorizing deity*,' [so] God could only be known through Scripture ..."[29] Protestant and Catholic sovereigns employed the Doctrine of Discovery themselves but did not recognize the *pope's* authority to grant rights to territory anywhere in the world. Both Protestant and Catholic nations then developed arguments to legitimize their actions.[30] Theorists justifying the doctrines of discovery and occupation grounded their international law arguments in the law of nature.[31] This **second version** of the Doctrine of Discovery solidified the principle that the first country to make an effective claim on a territory had a right to it, which other countries were bound to respect.

The doctrine thus became important to the practice and justification of establishing colonies.[32] But the Doctrine of Discovery was honored by Britain more in the breach than to the letter. For example, Britain forced the Netherlands out of the Hudson and Connecticut River valleys and Guiana, Sweden out of the lower Delaware River, Spain out of Florida, and France out of present-day Quebec.

John Marshall's use of discovery for the U.S. Supreme Court

U.S. Supreme Court Chief Justice John Marshall gradually articulated a **third version** of the Doctrine of Discovery for American Indian law in a series of decisions between 1810 and 1832. In contemporary U.S. law, the Doctrine of Discovery is used to infer how relations—including questions of territory, property, and natural resources—between indigenous peoples and the federal government are legally organized, and why. Although not formally a part of the U.S. Constitution, as a *legal theory* the Doctrine of Discovery significantly affects how the Constitution and statutes governing federal government-Indian relationships are *interpreted*.

Implicitly relying on the Doctrine of Discovery in *Fletcher v. Peck* (1810),[33] the Court ruled that the State of Georgia could legally grant land to speculators on which Indians were already living. Marshall's opinion held that the "seisin in fee" title Georgia gave to speculators and settlers was legally consistent with what he called "Indian title," which was valid and enforceable until it was extinguished. Thus, Indian title was qualified and different from the absolute fee simple title of settlers, with which it somehow legally coexisted. Marshall, notes Blumm, "did not explain how a proper extinguishment of Indian title could occur, nor who could extinguish it, nor what he meant by [the state's] 'seisin in fee.'"[34]

Although the British Proclamation of 1763 claiming the Crown's preemptive right to buy land from Indian tribes, and the taxes imposed to help enforce it, were among the "long train of abuses" denounced by the Continental Congress in its Declaration of Independence of 1776, the new American federal government continued this key British policy.[35] This was legitimized by the Supreme Court's decision in *Johnson v. McIntosh* (1823).[36]

The case contested a colonist's illegal private purchase of Indian land and resale to settlers under the Proclamation of 1763. To Marshall, *Johnson v. McIntosh* was about "the power of Indians to give, and of private individuals to receive, a title which can be sustained in the courts of this country."[37] Marshall explicitly invoked the Doctrine of Discovery as legal precedent in the case. Noting that European nations were "eager to appropriate to themselves so much of the world as they could respectively acquire," he stated the doctrine in a form that henceforth would influence American Indian law:

> This principle was that discovery gave title to the government by whose subjects or by whose authority it was made against all other European governments, which title might be consummated by possession. The exclusion of all other Europeans necessarily gave to the nation making the discovery the sole right of acquiring the soil from the natives and establishing settlements upon it.[38]

The territorial rights and sovereignty of the native peoples were "necessarily to a considerable extent impaired."[39] Native peoples had the rights of occupancy and use of the land, but had neither the full sovereignty of independent nations, nor complete freedom to sell or dispose of their territory because of "the original fundamental principle that discovery gave exclusive title to those who made it."[40] Marshall in effect assumed—incorrectly—that England had surrendered its discovery rights in the American colonies to the United States in the Treaty of Paris (1783) and implicitly assumed also that it surrendered its preemptive right in the Proclamation to purchase Indian land.[41] He therefore asserted that the United States government had the exclusive authority to extinguish Indian rights to land. "This is incompatible with an absolute and complete title in the Indians."[42]

Marshall could have based his opinion in relevant property law instead of the Doctrine of Discovery.[43] Although scholars have speculated about why he relied on it,[44] it seems most likely that Marshall believed the Doctrine of Discovery accounted entirely for the legal and factual history of the colonies (Pagden's view), and that through the Revolution, the colonists established property claims that made it impossible to acknowledge the Crown's claim or Indians' property interest (Fitzmaurice's view). Marshall's opinions based on the Doctrine of Discovery, however, beginning with *Johnson* also were anachronistic, rejected shortly before by England and Russia and later by the U.S. itself.[45] Nevertheless, Marshall continued to base decisions on discovery.

In *Cherokee Nation v. Georgia* (1831),[46] Marshall asserted that the United States, not the State of Georgia, had sovereignty over the Cherokee because they were "a domestic dependent nation" in a state of "pupilage," related to the U.S. government as a ward to a guardian.[47] Building on the *Johnson* decision, he reaffirmed the Cherokee's "unquestionable ... right to the lands they occupy" until extinguished by their voluntary cession to the federal government. Yet, "[t]hey occupy a territory to which," he said, "we assert title independent of their will ..." Therefore, the United States has the "sole and exclusive right" to manage all Indian trade affairs.[48]

Blake Watson argues that the Marshall Court gave up one of four possible models of indigenous land rights,[49] the "Limited Possessor" model of *Johnson v. McIntosh*, when it decided *Worcester v. Georgia* (1832).[50] In the "Limited Possessor" model, indigenous people have the right to occupy or possess the lands but no longer own them after "discovery." In the "Limited Owner" model of *Worcester v. Georgia*, however, the indigenous people have both possession and ownership rights subject only to preemption by the sovereign. In *Worcester,* Marshall argued that "discovery" merely "gave the exclusive right to purchase, but did not found that right on a denial of the right of the possessor to sell."[51] Affirming their limited political independence except for rights exercised by the European discoverer, Marshall argued that "the Indian nations possessed a full right to the lands they occupied until that right should be extinguished by the United States, with their consent [and] that their territory was separated from that of any State."[52]

Vine Deloria Jr., argues that "all efforts to revise, systematize, and comprehend the ... statutory and case laws dealing with the natives in the United States have been passed and decided under the shadow of [the *Johnson v. McIntosh*] doctrine."[53] Indeed, the Supreme Court has relied on precedents using the Doctrine of Discovery as recently as 2004 in *United States v. Lara*,[54] and it has been cited in cases in various other English-speaking countries, giving Marshall's interpretation of the Doctrine of Discovery continuing international legal influence.[55]

After the Marshall Court: further development of the Doctrine of Discovery

Though Marshall likely intended *Worcester's* "Limited Ownership" model to be the legal precedent going forward, President Andrew Jackson's refusal to enforce the *Worcester* decision solidified *Johnson* as precedent.[56] In a series of decisions following Marshall's death, the Court cited and reaffirmed *Johnson* on the question of Indian title to land.[57]

The federal government also used its pre-emptive power to acquire Indian land and extinguish titles of occupancy with the Indian Removal Act of 1830, designed to move Indians from the east to west of the Mississippi River.[58] By the mid-nineteenth century, almost all the land east of the Mississippi was owned by whites.[59] "From the Indians' perspective," Banner writes:

> removal, like earlier land sales, took place within circumstances constructed by whites to yield a state of affairs in which selling was the lesser of evils ... The Indians who removed to the west, like earlier Indian land sellers, were caught midway between force and consent. As in so many earlier transactions, the government had the power to make an offer the Indians could not refuse.[60]

Removal also yielded a **fourth version** of the Doctrine of Discovery emerging in *United States v. Rogers* (1846).[61] Chief Justice Roger Taney cited the Doctrine of Discovery, asserting that the Cherokee (now in Oklahoma) were living on land that "has been assigned to them by the United States, and they hold and occupy it with the assent of the United States, and under their authority." He also reiterated that native tribes "have never been acknowledged or treated as independent nations by European governments, nor regarded as the owners of the territories they respectively occupied."[62] This claim was "essentially a misinterpretation of the doctrine" that emerged from the Marshall Court, according to Newton.[63] Taney's opinion that the tribes were "subject to [U.S.] dominion and control" was used to justify federal intrusion into tribal affairs.[64]

In effect, Taney denied even the limited sovereignty and the "limited possessor" model of land occupancy of the *Johnson* decision. Newton notes that "[t]he more the government's interest was characterized as an ownership interest, the more it became possible to regard the ownership of land alone as giving the government power to govern Indians."[65] Invoking the "political question" doctrine, Taney argued that federal conduct of Indian affairs was beyond review by the courts.[66] This reflected the emerging international interpretation of the doctrine of occupation which stressed the use of sovereignty to control the land, labor, and capital of the colonized.[67]

The Court's reinterpretation of the Doctrine of Discovery began to have new consequences. In 1871, Congress ended the treaty-making process with Indian nations by statute, replacing it with formal agreements that did not have the same constitutional status, although obligations under existing treaties would remain.[68] Consequently, Congressional statutes would play a much more prominent role in Indian affairs. "Many of these statutes," Newton observes, "could not be viewed as either effectuating treaty promises or regulating trade. Thus, the Court was forced to develop new rationales to justify federal actions concerning Indians."[69] Newton notes that after 1871, "Indian law became more a matter of domestic law, with Indians regarded as subjects to be governed, rather than foreign nationals."[70]

The Court took major steps to develop a rationale justifying federal action regarding Indians. In *United States v. Kagama* Justice Samuel Miller established the doctrine that Congress has plenary power over Indian affairs and articulated a trust responsibility of the government for Indian tribes.[71] Indian tribes are "wards of the nation" now, completely "dependent on the United States ... largely for their daily food; dependent for their political rights." From this dependency and from treaty obligations, "there arises the duty of protection [by the United States], and with it the power."[72] These things were reaffirmed in *Lone*

Wolf v. sHitchcock along with *Rogers'* holding that Indian affairs were a political question not subject to judicial review.[73] To Pommersheim, these cases "fully incorporated tribes into the national system ..."[74]

Tribal natural resources, financial assets, and the Doctrine of Discovery

Another version of the Doctrine of Discovery is recognizable if we move from consideration of Indian land ownership and transfer our attention to four major cases on Indian natural resources, such as rights to fisheries and tribal financial assets. In *United States v. Washington* (1974),[75] the United States sued the State of Washington on behalf of 14 tribes, arguing that its regulations limiting off-reservation fishing violated rights in eleven treaties. Federal Judge George Boldt found that tribal members' right to fish off reservation along with citizens of Washington "cannot be qualified by the State."[76] However, Boldt ruled that Washington had legal authority to *regulate* tribal members' *off-reservation* fishing rights if the *only* reason for doing so is for conservation of a species[77] and the regulations are reasonable, do not discriminate against the Indians, and meet due process standards. Significantly, Boldt ruled that regulation of Indian fishing could involve the active, rather than merely passive, participation of the tribes themselves; they could join with the State to promote conservation of fish while reserving their treaty fishing rights with limited conditions.[78]

This **fifth version** of the Doctrine of Discovery emerged in *Tee-Hit-Ton Indians v. United States* (1955).[79] The Tee-Hit-Ton clan of the Tlingit Indians sued the U.S. government for loss of timber through government-contracted logging, and asserted either "full proprietary right" or a "recognized right to unrestricted possession" of their 350,000 acre aboriginal homeland in the Tongass National Forest of Alaska.[80]

The Court ruled that there was no evidence that Congress had granted the clan "permanent rights in the lands" which they occupied "by permission of Congress."[81] The tribe's "permissive occupation" did not constitute their formal recognition by Congress as a tribe with a legal right to occupy the land they lived on. Moreover, citing *Johnson v. McIntosh*, Justice Stanley Reed argued that the "original Indian title" the clan claimed was a right to occupancy at the will of the Congress, not title to the land.[82] Reed made this striking statement:

> No case in this Court has ever held that taking of Indian title or use by Congress required compensation. The American people have compassion for the descendants of those Indians who were deprived of their homes and hunting grounds by the drive of civilization ... Generous provision has been willingly made to allow tribes to recover for wrongs as a matter of grace, not because of legal liability.[83]

In this version of the Doctrine of Discovery,[84] the clan's "Indian occupancy, not fully recognized as ownership by action authorized by Congress, may be extinguished by the Government without compensation."[85] Hence, the clan's claim for loss of timber was not compensable, nor by implication was the loss of the area's natural habitat due to the logging activity upon which the clan depended for its livelihood.[86] Moreover, now that Congress exercised plenary power in Indian affairs, only tribes with congressionally "recognized" title could have a valid claim for compensation. This decision has not gone without scholarly challenge.[87] However, neither has the decision or its reasoning been reversed.[88]

of neighbors' *livelihoods* and not only their possessions.[115] It is a matter of "daily bread," of "everything that belongs to our entire life in this world, because it is only for its sake that we need daily bread."[116] The *Johnson* decision clearly deprived Indians of their "title," and along with *Worcester*, it justified the preemptive right of the federal government to buy their land, depriving Indians of the right to sell to whomever they wanted. By creating two different models of Indian land ownership, the Marshall Court opened the door both to legal confusion and to disagreement about what it did or intended.[117] Its decisions allowed later courts and Congress to choose the model that suited their current concerns or the precedent most restrictive to Indians.

Luther was especially critical of people who consider themselves upright but who scheme to get the possessions of others, often through lawsuits. He observed how

> they resort to anything that has the appearance of legality, so varnishing and garnishing it that the law must support them, and they gain such a title to the property that no one can raise an objection or initiate legal action.[118]

The decisions of the Marshall court would deeply disturb Luther, partly because Indian interests in their aboriginal lands were often at stake but Indians were rarely granted legal standing nor were they represented in court.

Because of his deep skepticism about human self-justification, Luther would not have been surprised at the government's use of Marshall Court opinions to exercise preemptive power to acquire tribal lands with offers tribes could not afford to refuse, a clear example of legalized scheming to get rights to their land and displace them with white settlers.[119] Taney's opinion in the *Rogers* decision not only misrepresented Marshall's arguments, but reinterpreted the Doctrine of Discovery in a way that deprived tribes both of their restricted rights to occupy their land and their restricted sovereignty, and subjected the tribes to arbitrary government policy and action. Subsequent federal policy innovations and court decisions repeatedly used this arbitrary power to deprive tribes of their land and livelihoods and impoverish them, especially through the scheme of allotments of Indian lands. The U.S. Supreme Court's later decisions in the *Kagama* and *Lone Wolf* cases merely validated these abusive federal policies.

More recently, natural resources and financial resources might have alleviated conditions for many Indians on their remaining land if they had been given the right to utilize them fully. Fortunately for some tribes, such as those in Washington State, the courts have upheld treaty rights to fisheries and enhanced the responsibility and power of qualified tribes to manage fishery resources on their reservations. However, Supreme Court precedent has exacerbated the predicament of others. Justice Reed's opinion in the Tee-Hit-Ton case not only extinguished the clan's claim of title to their aboriginal lands, but also expanded Congress's plenary power, holding that takings of land or resources, or destruction of habitat, are not compensable. This ruling and others have deprived Indian tribes of not only land but also customary livelihoods.

Similarly, the failed exercise of federal government trust responsibilities has only occasionally been remedied, as in the *Cobell* decision. The plaintiffs' demonstrations that the government lost or diverted individual Indians' and tribal income on a massive scale over many decades resulted in at least some return of tribal properties through settlement. Overall, however, settlement critic Ward Churchill argues that BIA malfeasance "is the principle source of poverty on the reservations, and … plainly results from federal policies sustained for over a century in full knowledge of their devastating effects on the people living on those reservations …" "Wealth simply gushed from the reservations" he argues, "while the Indians, whose wealth it was, received chump change."[120]

The alleged scope and nature of the federal government's violation of trust account responsibilities in these cases suggests a basic motivation of greed, often condemned by Luther. The government was eager to get Indian land into the hands of whites who could benefit from it economically while it appeared to act in Indians' interests. Luther might well accuse the BIA of "practicing wickedness under the guise of fair dealing."[121] He might claim that the federal government's intentional and negligent aiding and abetting of "*Finanz*," i.e., "usurious intrigue, fraud, and deception" by unscrupulous profit-minded dealers, violated its fiduciary responsibilities, forcing courts to step in and put matters right.[122] These federal actions were egregious examples of covetousness, harming individuals and tribes "by intending or scheming to take away" their assets "so that they suffer loss while [others] satisfy [their] greed" under the appearance of legality.[123] The government, and its white contractors and lessees, casually squandered individual and tribal assets and severely affected account holders' livelihoods. They are like the merchants Luther condemned who "deal with [other people's] own money and property without any risk, trouble, or labor, and … get rich."[124]

Conclusion

Luther contrasts such behavior by governors with that of the biblical figure of Joseph, who followed up on his interpretation of Pharaoh's dreams with faithful, efficient, and fair management of Egyptian agricultural supplies on Pharaoh's behalf in prudent preparation for famine.[125] "[Rulers] are to make *and administer* just laws," Luther argued, "so that the poor, the wretched, the widows, the orphans are not oppressed, but have their rights and keep them. [They are to] judge the poor and orphaned, and help the wretched and needy to justice."[126] This the U.S. government has seldom if ever done, with policy based on legal precedents justified by the Doctrine of Discovery.

Notes

1 The author thanks Howard J. Vogel, Ted Peters, and David Selden for their help in preparing this chapter; and Rev. Steven Charleston for his encouragement to write a *theological* critique of the doctrine.

2 Andrew Fitzmaurice, *Sovereignty, Property and Empire, 1500–2000* (Cambridge: Cambridge University Press, 2014), 33.

3 Vine Deloria Jr., *Behind the Trail of Broken Treaties: An Indian Declaration of Independence* (New York: Dell Publishing Co., 1974); Blake A. Watson, "The Doctrine of Discovery and the Definition of Indian Title," *Lewis & Clark Law Review* 15, no. 4 (2012): 997.

4 Philip P. Frickey, "Domesticating Federal Indian Law," *Minnesota Law Review* 81 (1996): 37.

5 Steve Newcomb, "Five Hundred Years of Injustice: The Legacy of Fifteenth Century Religious Prejudice," *Shaman's Drum* (Fall, 1992): 18–20. http://ili.nativeweb.org/sdrm_art.html (Accessed May 11 2014); Howard J. Vogel, "U.S.-Dakota War of 1862: Rethinking the Effect of the Abrogation of the Dakota Treaties and the Authority for the Removal of the Dakota People from their Homeland," *William Mitchell Law Review* 39, no. 2 (2013): 543; and George E. "Tink" Tinker, *American Indian Liberation: A Theology of Sovereignty* (Maryknoll, NY: Orbis Books, 2008), 5.

6 The Episcopal Church USA, "Repudiate the Doctrine of Discovery" (Resolution Number 2009-D035) (2009); Canadian Friends Service Committee (Quakers), """Repudiating the Doctrine of Discovery: Some references and resources," (2013); Anglican Church of Canada, "Repudiate the Doctrine of Discovery," Resolution A086 R1 (2010); Unitarian Universalist Association, "The Doctrine of Discovery—2102 Responsive Resolution," (2012); United Methodist Church,

55 *Wewaykum Indian Band v. Canada*, 4 S.C.R. 245 (2002); *Delgamuukw v. British Columbia*, 3 S.C.R. 1010 (1997); *Wik Peoples v. Queensland* (pastoral lease cases), HCA 40 (1996), 187 CLR 1 (1996), 141 ALR 129 (1996), 71 ALJR 173 (1996); *Mabo v. Queensland*, 174 CLR 1 (1992); *Mabo v. Queensland*, HCA 23 (1992), and 175 CLR 1 (1992) (*Mabo 2*); *Gerin v. The Queen*, 2 S.C.R 335 (1984); and *Calder v. Attorney General for British Columbia*, S.C.R. 313 (1973), 4 W.W.R 1. Robert A. Williams Jr. also cites four older cases dating back to at least 1847 in "Columbus's Legacy: Law as an Instrument of Racial Discrimination against Indigenous Peoples' Rights of Self-Determination," *Arizona Legal Studies*, Discussion Paper No, 09-36, 5n (2009).

56 Walter R. Echo-Hawk, *In the Courts of the Conqueror: The 10 Worst Indian Law Cases Ever Decided* (Golden, CO: Fulcrum Publishing, 2010), 110.

57 Watson, "The Doctrine of Discovery," 1008. These cases included *United States v. Fernandez*, 34 U.S. (9 Peters) 303, 304 (1836); *Clark v. Smith*, 38 U.S. (13 Peters) 195, 200–201 (1839); *Mitchel v. United States* (*Mitchel II*), 21 U.S. (15 Peters) 52, 89 (1841); and *Martin v. Lessee of Waddell*, 41 U.S. (16 Peters) 367, 406–418 (1842).

58 See also Robertson, *Conquest by Law*, 118, 129–135.

59 Banner, *How the Indians Lost Their Land*, 226.

60 Banner, *op. cit.*, 227.

61 Newton, "Federal Power," 209–210, citing *United States v. Rogers*, 45 U.S. (4 How.) 567 (1846).

62 *United States v. Rogers*, 572.

63 Newton, "Federal Power," 210.

64 *United States v. Rogers*, 572.

65 Newton, "Federal Power," 209.

66 *United States v. Rogers* at 572.

67 Fitzmaurice, *Sovereignty, Property and Empire*, 5–6.

68 Act of Mar. 3, 1871, Rev. Stat. § 2079, 16 Stat. 566, codified at 25 U. S. C. § 71; Banner, *How the Indians Lost Their Land*, 251–253.

69 Newton, "Federal Power," 207.

70 Ibid., 213.

71 *United States v. Kagama*, 118 U.S. 375, 383–384 (1886).

72 Frickey, "Domesticating Federal Indian Law," 35.

73 *Lone Wolf v. Hitchcock*, 187 U.S. 553, 565, 567 (1903). See also Echo-Hawk, *Courts of the Conqueror*, 434.

74 Frank Pommersheim, "Is There a (Little or Not So Little) Constitutional Crisis Developing in Indian Law?: A Brief Essay," *Journal of Constitutional Law* 5 (2003): 277–278.

75 *United States v. Washington*, 384 F. Supp. 312 (W.D. Wash. 1974).

76 *United States v. Washington*, 333.

77 Ibid., 339.

78 Ibid., 340–341.

79 *Tee-Hit-Ton Indians v. United States*, 348 U.S. 272 (1955). See also Echo-Hawk, *In the Courts of the Conqueror*, 359–394, for additional background and discussion.

80 *Tee-Hit-Ton Indians v. United States*, 277.

81 Ibid.

82 *Tee-Hit-Ton Indians v. United States*, 278–280.

83 Ibid., 281–282.

84 Newton, "Federal Power," 248–249.

85 Ibid. at 287–289.

86 Echo-Hawk, *Courts of the Conqueror*, 363–366.

87 Howard M. Friedman, "Interest on Indian Claims: Judicial Protection of the Fisc," *Valparaiso University Law Review* 5 (1970): 26, 39, 41–46.

88 Echo-Hawk, *Courts of the Conqueror*, 365.

89 *Cobell et al. v. Babbitt*, "Complaint to Compel Performance of Trust Obligations," U.S. Dist. Ct., District of Columbia (6/10/96) Civil Action No. unrecorded. http://www.indiantrust.com/docs/1996.06.10_Cobell_Complaint.pdf. (Accessed September 6 2016). The lawsuit went through several iterations over several years, finally being settled as *Cobell et al. v. Salazar et al.* in 2011.

90 Newton, "Federal Power," 220; and Francis Paul Prucha, *American Indian Treaties: The History of a Political Anomaly* (Berkeley and Los Angeles: University of California Press, 1994), 319–320.

91 *Cobell v. Babbitt*, "Memorandum Opinion: Findings of Fact and Conclusions of Law," United States District Court, District of Columbia, Civil Case No. 96-1285 (RCL), 2–3.
92 Public Law 103-412; 108 Stat. 4239; 42 U.S.C. 4001 et seq.; Echo-Hawk, *Courts of the Conqueror*, 211.
93 *Cobell, v. Babbitt*, "Memorandum Opinion: Findings of Fact and Conclusions of Law," United States District Court for the District of Columbia, Civil Case No. 96-1285 (RCL), 2.
94 Eric M. Weiss, "At U.S. Urging, Court Throws Lamberth Off Indian Case," *Washington Post*, July 12, 2006, A13.
95 *Cobell v. Kempthorne*, "Findings of Fact and Conclusions of Law," United States District Court for the District of Columbia, Civil Action No. 961285 (JR), Document 3505 Filed 1/30/2008, 2–3.
96 Ibid.
97 *Cobell v. Kempthorne*, "Findings of Fact," 163–164.
98 *Cobell v. Kempthorne*, "Memorandum Opinion," United States District Court for the District of Columbia, Case 1:96-cv-01285-JR, Document 3573 Filed 08/07/2008, 35.
99 *Cobell, et al. v. Salazar*, Class Action Settlement Agreement, United States District Court, District of Columbia, December 7, 2009, Case No. 1:96CV01285-JR, 6, 10, 15, 26, 27, 28-29, 38, and 42.
100 *Assiniboine & Sioux Tribes of Fort Peck Indian Reservation, et al., v. Norton, et al.*, Memorandum Order Filed December 19, 2007, U.S. District Court, District of Columbia, Case: 1:06-cv-02239-TFH, Doc. 43, 4.
101 *Nez Perce Tribe v. United States*, Opinion and Order, U.S. Court of Federal Claims, No. 06-910L, filed August 22, 2008, 2.
102 *Nez Perce Tribe v. Salazar*, "Joint Stipulation of Settlement Between Defendants and Plaintiff Nez Perce Tribe, and [Proposed] Order," U.S. District Court, District of Columbia, Case 1:06-cv-02239-TFH, Doc. 118, (Filed April 11 2012), 2.
103 Ronald W. Duty, "Law, Grace, Climate Change, and Water Rights in the American Southwest," *On Secular Governance*, 111–112.
104 Martin Luther, "The Ten Commandments" in *The Large Catechism, The Book of Concord: The Confessions of the Evangelical Lutheran Church*, eds. Robert Kolb and Timothy J. Wengert (Minneapolis, MN: Fortress Press, 2000), 410.
105 Luther, "Ten Commandments," 430.
106 Ibid., 425.
107 Ibid., 386–392.
108 See Paul Hinlicky, p. 33 in this volume.
109 Martin Luther, *Lectures on Genesis, Chapters 1–5*, *LW* 1, 56–62.
110 Luther, "Ten Commandments," 420 and 417.
111 John Locke, *Two Treatises of Government*, rev. ed. Peter Laslett (Cambridge: Cambridge University Press, 1963), 309–344.
112 Martin Luther, *Trade and Usury*, *LW* 45, 261.
113 Luther, *Trade and Usury*, 248.
114 Martin Luther, "The Lord's Prayer" in *The Large Catechism*, *op. cit.*, 449–450.
115 Luther, "The Ten Commandments," 417–419.
116 Martin Luther, "The Lord's Prayer," 450.
117 Watson, "The Doctrine of Discovery," 999.
118 Ibid., 426.
119 Luther, "The Ten Commandments," 426.
120 Ward Churchill, "There is Nothing 'Post' about Colonialism: On the Continuing Reality of Colonization and the Implications of Terminological Denial," *Counterpoints* 430 (2012), 28.
121 Luther, *Trade and Usury*, 245, 273.
122 Ibid., n. 1.
123 Luther, "Ten Commandments," 427.
124 Luther, *Trade and Usury*, 265, 270–272.
125 Ibid., 263–264.
126 Martin Luther, "Ten Commandments," 417; *Psalm 82*, *LW* 13, 57, emphasis added.

12 For the woman who yelled 'Fire!' in my backyard

Rape law and Lutheran theology

Mary J. Streufert

In June 1984, some friends and I went out for dinner and a movie. I have no idea where we went to dinner, much less what I ate. I do know, however, that we saw *Ghostbusters*. That night, I awoke to a woman's screams outside my open window, "Rape! Rape!" But then she yelled, "Fire! Fire!" Back and forth, her muffled screams came through my window with the summer breeze. I froze, listening. Then I rolled over and reached for the white princess phone next to my bed. First, the operator: "Is this an emergency?" Then the police: "What exactly are you hearing?" By then, I was shaking and went downstairs to my parents' room to tell them. We could tell that the screams were coming from the back yard.

We went to the front door as the police pulled up silently, but we discovered that my call might appear to be a prank. The trees in front were streaming with toilet paper. The front yard was full of forks, tines to the sky—and on every tine was a large marshmallow, a fond nod to a character we saw in the movie the night before. My friends were sending me off on my summer abroad program in high 1980s style. My dad wanted to go out the front door to tell the police exiting their squad cars in full riot gear, with rifles at the ready, that the call to them was no joke. My mom and I convinced him that was not a good idea, and the police entered the back yard from both sides of the house. We stayed inside and waited.

Soon an officer came to our back door to get my statement. I repeated what I heard through my open window—that a woman alternately screamed "Fire!" and "Rape!" That her cries were occasionally muffled. The officer had learned from the victim that the two had met at a bar at the end of our block and walked up our alley. Our yard was the first without a fence, so it was easy for him to pull her into it.

"Will you need me in court?" I asked. "Tomorrow morning, I leave for Germany." The officer said that because they caught the man in the act of raping the woman and they had my statement, they would not need me to testify in court, he was sure.

The next morning, I left. My parents and I never talked about what happened. I never heard back from the police. I never saw *Ghostbusters* again—at least, not until the summer of 2016 when I watched the original movie with my husband and children. The morning after, my oldest son declared how bizarre it was that I had never seen this "classic" movie again, so I told him my story. Only now have I begun to think about why I never saw the movie again. Or why my family never talked about what happened that night. Or that it was even a possibility that this rapist might not have gone to jail. However, I have thought about that night so very often since 1984—because I think about the woman who had to yell "Fire!"

The woman had to yell "Fire!" in my backyard because screaming rape didn't matter—the guy kept raping her.[1] Clearly, her voice did not matter. She had no authority to stop him. Well into the twenty-first century, we might assume that no one must scream fire to get help when raped. We might assume what women know and say is authoritative enough for the law to see that their perpetrators are charged and convicted. But we would be wrong.

Even in 2010, Kelsey Belnap, a senior at the University of Montana, was not able to see men who raped her charged. Neither the authority of her voice nor of her body mattered to our justice system; it paid attention only to the bodies and voices of the four college football players who she said gang-raped her.[2] These four players were on the University of Montana's beloved Grizzlies' team,[3] which holds an excruciatingly vigorous and exclusively loyal hold on fans. As described by writer John Krakauer, Grizzly fans are fervent; on game days, Missoula simply rocks with fever-pitched pride.[4]

In a confusing state of affairs after Belnap's complaint, the county prosecutor did not file criminal charges.[5] Her voice and the testimony of her body were apparently not enough for the office to prove this crime beyond a reasonable doubt. It was not enough that she explicitly refused the first man to assault her while she was so drunk she was incapacitated.[6] It was not enough that her bodily injuries were documented.[7] It was not even enough for the law that what others said and did corroborated Belnap's experience. The morning after Belnap was raped, her best friend Betsy Fairmont[8] and another friend of Fairmont's (also a football player) drove Belnap to the hospital, and Belnap later visited a rape clinic for evidence collection and treatment.[9] Soon after that, Fairmont texted Belnap this message: "'I am so sorry. I should have taken better care of you.'"[10] But then, the care and loyalty Fairmont and her boyfriend showed Belnap vanished; they later refused to testify against the football players, so that it became, in Krakauer's words, "Belnap's word against the word of six eyewitnesses"—her best friend, her best friend's boyfriend, and the four teammates who violated her.[11] It was also apparently not enough that police recordings of the four perpetrators revealed that they were not able to explain when or why they believed that Belnap had consented, even after detectives confronted them with the "implausibility of [their story that Belnap wanted to have] painful, injurious sex with four men she'd never met before that evening."[12] We may wonder, how was the moral authority of Belnap's body—the evidence of violence collected at the hospital—not enough to support a conviction? How is it that the four teammates' inability to identify when and how Belnap consented was legally sufficient to escape charges?

When Belnap's mom asked her if she wanted a lawyer to pressure the county prosecutor to file criminal charges, Belnap said, "'Mom, they're football players and nobody's gonna listen to me. They'll make my life hell.'"[13] She instinctively knew whose voice would have authority within the community as well as within the law.

What is at stake for Belnap and the many like her is our failure to recognize the moral authority of these women, not only in their relationships, but also in the law. One reason the law fails women is that rape law reflects and reifies a hierarchical gender binary. This hierarchical gender binary, which historically has been and continues to be at the root of U.S. rape and sexual assault law, is deeply connected to Christian views on gendered humanity. Because the law is governed by this gender ideal, the law denies the moral authority of women, girls, and gender non-conforming people.

For the law or society to believe and to act as if human beings simply *are* gendered "opposites" that exist in a hierarchy of authority and value is wrong. As I will demonstrate, this ideal both contributes to the incidence of rape and permeates the content and application of rape law. This theological anthropology—this understanding of humanity—is problematic not only from a contemporary democratic viewpoint but also from a Lutheran perspective because its models of gender hierarchy and gender binaries endanger the lives of women and girls as total persons.[14] The gender hierarchy embodied in rape law is the idea that males have authority and females must be obedient to them—or that men are leaders and women are followers. The working gender binary of the law is the idea that all persons are opposites based on their gender; an age-old assumption of this binary is that men are active and women are passive. This harmful model of gendered humanity is so strong in our religion and culture that it is the responsibility of those who shape the law to address this critical problem.

Because this Christian ideal of a hierarchical gender binary significantly distorts women's moral authority, we must create a Christian theological view of gender to serve as the analytical framework for the crime of rape.[15] Lutheran values and insights are fruitful in addressing this problem, and Lutherans have a responsibility to advocate for them because no one, no matter who they[16] are, should have to yell, "Fire!" when they are raped in order to get someone to pursue justice and care for them. I argue that feminist Lutheran theological anthropology disrupts these harmful Christian hierarchical gender binaries, including those embedded in U.S. rape and sexual assault law, and affords insight into possible legal reforms that could offer greater justice for women.

In Lutheran thought, the law serves justice by restraining harm within and among communities. Martin Luther's work demonstrates the understanding that law serves the common good by ordering society, preventing harm, and holding people accountable for crime. He writes, for example, that the law "restrain[s] civic transgressions."[17] From a Lutheran perspective, not only does the law restrain, but it also is to be a servant of justice.[18] As theologian Carl Braaten writes, "The core of justice is care for the neighbor. Justice is the form that love takes in the life of society."[19] This love is expressed through concern for the well-being of others in society, often through laws, whether or not one is emotionally motivated to serve their rights.

In expressing this concern, the law must protect and promote the well-being and safety—the total personhood—of all members of society. Specifically, the secular law at its best contributes to the creation of a society not ruled by rape, which generates fear, anguish, brokenness, terror, complicity, obedience, and further violence. Rather, at its best, the law fosters freedom (liberation), health, well-being, thoughtfulness, and peace. From a Lutheran perspective, the secular law is meant to be both preventative and responsive. Given what the law is meant to reflect about individuals' moral authority over themselves as total persons, the law ought to function to support the moral authority of women, both before they are harmed, and afterwards when they are victim-survivors of rape and other forms of sexual violence. A look at historical and contemporary law on rape in the United States is the first step in evaluating its effectiveness to foster justice in the ways that it protects and supports women's moral authority.

Legal rape: problems in rape law

Moral authority of one's body is the authority and freedom to decide how one will engage the world and others through and with one's body. It is the authority to ***know*** and to be believed when one speaks out of one's own knowledge. We know through our bodies and experiences, and we express moral authority through voice and body.[20] As ethicist Traci West argues, "Knowledge that we acquire through our bodily perceptions must not be discounted in ethics, for it is a crucial source of moral knowledge."[21] In Anglo-American rape law, women's moral authority has consistently been disputed and often denied.

As is well-known, the law in England, which strongly influenced American rape law, was inherently distrustful of women, as evidenced in the traditional legal requirements for proving rape. Formal substantive and procedural rules in effect in many states reflect this discounting of women's moral authority. As one egregious example, marital rape was not a crime until the 1970s.[22] For a woman not married to her attacker to claim rape, she must have resisted to her utmost, to the point of severe harm or death, as evidence that she was not consenting to intercourse. To be believed, the woman needed to report the rape immediately, which was called a "fresh complaint." The rape needed to be corroborated by other persons or by evidence such as physical injury or torn clothing. Information about women who had any history of sex outside of marriage was allowed in evidence. Finally, "'special cautionary instructions'" were to be read to juries "'to warn them of the fallibility of the testimony of those who complained of having been raped.'"[23] These rules were memorialized in John Henry Wigmore's influential treatise, *Evidence in Trials at Common Law*. Referring to psychiatric studies, Wigmore communicates the legal profession's view about the emotional defects and therefore the lesser credibility and status of females:

> [Women's] psychic complexes are multifarious, distorted by inherent defects, partly by diseased derangements or abnormal instincts, partly by bad social environment, partly by temporary physiological or emotional conditions.[24]

With such supposed faults, women were assumed to frequently make false charges of rape against supposedly innocent men. In these ways, women's moral authority was disputed and denied within the law.[25]

Rules and assumptions reflecting such gender-based distrust may now seem outrageous. However, as Michelle Anderson consistently argues, most statutes have not strayed significantly from common law assumptions, despite some legal reforms. Evidence of victim consent and victim resistance still dominate the legal analysis of rape. In terms of assumptions about victim consent, in the two models of consent currently debated in rape reform efforts, which Anderson describes as the "No" model and the "Yes" model, there are at least two problems. First, "[u]nder the No Model ... sexual penetration is legal unless the woman physically or verbally opposes it ... [U]nder the Yes Model[,] sexual penetration is illegal unless one's partner physically or verbally grants permission for it."[26] Not only does everything depend upon the victim, but "[b]oth models," according to Anderson, "reward willful blindness" on the part of the accused.[27] In this way, the law imputes permission of access for men and responsibility to prevent access by all means possible for women. Second, the idea of consent in rape law is tied to and reifies active-passive models of gendered sexual activities and relationships. According to Anderson, both the "No" and "Yes" models have reinforced the flawed ideal of what I have called a hierarchical gender binary.[28]

Moreover, the legal assumptions about perpetrator force and the victim's responsibility to resist it have carried over from historical law into contemporary law. As Susan Estrich points out, "[Rape] is the only crime that has required the victim to resist physically in order to establish nonconsent."[29] What is criminally prohibited, she further points out, is usually determined by the victim's response—but from a male perspective that a physical fight, not words, is resistance.[30] If a woman has injuries, she is more believable in the judicial system.[31] However, continuing to define rape in the law by evidence only of a particular kind of violence—blood, bruises, lacerations, and broken bones and teeth—does not sufficiently address how men actually act in rape since there is not necessarily evidence of physical violence in every rape.[32] Nor does it sufficiently address most women's experiences, since most are raped by acquaintances and intimates. As Estrich so famously put it, "Power will do," for force in rape comes not necessarily in the form of physical violence.[33] Much of this power that men hold in rape, at least in the United States, comes from a deeply embedded, deeply faulty Christian theological anthropology, to which I will now turn.

Who is rape-able? Christian theological anthropology and a feminist Lutheran critique

While most Christians in the United States might agree in theory that all people are equal before God, many predominant Christian views of gendered humanity are in fact highly problematic. Teachings of major streams of Christianity in the United States advance the idea that humans are created in gender binaries that are arranged by God in a hierarchy, men over women.[34] These gendered ideals not only restrict the flourishing of all people as total persons, but they also can contribute to spiritual as well as physical death.

Prevailing Roman Catholic and Protestant teachings advance theological anthropologies rooted in binaristic gender essentialism and gender-based hierarchy. Four key commonalities stand out, for example, in central teachings of the Roman Catholic Church, the Lutheran Church-Missouri Synod, and as a sample of evangelicalism, the Promise Keepers movement; collectively, they represent the predominant Christian view in the United States.[35] The first commonality is that a gender hierarchy of males over females is God-ordained. Second, according to this view, God creates humans to be opposites based on their gender; they are "essentially" this way. The third commonality is that gender roles are inherent to Christian vocation, which requires male headship and female subordination and obedience. Fourth, moral responses to female oppression are the responsibility of individuals, and state or institutional structures have little role to play.[36]

From a feminist Lutheran perspective, these views are theologically problematic because they are idolatrous: they elevate male humans into the roles and place of God, justifying and enforcing a world that is male-dominant, male-identified, and male-centered.[37] The social enforcement of these views results in foreclosed lives, not only for women and girls, but also for any person who is lesbian, gay, bisexual, transgender, queer or intersex and for men and boys, because there is only one "approved" model of being and acting male and one model of being and acting female. There is thus precious little room for recognizing God's work in creation through human variation, human imagination, and human expression in gender.

Feminist Lutheran theology disrupts these hierarchical gender binaries and offers insights into gender-equitable values and practices. A Lutheran priority of grace helps to confront problematic hierarchical gender binaries. Justification by grace through faith was the central wager of the Protestant Reformation, and it serves as a central interpretive and guiding principle of Reformation theologies. As Martin Luther saw it, justification is the primary focus of the Gospel and therefore is the basis and guide for all Christian thought.[38] Central to Luther's understanding of the Gospel is the good news that believers receive grace *freely* from God and not through our own actions or inactions, which is the contrary view to a theology famously known as "works righteousness." From a feminist perspective, "works righteousness" includes what I call "gender righteousness." In other words, I argue that fulfilling idealized gender roles does not earn us God's love and grace. Conversely, *not* fulfilling gender ideals is not sinful.

A feminist priority on the well-being of women, girls, and gender non-conforming persons allows new understanding of the doctrine of justification. It challenges hierarchical gender binaries[39] by upending the idolatry of male supremacy. Moreover, the doctrine of justification declares freedom from the bondage of what gets in the way of the Gospel, including gendered assumptions about required roles for men and women. God's alien righteousness affirms human equality and alters human relationships. The doctrine of justification clarifies our common human vocation in both individual and systemic realms.

While the Christian teachings I refer to emphasize spiritual gender equality before God, they each emphasize **God-ordained earthly hierarchy**. In these teachings, God creates humans in a hierarchy of headship and subordination and intends for people to live within this hierarchy of gendered status, particularly in the family and church. In one way or another, this theology grounds gendered hierarchy in the doctrines of creation and redemption, thus multiplying the weight of their arguments, lest anyone ever claim it is right to go against what God has ordained from the beginning of time and in the healing of creation. Such theology can lead to idolatry.

From a feminist perspective, the doctrine of justification challenges this idolatry of male supremacy because it is thoroughly theocentric and christocentric. This means that God acts in and through Christ to make us righteous; we are not able to make ourselves righteous before God. God through Christ at the center of human existence unmasks human male supremacy for the idolatry that it is because in this ideology, the male is made a god, something "good" to be protected and celebrated.

Within this earthly hierarchy, the theology goes, humans are created in a binary according to gendered essences. The teachings rarely emphasize identities or qualities common to humanity regardless of gender; rather, they emphasize that men and women are created with their own "special" qualities. For example, one assumption is that women are created to be passive and men are designed to be active. The papal encyclical *Mulieris Dignitatem* evidences this assumption when it emphasizes that women live best for others as virgin, spouse, and mother and that they have a feminine "'originality'" that it is sinful to ignore.[40] The essence of women and girls, their self-giving and passivity, is then tied directly to the proper role of females in domestic relationships. Pope John Paul II suggests that if people behave correctly according to the principles of this binaristic gender essentialism, "the inheritance of sin" can be overcome. In other words, he claims that if women behaved according to their God-given vocation as "feminine," domestic strife, violence, and domination by men of women would dissipate. In a different vein, but using the same gendered active-passive model, the Promise Keepers teach that God empowers men to be the saviors of the family, church, and society if they outdo their wives in service within the family and fix the problems of the nation. While Promise Keeper teachings often reflect a high regard for the well-being of women and children, they remain primarily wedded to an oppositional understanding of males as active and females as receptive.

Alternatively, the doctrine of justification declares freedom from bondage. Luther argues that justification frees the whole person from what gets in the way of the Gospel. For example, he condemns a hierarchy of human value that places clergy over laypeople as "an unbearable bondage of human works and laws."[41] A number of contemporary Lutheran theologians extend Luther's explication of freedom from bondage, seeing freedom in Christ as both eschatological and ethical. Theologian Lois Malcolm describes the ethical implications of freedom in Christ most succinctly:

> The wager of the Lutheran movement is precisely that the heart of Jesus' gospel lies in its promise of liberation from oppression of all sorts and that this promise provides the church with a criterion for distinguishing what is Christian from what is not in its beliefs and practices.[42]

15 For a similar argument that colonialism must be an analytical framework on rape related to rape and rape law affecting indigenous women, see Sarah Deer, "Toward an Indigenous Jurisprudence of Rape," *Kansas Journal of Law & Public Policy* 14, Fall (2004): 125, 134.
16 It is now common usage to use the pronoun "they" to write without gender specificity. At strategic points in this chapter, I use this practice to emphasize the fact that not only women are raped for gender-based reasons.
17 Luther, *Lectures on Genesis*, *LW* 26, 312–313.
18 Carl E. Braaten, *Principles of Lutheran Theology* (Philadelphia, PA: Fortress Press, 1983), 127.
19 Ibid., 132.
20 See Traci C. West, *Disruptive Christian Ethics: When Racism and Women's Lives Matter* (Louisville, KY: Westminster John Knox Press, 2006), 36–71.
21 Ibid., 42.
22 Marital rape did not become a crime in all states until 1993. On the history and relevance of the law of coverture, see Jill Elaine Hasday, "Contest and Consent: A Legal History of Marital Rape," *California Law Review* 88, no. 5 (2000): 1386–1418.
23 Deer, "Toward an Indigenous Jurisprudence," 124–125, quoting Michelle J. Anderson, "Women Do Not Report the Violence They Suffer: Violence against Women and the State Action Doctrine," *Villanova L. Rev.* 46 (2001): 924–925.
24 Richard Klein, "An Analysis of Thirty-Five Years of Rape Reform: A Frustrating Search for Fundamental Fairness," *Akron Law Review* 41 (2008): 985–986, quoting John Henry Wigmore, *Evidence in Trials at Common Law*, rev. ed. James H. Chadbourn (Boston, MA: Little Brown, 1970).
25 Note the contrast related to public trust of women about rape when racism is involved in Estelle Freedman, *Redefining Rape: Sexual Violence in the Era of Suffrage and Segregation* (Cambridge, MA: Harvard University Press, 2013). White women in the last two centuries were easily able to accuse black men of rape or sexual assault, which often led to the injustices of prosecution and execution of innocent men or of lynchings.
26 Michelle Anderson, "Negotiating Sex," *Southern California Law Review* 78, no. 6 (2005): 1411.
27 Anderson, "Negotiating Sex," 1420.
28 See ibid., 1405–1409.
29 Susan Estrich, "Rape," *Yale Law Journal* 95 (1986): 1090.
30 See ibid., 1094.
31 Belief of a rape victim has been tied to physical resistance to establish non-consent. See ibid., 1090.
32 See Christina E. Wells and Erin Elliott Motley, "Reinforcing the Myth of the Crazed Rapist: A Feminist Critique of Recent Rape Legislation," *Boston University Law Review* 81 (2001): 153, quoting Dorothy Roberts, "Rape, Violence, and Women's Autonomy," *Chicago-Kent Law Review* 69 (1993): 359, 362.
Estrich, "Rape," 1150.
33 Ibid.
34 For a fuller argument of my points here, see Mary J. Streufert, "Idolatry—Critical Justification and the Foreclosed Gendered Life," in Carl-Henric Grenholm and Göran Gunner, *Lutheran Identity and Political Theology*, Church of Sweden Research Series vol. 9 (Eugene, OR: Pickwick Publications, 2014), 134–152 (hereafter, "Idolatry").
35 In terms of sheer numbers, Roman Catholics, evangelicals, and other Protestants with theology similar to Promise Keepers and the Lutheran Church-Missouri Synod outstrip the historical mainline denominations, whose official church teachings on gender and sexuality tend to be more equitable. This is not to say, however, that individuals or single congregations within each of these Christian denominations in the U.S. adhere to church (e.g., Roman Catholic or Lutheran Church-Missouri Synod) or organizational (e.g., Promise Keepers) teaching.
36 See Streufert, "Idolatry," 136.
37 See ibid.
38 See Luther, *Lectures on Genesis*, *LW* 26, 312–313 (discussion of futility of "active righteousness" vs. salvation related to "passive righteousness").
39 As stated elsewhere, I fully acknowledge that Luther's doctrine of justification, *Lectures on Genesis*, *LW* 26, 312–313, is highly problematic from various perspectives and deserves ongoing critical work. See generally Streufert, "Idolatry."

40 Ibid., 141.
41 Luther, "The Freedom of a Christian," *The Career of the Reformer I*, *LW* 31, 356–357.
42 Lois Malcolm, "The Gospel and Feminism: A Proposal for Lutheran Dogmatics," *Word & World* 15, no. 3 (1995): 298.
43 For further social analysis of cultural hierarchical gender binaries and a feminist Lutheran scriptural response, see Mary J. Streufert, "Gender and Justice within Empire: Toward a Christian Ethic of Gender Justice," *Journal of Lutheran Ethics* 13, no. 5 (2013). Accessed November 2, 2017. www.elca.org/What-We-Believe/Social-Issues/Lutheran-Ethics.aspx.
44 There are, however, Christian leaders who support female acquiescence in male violence. See Erin Parks, "Dropping the Crystal Goblet: Evangelical Complementarian Responses to Domestic Abuse" (Capstone project, Pacific Lutheran University, 2014) regarding John Piper and Debi Pearl.
45 See Evangelical Lutheran Church in America, "The Church in Society: A Lutheran Perspective," (1991). Accessed October 21, 2016. http://download.elca.org/ELCA%20Resource%20 Repository/Church_SocietySS.pdf. See also Luther, "The Freedom of a Christian," *LW* 31, 309.
46 Kristen E. Kvam, "God's Heart Revealed in Eden," in Mary J. Streufert, *Transformative Lutheran Theologies* (Minneapolis, MN: Fortress Press, 2010), 66.
47 See Streufert, "Idolatry," 150–151.
48 Wells and Motley, "Reinforcing the Myth of the Crazed Rapist," 128–129, 153.
49 Ibid., 153.
50 See Estrich, "Rape," 1094. Estrich starts from the basic premise of criminal law, which defines crime as composed of two elements: the prohibited act (*actus reus*) and "the prohibited mental state (*mens rea*)" of the defendant.
51 Ibid., 1098.
52 Deer, "Toward an Indigenous Jurisprudence of Rape," 124.
53 Ibid., 122.
54 See ibid., 123, 129.
55 Freedman, *Redefining Rape*, makes similar links in her analysis of the history of rape in slavery and segregation.
56 Deer, "Toward an Indigenous Jurisprudence of Rape," 137.
57 For state-by-state information, see Affirmative Consent. Accessed November 1, 2017. http://affirmativeconsent.com/affirmative-consent-laws-state-by-state/.
58 Estrich, "Rape," 1096.

13 Re-creating the law of the family

A Lutheran perspective

Marie A. Failinger and Patrick R. Keifert

Introduction

Despite the many paradoxes of human nature and human relationships, according to the Christian witness, we are made in and for community, both with other human beings and with God. One expression of community is the family, within which all these paradoxes manifest themselves over time. Because families exist within the larger communal context of civil society and the state, as the Lutheran Reformation underscored, society has an interest in how communal life in families is lived, in the social reasons for creating families, and in the use of family law in ordering this gift for living.

The Lutheran Reformation was a profoundly innovative moment in the Western understanding of secular law that influences our current day-to-day reality, and its influence was never more profound than in the life of families in the lands most transformed by that Reformation.[1] Only in the last century have historians and social scientists uncovered the deep theological undersides of the connection between the Lutheran Reformation and the emergence of modernity, especially in countries identified with the Enlightenment. One likely unavoidable outgrowth of this development assumes a great chasm, called the "modern dogma" by Wayne Booth,[2] between public, objective discourse and private, relative and subjective discourse. On one extreme, this modern dogma sentimentalizes public discourse on the family; on the other, our modern social imagination represents the Lutheran confession in a decidedly authoritarian and reactionary way.

As Lutherans, we take our chief clue for understanding ever-emerging varieties of family life, their social and cultural forms, and the ways in which the state can help families from the explanation of the commandments found in Luther's Large and Small Catechism, and especially its repetitious call to "fear, love, and trust in God." Luther's catechetical explanations can hardly be called either authoritarian or sentimental. Indeed, his explanations deliver a rather strong "reality therapy" to help us rediscover a social imaginary for family life that counteracts both sentimentalization of the family, and authoritarian understandings of our relationship with God that neglect the deep promise, conditional to be sure, embedded in his explanation of what it means to fear, love, and trust in God.

Lutherans might thus propose that secular law has to be designed with dual purposes: first, protecting the role of the family in working toward a preferred future for the human community—e.g., in providing the basic physical needs of life such as food, clothing and shelter; but equally importantly, in meeting educational, affectional, spiritual and other needs required for all to thrive according to that preferred future. Second, secular law must protect against the reality of sin, because even family members use loved ones to achieve their own desires rather than cherishing each family member with respect for the One who created him or her.

Lutherans would thus critique two imaginaries—status (reflecting the authoritarian and reactive interpretation of the commandments) and contract (reflecting the sentimentalization of the family)—that have shaped the way in which family law jurisprudence has been debated. As family law historian Jill Hasday has argued, one consistent theme in contemporary family law jurisprudence is that family law has moved from status to contract.[3] That claim suggests that the traditional institution of the family was premised on the idea that each member of the family was born into a role—son or daughter, husband or wife, mother or father, servant or head of household—with distinct and non-negotiable obligations. In the status-to-contract story, modern social life has "progressed," abolishing obligatory roles based on one's status in the family, and the law should reflect that reality. One extreme "progressive" modern view would claim that that every aspect of the family, from composition to individual roles should result only from bargained-for agreements between autonomous adult members of the family, respecting children's rights.

While history certainly reflects clear resonances of the status-to-contract story, Lutherans would agree it is much too simple to describe the law of the family either as a reality or as a normative ideal.

A status-based model of the family

The status-based model of the family is neither historically accurate nor normative for Lutherans and most Christians. As legal historians John Noonan, Mary Ann Glendon and John Witte have shown, marriage law in the Christian tradition has always emphasized the essence of agreement in the required consent of the two parties to the marriage. Indeed, by the end of the third century B.C., even pre-Christian Roman marriage was largely consensual, with those who regarded themselves as married simply setting up their household.[4] Later, Glendon notes, "the Church's consistent position (with some diversity of opinion) was that consent of the parties alone sufficed to constitute a valid marriage, and no particular form was required for the exchange."[5]

Similarly, with some historical fluctuations, divorce by mutual consent of the parties was also acceptable practice until canon law took hold in the late medieval age and its view on the indissolubility of marriages triumphed.[6] Glendon argues that the Church's doctrine "that Christian marriages could be formed by the parties' consent alone" caused problems for the transmission of family wealth in the late medieval period, which led the Church to insist on a more public display of the parties' permanent consent to marriage through a compulsory church rite and public banns and registration for marriage.[7] Even if often honored in the breach by families who made beneficial alliances by arranging their children's marriages, the basic requirement of the parties' consent continued to be at the heart of medieval church law on marriage.

Today, there are those who yearn or advocate for a return to a status-based model of the family, often suggesting that God has designed specific roles for different members in the family. Some of these status advocates argue that Scripture is clear about the duty of children to obey their parents and the duty of wives to submit to their husbands, as examples. Others make natural law arguments to justify setting static parameters around each family member's role in the family community.

The Lutheran witness recognizes that God's will for the Creation is critical in understanding the nature and structure of marriage and family, but rejects rigidly static, status-based understandings of family roles. For Lutherans, the family is one of the foundational "orders of creation," yet one that God is continuously creating and re-creating (*creation continua*). Theologian Bill Lazareth underscores that to create is always to do something new—*creare est semper novum facere.*[8] Indeed, *creation continua* is a necessity in a world in which human beings and their communities are constantly undergoing change. Even children, who are placed without choice into those families by God, constantly experience the changing nature of their relationship with others in their families.

As co-creators of these orders with God, we have choices in "making something new"—choosing to flourish and take responsibility for the flourishing of the whole family, or refusing to thrive as God intended, creating damage to ourselves and our families. This reality of the continuous creation of God necessarily rejects a family law that assigns duties based on gender, age, etc. Our attempts to reify family life deny God's creativity and God's plan that our families shape and are shaped by our unique individual gifts and purposes.

A status-based model of marriage and family also fails to recognize a key Reformation doctrine—that we are always, irrevocably, even unconsciously sinful. As sinners, we will abuse the Creator's ordainings[9] about the family in order to achieve our own selfish and short-sighted desires, including our beliefs that our own needs and value are more important than those of others, sinfully justifying the harms that we cause others in the family. There is no better modern example of this self-justificatory abuse of the orders of marriage and family than domestic violence. In the traditional Christian model of marriage, Scripture tells us that the husband should give his life for his wife.[10] Because of sin, in domestic abuse, this instruction is turned upside down: the husband claims his right, as head of the household, to take the very life of his wife, forcing her to do his bidding, disrespecting her body through physical and sexual abuse, and disrespecting her heart and soul through threats and verbal diminishment. Indeed, in typical cases, the abuser engages in deep self-justification, claiming that it is his right to abuse her because of his wife's faults and his standing as household head. This divine order becomes its very opposite, the site for the degradation of the human person.

The contract model of the family

Lutherans would also reject the story that modern family law has resolved the difficulties with the status model through a purely contractual model of marriage and family duties. Noting that the family law "story celebrates the rise of contractualization as a triumph of individual freedom and equality," Hasday notes the many "status" rules that continue to define the creation and breakup of most modern families; we might note mostly non-negotiable duties of parents toward their children and non-waivable rights that spouses have against each other, including the right to "necessities."[11] And, while more property and custody rights of spouses are considered negotiable in modern American marriage and divorce law, most married people fail to exercise the opportunity to negotiate terms for their marriages, thus triggering default rules in family law. Indeed, the clearest rejection of the pure contract model is that no American jurisdiction has embraced repeated scholarly proposals to abolish marriage as an institution in favor of legal contracts, with religious communities setting other expectations for their members.[12]

In the Lutheran witness, a purely contractual model for family law is not normatively desirable either. In the contemporary Western tradition, courtship and marriage bely contract law assumptions that parties can get adequate information about each other, identify terms of the marriage to satisfy their self-interested goals, and bargain dispassionately to achieve a compromise. The rise of romantic love disrupts these arms'-length processes: the hopes and emotions that partners invest in mates often make them partially oblivious to the prospective partner's undesirable traits, as well as their own. And there may be a substantial disparity in marital "bargaining power" because of one party's desire to be married, economic imbalances, and other factors, as evidenced by the number of cases in which prenuptial agreements are challenged. Moreover, because marriage partners generally invest an enormous amount of their emotional and physical lives in their mates, the violation of a marriage "contract," for example by desertion, is such a profound breach of trust that it cannot be repaired through traditional contract means, such as money damages.

Lutheran "reality therapy" demands that secular law respond to the human condition as it is, not as we might wish it to be. In reality, in conditions of sin which affect all human beings, spouses are likely to misuse their partners and children to satisfy their own desires.[13] Martin Luther was coldly realistic in arguing that marriage "may be likened to a hospital for incurables which prevents the inmates from falling into grave sin."[14]

Recognizing that even fully consensual marriages often quickly lose any initial egalitarian character, post-Reformation law emphasized that the community is vital to supporting new family formations, and the family's health also affects the surrounding community, for good or ill. Because they understood that marriage and family were **public callings from God** within the larger community,[15] Reformation countries enhanced the "publicness" of this institution, requiring a public marriage ceremony, government registration of the marriage, and parental consent for minors.[16] They also placed marriage and divorce within the order of the state, not the church; the state, with its monopoly on legitimate coercion to deter and punish human wrongdoing, governs all human beings, Christian or not.

Even today, the post-Reformation understanding that marriage is a public institution is evidenced in requirements that partners obtain a state-issued license and solemnize their consent through a ceremony conducted by a state-approved official.[17] Subject to constitutional constraints, states continue to set rules for marriage eligibility and "fault" or "no-fault" rules for divorce.[18] At the same time, the emphasis on the free consent of the parties continues to be honored through annulment law doctrines such as the lack of capacity to consent because of age or severe mental disability or mental illness,[19] as well as coercion, duress or substantial fraud going to basic aspects of marriage, such as a party's impotence or sterility.[20]

Reformation themes in marriage and divorce law

Prizing the reasoning of all of God's created persons about how the secular world should be governed, Lutherans hold that solutions to family law issues are properly debatable and should reference specific social contexts and political communities. Lutherans will, however, pose questions to democratic governance that reflect the insights of their tradition.

A Reformation model for marriage will especially emphasize that family law must properly balance two important values necessary for human flourishing: human freedom and responsibility, values often in a tension that will take a different shape from age to age and culture to culture. The very act of marriage is an exercise in human freedom that builds a legal institution on relationships that did not exist before, relationships that affect even children and in-laws who did not consent to these potentially disruptive changes in their lives. Even the consenting couple experiences surprising life-opportunities that were not possible before each had a helpmeet, and unexpected responsibilities in establishing a home, an occupation, a shared social life, and perhaps a shared spiritual life.

In the Lutheran tradition, this yoking of freedom and responsibility is captured in a key commandment:

> "Love the Lord your God with all your heart and with all your soul and with all your mind"--This is the first and greatest commandment. And the second is like it: "Love your neighbor as yourself." All the Law and the Prophets hang on these two commandments.[21]

This commandment reflects a vision of human existence that is essentially ethical, that understands that we do not exist except in relation to others and we do not exist except to serve those others. Philosopher Emmanuel Levinas graphically represents our existence as an encounter with the face of the Other, standing over us in His need.[22] That reality rejects a sentimentalized notion that the "oneness" of marriage erases the irreducible otherness of the spouse and assures unconditional trust between partners. For Lutherans, both partners remain strangers who present to each other the demand and promise of God. Lutheran theology reminds us that we are to fear, love, and trust in God above everything and everyone else, including our spouses or ourselves.

As the Lutheran theory of continuous creation suggests, Lutheran theology calls for a family law that is dynamic, reflecting the ongoing work of God in the world, while being candid and humble about the limits of orders of creation co-managed by sinful human beings. We recognize that God expects us individually and as families to help preserve and heal the world.

Most critically, we are called to raise children to be healthy adults who can contribute to that preservation and healing. Not that children are the sine qua non of marriage, or that the state should refuse to marry individuals who cannot or will not bear or raise children: that would disrespect God's calling to many childless families to contribute to repairing the world according to their gifts. Rather, the demand to put the lives and wellbeing of children first is both literal and metaphorical: it represents the divine call to prioritize the needs of those who are most vulnerable, children or the elderly, the disabled or the emotionally fragile. This vision also challenges the contemporary assumption that children, and those like them vulnerable, are only the responsibility of parents. Whether born into healthy marriages, born into unhealthy relationships, or abandoned while young, these vulnerable persons are the responsibility of all families and communities to care for.

A particularly important responsibility of parents and communities in the Lutheran tradition is teaching children. While for Christians, the most critical aspect of this responsibility is to teach children the Gospel, the Lutheran tradition also expects all adults to provide the knowledge and skills children need to make their contribution in this world. While adults inculcate a moral foundation of neighbor-love for others in this secular life, children also need to learn by study and example that "being good" is not in any way a means to salvation. Rather, morality is only our best and current understanding about God's desire that we live together in peace and justice in this secular age. As "the best we can understand and the best we can do," these moral understandings are always subject to reflective critique, revision and reformation as the conditions in this earthly life warrant.

Given these responsibilities, the limits of proper parental authority must be resolved by secular law. For example, modern societies have had to draw a line between permissible (if ever permissible) and abusive corporal punishment, and consider whether parents may substitute faith healing for Western medicine when their children are gravely ill. They have had to determine how to regulate homeschooling, and how to respond to religiously-informed pedagogy that teaches non-mainstream values (e.g., views that the white race is superior, or that the genders should not mix). They have had to consider whether children should be exempt from child labor laws or child marriage bans based on their parents' religious beliefs. Indeed, they have had to decide whether children have rights at all, e.g., whether minors should be able to get contraceptives or abortions without parental consent, and when they should be granted access to adult privileges such as driver's licenses and alcohol. Similarly, the issue of when children should be held legally responsible for crimes they commit or contracts they sign must be re-considered in every generation and every society.

In the Lutheran view, God has *entrusted* children to their parents and other adults because our experience makes us wiser about what is best for them. But it also suggests that any legal regime that gives unrestrained "power over" to parents or "rights to" children cannot preserve the delicate balance between the freedom and the self-giving expected of parents and children for this *entrustment* to work without sliding into serious sinful behavior by either parent or child. As Lutheran theologian Edward Schroeder describes it:

> Just as children need to learn how to speak, and then read and count, so also living with authority must be learnt. That includes learning both how to live under someone else's authority and how to exercise authority when it is in your own hands. If such bilateral living with authority ... is not learnt in the family, along with all the other elements in the network of socialization and maturation, where can it be learnt? ... If authority figures are to be acknowledged as such, they must be seen as trustworthy. Trustworthiness is established by experience, the experience that some person indeed has my welfare at heart. Once that has been learnt ... other family members, school teachers, public officials, etc., can be acknowledged as authorities from this primal foundation of positive parental experiences.[23]

Acting as trustees for their children means that parents must exercise sacrificial love, which will include discipline, sanctions, and saying no when saying yes or ignoring their behavior would do harm.[24]

The state also plays two important roles in responding to this vulnerability of children and others in the family. Schroeder describes God's activity or "agenda," as conceived by the Reformers, as the law of preservation and the law of recompense:

> Preservation is God's organizing things so that life—human and all other things living—doesn't die out, but keeps on going. Recompense was God's organizing things so that rightful actions (the preservation agenda) got rewarded and wrongful actions (destruction) got their come-uppance to make them stop.[25]

Thus, God's work in the world through the family law of the state is not limited merely to the law of recompense, or in modern rights language, negative rights. The Lutheran tradition also rejects a vision of family law that assumes that family business is private business unless members of the family create public harm. This privatized vision of the family has justified state non-intervention into spousal and child abuse and neglect of suffering vulnerable children and fragile families who do not have the resources to care for themselves. The Lutheran tradition demands that the state take those affirmative actions that preserve the family, whether they may be regulatory or distributional.

This dual role of the state in implementing God's laws of preservation and recompense implies that taxation properly provides financial and other assistance to families when it

Notes

1 Trevor O'Reggio, "Martin Luther on Marriage and Family," *Andrews University Faculty Publications* (2012): 196. Accessed November 13, 2017. http://digitalcommons.andrews.edu/church-history-pubs/20.
2 Wayne Booth, *Modern Dogma and the Rhetoric of Assent* (Chicago, IL: University of Chicago Press, 1974), 87–89.
3 Jill Hasday, "The Canon of Family Law," *Stanford Law Review* 57 (2004): 825, 835–38.
4 Mary Ann Glendon, *The Transformation of Family Law: State, Law, and the Family in the United States and Western Europe* (Chicago, IL: University of Chicago Press, 1996), 21.
5 Ibid., 25.
6 Ibid., 22.
7 Ibid., 28–29.
8 William H. Lazareth, *Christians in Society: Luther, The Bible, and Social Ethics* (Minneapolis, MN: Augsburg Press, 2001), 66.
9 See Edward H. Schroeder, "Homosexuality and Reformation Theology." Accessed October 27, 2017. www.crossings.org/homosexuality-and-reformation-theology/
10 Eph. 5:25 (N.I.V.); William Lazareth, *Christians in Society*, 150.
11 See Jill Hasday, "The Canon of Family Law," 835.
12 See Anita Bernstein, "For and Against Marriage: A Revision", *Michigan Law Review* 102 (2003–04): 129, 132–43.
13 O'Reggio, *Martin Luther on Marriage and Family*, 202 (quoting Martin Luther, "A Sermon on the Estate of Marriage" (1519)).
14 Ibid., 202; William H. Lazareth, *Luther on the Christian Home: An Application of the Social Ethics of the Reformation* (Philadelphia, PA: Muhlenberg Press, 2011), 181–82, 208 (quoting Martin Luther, *A Sermon on the Estate of Marriage* (1519)).
15 Lazareth, *Christians in Society*, 68.
16 Glendon, *The Transformation of Family Law*, 29.
17 Thomas Oldham, "Model Marriage and Divorce Act," in *Family Law: Uniform Laws Affecting the Family* (St. Paul, MN: Thomson Reuters, 2012), 540–42.
18 See e.g., Allen M. Parkman, "Reforming Divorce Reform," *Santa Clara Law Review* 41 (2001): 379.
19 See Ira Mark Ellman et. al., *Family Law: Cases, Examples, Problems*, 5th ed. (Providence, RI: Lexis Nexis, 2010), 122, 183–85, 187–90, 193–95; Thomas Oldham, *Family Law*, 540; Douglas J. Abrams et al., *Contemporary Family Law*, 3rd ed. (St. Paul, MN: Thomson Reuters, 2012), 167.
20 Ira Ellman, *Family Law*, 193–95.
21 Matthew 22:37–40 (N.I.V.).
22 See Emmanuel Levinas, *Totality and Infinity: An Essay on Exteriority*, trans. Lingis (Pittsburgh, PA: Duquesne University Press, 1969), 197, 199–200.
23 Edward H. Schroeder, *Relocating Authority: A Perennial Family Issue*, in *The Changing Face of the Family* (Adelaide: Dietrich Bonhoeffer Institute, 1994), 54–58. Accessed October 27, 2017. http://digitalcommons.andrews.edu/church-history-pubs/20.
24 Ibid.
25 Edward H. Schroeder, "Reformation Resources: Law/Promise Hermeneutics and the Godly Secularity of Sex:" 5. (Presentation at SW Minnesota Synod ELCA Fall Theology Conference, Sept. 29, 2001.) Accessed October 27, 2017. www.crossings.org/library/schroeder2/ReformationResources.pdf
26 Evangelical Lutheran Church in America. *A Social Statement on Human Sexuality: Gift and Trust*, 12. Accessed October 27, 2017. http://download.elca.org/ELCA%20Resource%20Repository/SexualitySS.pdf?_ga=2.56627306.1150282620.1499299569-1928962704.1499299569.
27 ELCA, "Human Sexuality: Gift and Trust" Social Statement Summary, 1–2. Accessed October 27, 2017. http://download.elca.org/ELCA%20Resource%20Repository/SexualitySS_Summary.pdf.
28 See Schroeder, *Relocating Authority.*

Part VI

Professionals, law and neighbor-love

14 Professional responsibility, informed consent, and neighbor love in cancer trials

Theological, ethical, and legal dimensions

Deanna A. Thompson

Can a person flee a deadly plague? That is the question Martin Luther wrestled with in the 1520s as the plague intensified its grip on Central Europe. Luther frames his pastoral response about whether one can flee in terms of love of neighbor, stressing Christians' obligation to serve their neighbors just as they serve Christ. It is incumbent upon those "who stand in a relationship of service or duty toward one another"—people like "physicians, clerks, and constables"[1]—not to flee, Luther writes, but to stay and serve the neighbor by fulfilling their roles as ministers, doctors, or even the town lawyer.

Central to Luther's ethical vision is the commitment to love of neighbor. But because we live in a finite, fallen world, Luther acknowledges that loving the neighbor often takes on a cruciform shape. In the instance of the plague, Luther stresses how easy it is to become repulsed by those who are sick. The intense desire to get away from those who are ill is the devil's work; Satan constantly tempts us to abandon those most in need of care. But in making the case for remaining with those who suffer from this epidemic, Luther repeatedly invokes Matthew 25, reminding Christians that caring for the least among us—in this case, *the sick*—is caring for Christ.

Luther also takes on those in his midst who propose that all healing from disease should be left up to God, the Great Physician. His response is crystal clear: while God is indeed our Healer, God also "created medicines and provided us with intelligence to guard and take good care of the body." Therefore, Luther urges,

> [u]se medicine, take potions which help you … and act like a [person] who wants to help put out the burning city. What else is the epidemic but a fire which instead of consuming wood and straw devours life and body?

Ask God to protect you, Luther encourages, but then "administer medicine, and take it." It is nothing less than an offense against God and neighbor to ignore the tools God has enabled humans to create to love the neighbor amid tragedies like the plague.[2]

In addressing concerns over how to be a Christian in the middle of a health care crisis, Luther provides a framework for thinking about medical ethics, even in issues that continue to confront us today. While one of the epidemics of Luther's day was the plague, cancer is one of the most significant epidemics of our age. Even as great strides are being made to treat people living with cancer, just as in Luther's day, a host of ethical and legal issues face those who have a professional duty to treat the sick and those of us who care for and about such people in our professional and personal lives.

One reason for significant recent advances in cancer care is the existence of medical trials that allow for the development and promotion of more effective treatments. At the same time, the ethical and legal issues surrounding especially the physician's role and informed consent in medical trials are many. Before we can assess whether Luther's insights into one's professional duty of neighbor love are helpful in thinking about these issues, we need to understand something about the evolving nature of the physician-patient relationship and how that evolution impacts current views of the physician's role in the relationship.

Paradigms of the physician-patient relationship

Until the last several decades, the dominant model of the physician-patient relationship was that of paternalism. This model views the doctor as the expert and the one charged with making decisions on behalf of the patient, who defers to the expertise of the physician and expects the doctor to make the most beneficial decision for the patient.

Under this paradigm, there has often been little to no appreciation of a patient's right to consent to a particular course of treatment. But in the aftermath of the human research atrocities during WWII, the creation of the Nuremburg Code in 1947 set forth three fundamental tenets: (1) that voluntary consent is essential for human participants in research; (2) that human subjects must be free to discontinue the research; (3) that the researcher must be prepared to halt the research if there's probable cause that further research will result in injury, disability, or death of the human subject.[3] Building on the Nuremburg Code, U.S. courts put forward a number of significant verdicts from the 1950s to the 1970s that helped develop what is now known as the doctrine of informed consent.[4] These rulings resulted in a dramatic solidification of the view that both physicians and biomedical researchers have a moral and legal duty to obtain informed consent for certain procedures.

These legal decisions helped precipitate a paradigm shift in the physician-patient relationship from paternalism, where the physician is seen as the decision-maker on behalf of the patient, to a relationship that focuses on patient autonomy and the patient's ability to decide for themselves on their own course of treatment.

In the second decade of the twenty-first century, informed consent is a legal doctrine that governs physician-patient relationships; all 50 states have legislation that requires some level of informed consent. Details vary by state, but what remains consistent is the insistence that the physician must provide *full disclosure* to the patient of the diagnosis, recommended treatment and its alternatives, and the risks and benefits of treatment or not being treated, along with any possible financial gain the physician might receive if certain treatments or trials are pursued.[5] While there is broad agreement that the paternalism paradigm should no longer govern physician-patient relationships, there continues to be considerable discussion by bioethicists about the inability of the legal doctrine of informed consent, on its own, to create a moral framework robust enough to address the complex nature of the physician-patient relationship.

Moreover, as bioethics philosopher Tom Beauchamp observes, while the development of the doctrine of informed consent was "sudden and impressive," getting to "high quality consents" has been much more difficult. Beauchamp notes that if the criteria for informed consent are overly demanding—emphasizing *complete* understanding, for instance—then such consent will rarely be obtained. On the flip side, however, if informed consent becomes *pro forma* and easy and quick to obtain, it loses its moral significance.[6] Mere disclosure, it must be acknowledged, does not by itself indicate informed consent.

One of the most persistent challenges for physician-patient relationships, therefore, especially when dealing with serious and complex diagnoses that involve serious and complex treatments, is how "informed" consent can actually be. Much has been written about the vulnerable position those who are very sick are in. As medical ethicist Terrence Ackerman observes, the legal framework, while important, fails to adequately account for the impact of an illness upon the patient's autonomous behavior.[7]

And while the question of *informed* consent is often made more challenging by the vulnerabilities that accompany serious illness, informed consent becomes even more challenging for those undergoing clinical trials for cancer treatment. Regulations still rely heavily on written informed consent documents to achieve full disclosure of all the aspects of the trial, and many of those documents can be lengthy and difficult for a lay person to understand.[8] Research has also shown that hope and optimism often accompany the signing up for a clinical trial.

In addition, research has demonstrated that a discrepancy exists between what patients think they understand about the trial in which they are enrolled and what they actually understand. One study revealed that only 33% of cancer patients enrolled in a particular clinical trial were able to correctly state the purpose of the trial.[9] Further, for cancer patients currently involved in clinical trials, the majority—especially in randomized trials where they may receive only a placebo—will not see significant benefit from the trial for their own condition.

While patients should have the opportunity to choose to participate in clinical trials for altruistic reasons, many medical ethicists observe that the process of making such a decision is ripe for possible abuse. Many patients have great faith in the medical system and they know new treatments are emerging virtually every day; therefore, the possibility of participating in a trial understandably creates hope that those who enroll will benefit personally from participation. All of these dynamics become part of the physician-patient relationship when a patient is faced with the decision of whether or not to participate in a clinical trial.

Ethical challenges like these have prompted bioethicists and others to continue interrogating the paradigms and metaphors governing the physician-patient relationship. While some see the paradigm of patient autonomy as primarily a negative concept—i.e. focused on the limits of the physician's authority to determine patient care—medical ethicist Edmund Pellegrino argues that in order to appreciate the robust meaning of patient autonomy, the concept of "autonomy" must be understood within the context of the mutual obligation of the physician and the patient to one another. Pellegrino is worth quoting at length on this point:

> [T]otal independence is unrealistic in any walk of life. Human beings live in community and personal association, especially when they are patients. Patients especially need input of others if their own choices are to be genuine ones. Physicians are needed to provide information and to discuss this information with patients to enable and empower them to use their autonomy wisely. Patients must compare their values with those of others in the context of some community of belief which they accept in whole or in part. Patients cannot identify with their current choices without reference to some structure of values which they formed in the past and which they reaffirm or reject at the moment of choice. This is part of knowing ourselves, and we know ourselves largely in relation to others.[10]

Even as Hansen acknowledges Luther's sixteenth-century, patriarchal ways of envisioning a Christian living out one's role as father, doctor, mayor, mother, wife, or teacher, he nevertheless counsels us against overlooking

> the revolutionary shift produced by Luther's theology in his particular context: these are the fields where the other, who is normally regulated by the law as a potential agonistic pole, appears now as a neighbor inscribed in one's own (Christian) subjectivity. These are not just secular realities, but ways of life that embody the fruits of the Spirit (*fructus spiritus*) socially, politically, and economically.... To love your neighbor is to be ready to surrender money, property, life, everything one has for the health and welfare of the other.[28]

In listening to the women she interviewed, Vigen states that what they wanted most from their physicians is to be seen as a person.[29] When physicians see their role of loving neighbors as themselves within the larger framework of the subjectivity of Christ, then the patient's subjectivity and personhood is allowed to take center stage.

Physician and palliative care specialist Harvey Chochinov encourages physicians to adopt this broader notion of autonomy by realizing that "[t]here is very little that separates us from our patients other than time and luck.... And if we can see ourselves in that way, we are more likely to be able to practice compassionate medicine."[30] For physicians to envision themselves and their patients as neighbors invites an appreciation of the patient's vulnerability as well as their agency.

But we simply cannot ignore the reality that, for patients trying to decide whether or not to enroll in a trial, "physician's influence" is the single most significant factor.[31] Studies also indicate that "lack of encouragement" by physicians is a major reason for refraining from enrolling in a trial, as is misinformation about how likely it is that participants will receive no treatment, and the mistaken view that enrolling in a trial signifies a last-ditch effort to treat the cancer.[32] Taking on the patient's subjectivity as one's own, the physician must hold that notion of vulnerability in tension with the reality that the patient-neighbor will look to the physician for insight on whether a trial is the best choice.

How far should taking on a patient's subjectivity go, especially when a patient like Sophia is struggling with the severe effects of experimental treatment? Given the outcome of her case, it could be argued that Sophia's physician imagined the kind of encouragement he thought he would need if he were the patient and acted accordingly. At the same time, physician Atul Gewande suggests that in the current medical climate, physicians often see their role as ensuring health and survival instead of, as he would hope, enabling well-being.[33] And well-being may, for the patient facing an aggressive form of cancer and harsh treatments, include saying "enough is enough."

Before we leave it there, it's worthwhile to turn one last time to Luther's vision of treating those with the plague. He writes about the duties of doctors, pastors, and lawyers to tend to those who are ill. But he also commends any and all who are able to embody neighbor love and remain with the sick. Similarly, the proposal by Sophia's oncologist to hospitalize her if need be to help her get through the final leg of the trial hints at an awareness that Sophia needs additional support—other neighbors—to encourage her and help her make decisions about her future that could well determine whether she lives or dies. The neighbor metaphor is open to being expanded to potentially include a whole host of neighbors who can help patients articulate and embrace treatment regimens that are consonant with their values.

Additional neighbors whom the patient trusts can help her take in what the physician-neighbor has to say, weigh the pros and cons, and move forward in a way that honors her values, decision-making process, and vision for her life.

The invocation of the neighbor image for patient and physician alike cannot fully put to rest every challenging ethical issue facing the current practice of informed consent. At the same time, Martin Luther's use of the neighbor image in his 1527 treatise continues to have resonance today as we think through the ethical issues facing the doctrine of informed consent and its potential to help patient-neighbors in their attempts to access treatment for the epidemic of cancer.

Notes

1 Martin Luther, "Whether One Should Flee the Deadly Plague," *Martin Luther's Basic Theological Writings*, eds. Timothy F. Lull and William R. Russell, 3rd ed. (Minneapolis, MN: Fortress Press, 2012), 483.
2 Ibid., 483.
3 "The Nuremberg Code," National Institute of Health. Accessed December 5, 2016. https://history.nih.gov/research/downloads/nuremberg.pdf.
4 The first time the term "informed consent" appeared publicly was in *Salgo v. Leland Stanford, Jr. University Board of Trustees*, 317 P.2d 170 (1957), where the court ruled that the duty to disclose risks and alternatives of treatment was an already established duty of physicians. Then in 1972, three landmark decisions in three separate state courts solidified the place of informed consent in the law. Those three cases were *Canterbury v. Spence*, 464 F.2d 772 (D.C. Cir., 1972); *Cobbs v. Grant*, 104 Cal. Rptr. 505, 502 P.2nd 1 (1972); and *Wilkinson v. Vesey*, 295 A.2d 676 (R. I. 1972.) All of them demanded a more patient-oriented standard of disclosure.
5 The basic features of everyday informed consent: the physician (not a delegated representative) should disclose and discuss the diagnosis, if known; the nature and purpose of a proposed treatment or procedure; the risks and benefits of proposed treatment or procedures; alternatives (regardless of costs or extent covered by insurance); the risks and benefits of alternatives; the risks and benefits of not receiving treatments or undergoing procedures. "Code of Medical Ethics," *American Medical Association* (1998). Accessed December 15, 2016. www.ama-assn.org/about-us/code-medical-ethics.
6 Tom L. Beauchamp, "Informed Consent: Its History, Meaning, and Present Challenges," *Cambridge Quarterly of Healthcare Ethics* 20 (2011): 515–517.
7 Terrence F. Ackerman, Why Doctors Should Intervene," *Hastings Center Report* 12, no. 4 (August 1982): 16.
8 Christopher K. Daugherty, M.D., "Informed Consent, the Cancer Patient, and Phase I Clinical Trials," *Ethical Issues in Cancer Patient Care*, eds. Peter Angelos and Robert H. Lurie (Norwell, MA: Kluwer Academic Publishers, 2000), 78.
9 Daugherty, "Informed Consent, the Cancer Patient, and Phase I Clinical Trials," 83.
10 Edmund Pellegrino, "Patient and Physician Autonomy: Conflicting Rights and Obligations in the Physician-Patient Relationship," *The Philosophy of Medicine Reborn: A Pellegrino Reader*, eds. H. Tristram Engelhardt Jr, and Fabrice Jotterand (Notre Dame, IN: University of Notre Dame Press, 2008), 208.
11 William F. May, *The Physician's Covenant: Images of the Healer in Medical Ethics*, 2nd ed. (Louisville, KY: Westminster John Knox, 2000).
12 Martin Luther, *The Sermons of Martin Luther*, ed. John Nicholas Lenker, 8 vols. (Grand Rapids, MI: Baker, 1983), vol 1: 112.
13 William F. May, *The Physician's Covenant*, 9.
14 "The Ethics of Randomized Clinical Trials," *Ethical Issues in Modern Medicine: Contemporary Readings in Bioethics*, eds. Bonnie Steinboch, John D. Arras and Alex John London, 7th ed. (New York City: McGraw Hill Companies, 2008), 774.
15 American Cancer Society, "Clinical Trials: What You Need to Know." Accessed May 3, 2016. www.cancer.org/acs/groups/cid/documents/webcontent/003006-pdf.pdf
16 "The Ethics of Randomized Clinical Trials," 775.

17 Ibid., 776.
18 The issue of full disclosure of possible financial gain for physicians has become perhaps the primary focus of the doctrine of informed consent in the second decade of the twenty-first century. See "Physician Financial Transparency Reports (Sunshine Act)," American Medical Association. Accessed October 13, 2016. www.ama-assn.org/ama/pub/advocacy/topics/sunshine-act-and-physician-financial-transparency-reports.page/
19 Robert Arnold and Charles Lidz, the "Yes" response to "Is Informed Consent Still Central to Medical Ethics?" *Taking Sides: Clashing Views on Biomedical Issues*, ed. Carol Levine, 12th ed. (Dubuque, IA: McGraw Hill, 2008), 4.
20 William May, "Beyond Paul Ramsey's Beecher Lectures," in *The Patient as Person: Explorations in Medical Ethics*, ed. Paul Ramsey, 2nd ed. (New Haven, CT: Yale University Press, 2012), xli.
21 May, "Beyond Paul Ramsey's Beecher Lectures," xxxvi.
22 See, for example, Luther's claim that, "[w]e are bound to each other," in "Whether One May Flee From the Deadly Plague," and "we live for others and for ourselves," in "On the Freedom of a Christian," in *Martin Luther's Basic Theological Writings*, 477, 418.
23 Aana Vigen, *Women, Ethics, and Inequality in U.S. Healthcare: "To Count among the Living,"* (New York: Palgrave McMillan, 2006), 72.
24 Ibid., 84.
25 Ibid., 142.
26 Ibid., 145.
27 Luther, "Whether One May Flee From the Deadly Plague," 480.
28 Guillermo Hansen, "Luther's Radical Conception of Faith: God, Christ, and Personhood in a Post-Metaphysical Age," *Dialog: A Journal of Theology* 52, no. 3 (Fall 2013): 217.
29 Aana Vigen, *Women, Ethics, and Inequality in U.S. Healthcare*, 183.
30 Meg Barbor, "Dignity, Personhood, and the Culture of Medicine," The ASCO Post. Accessed December 5, 2016. www.ascopost.com/issues/august-15-2014/dignity-personhood-and-the-culture-of-medicine/.
31 "Transforming Clinical Research in the United States: Challenges and Opportunities: Workshop Summary," Institute of Medicine (US) Forum on Drug Discovery, Development, and Translation (Washington, DC: National Academics Press, 2010). Accessed December 5, 2016. www.ncbi.nlm.nih.gov/books/NBK50895/.
32 "Transforming Clinical Research in the United States: Challenges and Opportunities: Workshop Summary."
33 Atul Gewande, *Being Mortal: Medicine and What Matters in the End* (New York: Metropolitan Books, 2014), 259.

15 Role morality, dirty hands, and the theology of vocation

W. Bradley Wendel

The central issue in the theory of lawyers' ethics is the justification of role-differentiated moral duties and permissions. Roles and role-differentiated obligations and permissions are a pervasive feature of ethics.[1] Roles frequently do not present substantial difficulties for moral theory. A parent, for instance, may prefer the interests of his or her own children, even if other children have more urgent needs.[2] In many other cases, however, role-differentiated obligations are more difficult to square with the moral agency of the actor in the role. As Arthur Applbaum has argued, "[r]oles cannot filter out morally pertinent pre-conventional descriptions of acts and actors."[3] If an act can be described as "killing," then it remains killing even when a soldier or police officer kills in the line of duty. The act may be justified, but it remains a killing, not a something-else that can be re-framed as not-killing because of the actor's role. Euphemisms like "officer-involved shooting" are frequently used to obscure the descriptions that would be given in ordinary moral terms.

Some lawyers and philosophers have grasped the nettle and admitted forthrightly that carrying out their professional duties necessarily involves them in tragic choices and moral wrongdoing. In an article that provoked outrage when it was published in 1951, a distinguished Boston lawyer quoted Montaigne on the ethics of public callings:

> The mayor and Montaigne have always been two people, clearly separated. There's no reason why a lawyer or a banker should not recognize the knavery that is part of his vocation. An honest man is not responsible for the vices or the stupidity of his calling, and need not refuse to practise them. They are customs in his country and there is profit in them. A man must live in the world and avail himself of what he finds there.[4]

Notice, however, a subtle shift in this position. Montaigne is not saying that he was a virtuous mayor. Rather, he disclaims accountability for actions he may have taken within the role of mayor. "Knavery" may be part of the exercise of public office, but it is not *personal* knavery. It belongs to the role itself, not to its occupant. (As the saying goes, "Don't hate the player—hate the game.")

We should recognize Montaigne's attempt at justification as the transparent evasion it is. A person remains a moral agent even when he or she is acting in a professional role, and wrongdoing attaches to the actor, not the role.[5] Conceding this point, a few hard-nosed realists have emphasized Montaigne's observation that knavery may be part of one's vocation, but have also maintained that an honest person *is* responsible for the vices of her calling.[6] An honest person should recognize the hard truth about public life, that sometimes doing the right thing requires getting one's hands dirty. Machiavelli put it bluntly when he counseled

The concept of a vocation should also not be understood uncritically to baptize the power of public authorities (or lawyers who represent clients in legal proceedings) in the name of God, or to justify acquiescence in existing distributions of power.[25] Human institutions, caught up in the power of sin, are susceptible to corruption and abuse. "The doctrine of vocation can be easily abused to… encourage inaction in the face of injustice, and actions that harm neighbors."[26] Thus, the further challenge is either to discern, ***within*** vocations constituted by human institutional forms like law and government, how one is to love and serve one's neighbor, or to seek to reform legal institutions to God's work in the world. Recent ELCA social statements recognize that our vocations of service require us to live out our responsibilities to serve the neighbor in complex and sometimes tragic circumstances.[27] The complexity and tragedy of public callings is a theme quite familiar to lawyers.

Service to one's neighbor through the law can sometimes result in harm to others, and these others might plausibly also be one's neighbors. The law can be understood as a means of securing justice, order, or civil peace, but it can also be an instrument of violence, discrimination, and injustice. Thus, it is not enough simply to assert that one's vocation as a lawyer can be understood as a way of serving one's neighbor, where the result of this service may be to impoverish or harm other neighbors.[28] But what does that require, exactly, in the context of a professional role that is connected with an institution that, by its very nature, deals with conflict and violence? As Douglas Schuurman asks, in his study of vocation,

> Can it be a divine calling to work for an enterprise that appears to have either no connection to the common good or a deleterious effect upon it? What degree of complicity in the exploitive procedures and consequences of a given corporation should be tolerated if work is to serve the neighbor?[29]

In its social statement on criminal justice, the ELCA adopted a stance of modesty toward law reform efforts: "Not possessing special insight into matters of reason, this church does not presume to instruct the public authority how, in detail, the justice system should be shaped."[30] That is a reasonable position for a social statement pitched at a fairly high level of abstraction. Individual Lutheran lawyers, however, are in a position of having to discern whether action within their vocation, in its concrete form, harms rather than serves the neighbor. This problem is particularly difficult for lawyers, for whom the relevant neighbor may be not only the client, but also other members of the civil community served by the law. Just as we may seek a general doctrine of vocation that avoids withdrawal from social engagement, triumphalism, cynicism, and moral paralysis,[31] we must have something concrete to say to a person called to a particular vocation who wishes to know how to act within that role, and how to reform it if necessary, to respond rightly to the call to serve "God's ongoing creative work in upholding and directing all that is."[32]

The defense lawyer's dilemma

Take, for example, a wrenching ethical problem for a criminal defense lawyer.[33] In this story that took place not long ago in Chicago, a security guard was murdered and another guard seriously injured during the robbery of a store. The surviving guard identified two men, Logan and Hope, as the perpetrators. A week later, a man named Wilson was arrested for an unrelated crime, the murder of two police officers. Hope heard about the arrest of Wilson, and told his lawyer that he had committed the robbery with Wilson, not Logan. Hope's lawyer informed Wilson's lawyers about this conversation, and they went to see

Wilson at the jail. Wilson confessed to his lawyers that he, not Logan, had in fact shot the security guards. The lawyers made a written record of the confession, which Wilson signed. Meanwhile, not knowing of Wilson's admission of responsibility, prosecutors filed murder charges against Logan and Hope. Based on the testimony of the surviving guard, both were convicted at trial and sentenced to lengthy prison terms. Wilson was convicted in a separate trial of murdering the two police officers and was sentenced to two life sentences without possibility of parole.

Imagine that you are one of the lawyers representing Wilson, having observed these events and in possession of Wilson's confession. What do you do with the knowledge that an innocent person will be spending the rest of his life in prison for a crime committed by your client? Perhaps the answer is to be found in a code of professional ethics, applicable to lawyers representing clients in a situation like this one. The rules of professional conduct in your jurisdiction would likely provide as follows:

> A lawyer *shall* not reveal information relating to the representation of a client unless the client consents after consultation ... A lawyer may reveal such information to the extent the lawyer reasonably believes necessary ... to prevent reasonably certain death or substantial bodily harm.[34]

You have made repeated attempts to convince Wilson to consent to disclose his statement that he committed the restaurant robbery and murders, but he has consistently refused to agree. Now you try a fallback strategy—does the confidentiality rule really cover the confession? Yes, as it turns out. The communication from Wilson is "information relating to the representation" because you learned it in the course of defending Wilson in the separate murder case; it does not matter that the communication relates to a separate crime. You might argue that Logan's continued imprisonment constitutes "substantial bodily harm" because he is quite corporeally stuck in prison. That is not a bad argument, but assume the authority responsible for interpreting the ethical rules in your jurisdiction has essentially rejected it in a similar case.[35]

You might then reason that the duty does not apply because disclosing Wilson's communication cannot possibly harm him because he is already serving two life sentences for the other murders. The rule defining the duty of confidentiality does not make reference to harm to the client, however, and, upon reflection, you realize that there might be harm to Wilson if you disclose. What would happen, for example, if his convictions for the other murders were reversed on appeal? He might then face prosecution for the robbery of the store and the murder of the security guard. Thus, as a matter of professional ethics, your duty is clear: you must not disclose Wilson's statement even if it would result in freeing an innocent man from prison.

Thematically this ethics problem raises two issues. One, already mentioned, is the problem of integrating obligations to specific persons or communities with the universal demands of morality.[36] Detachment from one's parochial concerns seems basic to the methods of ethics, yet ethics also must make room for particular ties and commitments. Lawyers who have a fiduciary relationship with a specific client, and yet serve as instruments of impartial state law, exist at the intersection of these objective and subjective points of view.

The defense lawyer's role, including the stringent obligation of confidentiality, is often justified with reference to the fiduciary relationship that exists between lawyers and clients. Wilson is extraordinarily vulnerable to his lawyers, owing to both the background imbalance of power between himself and professionals with specialized knowledge and expertise, an occupant of one of these roles must take great care not to become cynical or inured to the harm that results from the exercise of public power.

As applied to the ethical problems confronting lawyers, the Lutheran approach is a dialectical, paradoxical conception of ethics, which seeks to maintain two beliefs simultaneously: first, that acting for others in the public domain (that is, in politics) requires working through institutions that at best only partially instantiate a truly just legal order and second, that since God continues to be active in creation, human institutions are nevertheless normed by ideals such as justice and the equal dignity of all persons. The claim that an institution can be both the instrument of God's left hand for regulating creation, while simultaneously being corrupted by human sinfulness, is a basic Lutheran insight. The Lutheran tradition also strongly warns against seeing the action of law and government in this world as redemptive. "The extravagant love revealed in the gospel cannot become the guiding principle for ordering life in the rough and tumble of this world."[45]

Yet our unrighteousness before God does not mean that it is impossible to strive to make human institutions better. Though radically fallen, humans are capable of civil righteousness. The history of American law in the twentieth century can be understood as a gradual lurching, in fits and starts, toward an order in which equality and justice are more fully instantiated. We should not overlook the partial goods that have been made possible by state law.[46] Significant injustice remains, however, and it may be impossible to work within the legal system without taking part in the wrongs it enables. As a lawyer, one must be committed to loyal client service and to justice. The Alton Logan case is only one example of the ordinary ways in which service to one neighbor necessarily involves complicity in harm to another.

A Lutheran approach to the lawyer's dilemma

Duly warned not to interpret the two kingdoms doctrine as sanctioning passivity in the face of injustice, but also not to expect worldly institutions to enact God's justice, how would a Lutheran lawyer be different from any other decent, conscientious person in the same role? The pressing question for legal ethics is not whether one may be a lawyer, but how one is to go about performing that role. At this point, however, the theological concepts of vocation and service to neighbor seem to do relatively little to guide discernment. There are two general issues on which an ethical theory can be expected to provide guidance. The first is in determining when the conditions are no longer satisfied which make service as a lawyer a suitable vocation for a Christian. This requires evaluating the extent of injustice that is tolerable within an institutional role whose end is justice. The second question is, even on the assumption that the legal system as a whole is functioning reasonably well, what should a lawyer do if an act permitted or required by applicable legal norms will lead to injustice in a particular case?

This question can be asked: is punctilious adherence to the norms of an unjust system required, or are lawyers permitted to transgress law in pursuit of justice? William Simon has argued that the lawyers we regard as moral heroes are not those who blindly conform to state law; rather, the praiseworthy lawyers are those who use cleverness and initiative to work around official authority, and sometimes even engage in outright defiance of the law—a quality he calls "moral pluck."[47] He cites the decision by Atticus Finch, the fictional lawyer hero of *To Kill a Mockingbird*, to collude with the sheriff of Maycomb County in telling a patently false story to explain the death of Bob Ewell, thereby shielding his disabled neighbor Boo Radley from prosecution.[48] Atticus's decision is the opposite of blind obedience to state law, yet he sits securely near the top of the pantheon of sainted fictional lawyers.

In my view, however, it is a serious misreading of the dirty hands literature to conclude that lawyers should—or even are permitted to—ignore the obligations imposed by law because they believe following the law would lead to injustice in a particular case. As the previous example of President Obama's justification of drone strikes shows, when the rubber hits the road for political ethics, the obligation of the role takes priority over what decent, conscientious people might otherwise have reason to do. The ethical obligations of the professional role do not, however, and cannot eliminate the qualms that ordinarily-decent people would have. Particularly with respect to the institution of law, which is needed precisely because we cannot rely on all people to be equally virtuous, professionals will be unable to reconcile completely their desire for justice with their recognition of the persistence of injustice.[49] The result will be unease and tension—precisely the kind of paradoxical vision of ethics with which Lutherans are so familiar. These "moral remainders" caution lawyers against too readily accepting the necessity of the injustices sustained by the legal system, even while they work within it, and provide a safeguard against self-deception and the sorts of consoling myths that people are apt to tell themselves to avoid facing up to the consequences of human sinfulness.

These qualms also provide resources for imagining a better world and may suggest strategies for mitigating injustice. Some participation in injustice may be inevitable, however, which is only to be expected given as-yet uncompleted fulfillment of the promise of God's kingdom.[50] The result, for lawyers, is that the unification of public and private selves sought by the Stoics will continue to be elusive. But Lutherans are, if anything, comfortable with ambiguity. Although Luther himself was not particularly fond of lawyers,[51] it may turn out that Lutherans are particularly well-suited to a vocation in the law.

Notes

1 See, e.g., Michael Hardimon, "Role Obligations," *Journal of Philosophy* 91 (1994): 333–363; Judith Andre, "Role Morality as a Complex Instance of Ordinary Morality," *American Philosophical Quarterly* 28 (1991):73–80; Mike W. Martin, "Rights and the Meta-Ethics of Professional Morality," *Ethics* 91 (1981): 619–625.

2 Richard Wasserstrom, "Lawyers as Professionals: Some Moral Issues," *Human Rights* 5, no. 1 (1975): 5; Tim Dare, *The Counsel of Rogues? A Defence of the Standard Conception of the Lawyer's Role* (Farnham: Ashgate, 2009), 31–32; Alan Goldman, *The Moral Foundations of Professional Ethics* (Totowa, NJ: Rowman & Littlefield, 1980), 4.

3 Arthur Isak Applbaum, *Ethics for Adversaries* (Princeton, NJ: Princeton University Press 1999), 109.

4 Charles P. Curtis, "The Ethics of Advocacy," *Stanford Law Review* 4, no. 1 (1951): 20.

5 Applbaum, *Ethics for Adversaries*, 75.

6 Stuart Hampshire, *Innocence and Experience* (Cambridge: Harvard University Press, 1989); Michael Walzer, "Political Action: The Problem of Dirty Hands," *Philosophy & Public Affairs* 2, no. 2 (Winter, 1973): 160–180; Bernard Williams, "Professional Morality and Its Dispositions," in *Making Sense of Humanity* (Cambridge: Cambridge University Press, 1995); Bernard Williams, "Politics and Moral Character," in *Moral Luck* (Cambridge: Cambridge University Press, 1981); Thomas Nagel, "Ruthlessness in Public Life," in Stuart Hampshire, ed., *Public and Private Morality* (Cambridge: Cambridge University Press, 1978).

7 Niccolò Machiavelli, *The Prince*, ed. E.R.P. Vincent, trans. Luigi Ricci (London: Oxford University Press, 1935), 84.

8 Max Weber, "Politics as Vocation," in Hans H. Gerth and C. Wright Mills, eds., *From Max Weber: Essays in Sociology* (New York: Oxford University Press, 1946), 121, 123.

9 Jonathan Chait, "Five Days That Shaped a Presidency," *New York Magazine* (October 2, 2016). Accessed October 21, 2017. http://nymag.com/daily/intelligencer/2016/10/barack-obama-on-5-days-that-shaped-his-presidency.html.

10 Williams, "Politics and Moral Character," 66.

11 i> Ibid., 62–63.
12 Gerald J. Postema, "Moral Responsibility and Professional Ethics," *New York University Law Review* 55 (1980): 63–89.
13 Alasdair MacIntyre, "Social Structures and Their Threats to Moral Agency," *Philosophy* 74 (1999): 311–312.
14 Kathryn Kleinhans, "The Work of a Christian: Vocation in Lutheran Perspective," *Word & World* 25 (2005): 394–402.
15 See Evangelical Lutheran Church in America, "The Church in Society: A Lutheran Perspective" (1991): 4. Accessed October 21, 2016. http://download.elca.org/ELCA%20Resource%20Repository/Church_SocietySS.pdf.
16 Marc Kolden, "Luther on Vocation," *Word & World* 3, no. 4 (1983): 383.
17 William Lazareth, "Love and Law in Christian Life," *Journal of Lutheran Ethics* 1, no. 3 (2001), para. 21–23.
18 Robert Benne, *The Paradoxical Vision* (Minneapolis, MN: Fortress Press, 1995), 63–68, 77–78.
19 Otto Hermann Pesch, "Free by Faith: Luther's Contribution to a Theological Anthropology," in Manfred Hoffman, ed., *Martin Luther and the Modern Mind* (New York: Edwin Mellen Press, 1985), 24.
20 Robert Benne, *Good and Bad Ways to Think About Religion and Politics* (Grand Rapids, MI: William B. Eerdmans Publishing Company, 2010), 19–22.
21 H. Richard Niebuhr, *Christ and Culture* (New York: Harper, 1956).
22 Kleinhans, "The Work of a Christian," 396; see also Benne, *Paradoxical Vision*, 91–96.
23 Douglas J. Schuurman, *Vocation: Discerning Our Callings in Life* (Grand Rapids, MI: Eerdmans, 2004), 53–55, 79, 90–91.
24 Evangelical Lutheran Church in America, "The Church and Criminal Justice: Hearing the Cries" (2013): 19. Accessed October 21, 2017. http://download.elca.org/ELCA%20Resource%20Repository/Criminal_JusticeSS.pdf.
25 Ibid.
26 Schuurman, *Vocation*, 97–98.
27 Evangelical Lutheran Church in America, "Human Sexuality: Gift and Trust," (2009): 4. Accessed October 21, 2017. http://download.elca.org/ELCA%20Resource%20Repository/SexualitySS.pdf?_ga=2.252575489.929358192.1508605423-889091389.1502033567.
28 Cynthia Moe-Lobeda, "Neighbor-Love's Moral Framework: From Markets That Concentrate Wealth to Markets That Serve Abundant Life for All," *Journal of Lutheran Ethics* 14, no. 1 (2014), para. 7.
29 Schuurman, *Vocation,* 12–13. Later in the book he gives the example of working for a tobacco company, and suggested that a Christian seeking "unity of his or her faith and paid work" would not be able to find it in such an occupation with a company whose activities harm the neighbor. Ibid., 132–33.
30 Evangelical Lutheran Church in America, "The Church and Criminal Justice," 22.
31 Schuurman, *Vocation*, 99–100.
32 Kolden, "Luther on Vocation," 386.
33 I used the Alton Logan case as the lead problem in Chapter 1 of W. Bradley Wendel, *Ethics and Law: An Introduction* (Cambridge: Cambridge University Press, 2014). The case is the subject of a number of articles in the local press, including Fran Spielman, "Chicago to Pay $10.25 Million in Another Burge Case," *Chicago Sun-Times*, (January 14, 2013), and "After 26 Years, 2 Lawyers Reveal a Killer's Secret," *USA Today* (April 13, 2008). Logan was released from prison in 2007 after Wilson died and his lawyers disclosed the affidavit they had written memorializing Wilson's statement. Logan filed a lawsuit claiming that evidence of his innocence had been covered up by state prosecutors. Wilson's lawyers were not charged with any wrongdoing in connection with the case.
34 Model Rules of Professional Conduct § 1.6(b)(1) (American Bar Association, 1983). Some version of this rule is in effect in all United States jurisdictions.
35 Indeed, this is the position taken by courts that have considered this issue. See, e.g., *State v. Macumber*, 544 P.2d 1084 (Ariz. 1976) (recognizing that the attorney-client privilege applies after a client dies, even when two attorneys of that client offer to testify that he confessed to the murder that another defendant is being tried for.)
36 See Thomas Nagel, *The View from Nowhere* (New York: Oxford University Press, 1986).

37 Dare, *The Counsel of Rogues*, 94–96.
38 Evangelical Lutheran Church in America, "The Church and Criminal Justice," 21–22.
39 H.L.A. Hart, "Commands and Authoritative Legal Reasons," in H.L.A. Hart, *Essays on Bentham: Jurisprudence and Political Philosophy* (Oxford: Oxford University Press, 1982): 254–255.
40 See, e.g., John H. Blume, "Killing the Willing: 'Volunteers,' Suicide and Competency," *Michigan Law Review* 103, no. 5 (2005): 939–982. According to a report from the Bureau of Justice Statistics, over half of the prison population has mental health problems. Doris J. James and Lauren E. Glaze, *Mental Health Problems of Prison and Jail Inmates* (U.S. Department of Justice, Bureau of Justice Statistics, 2006.) Accessed October 21, 2017. www.bjs.gov/content/pub/pdf/mhppji.pdf.
41 See, e.g., *In re Schafer*, 66 P.3d 1036 (Wash. 2003) (suspending a lawyer from practice for disclosing confidential information that led to conviction of a corrupt judge).
42 See, e.g., David Luban, *Lawyers and Justice: An Ethical Study* (Princeton, NJ: Princeton University Press, 1988) 217–220; Fred C. Zacharias, "Rethinking Confidentiality," *Iowa Law Review* 74 (1989): 351–411.
43 Benne, *Paradoxical Vision*, 87–89, 95–96.
44 C.A.J. Coady, "Dirty Hands," in Robert E. Goodin et al., eds., *A Companion to Contemporary Political Philosophy* (Malden, MA: Wiley-Blackwell, 2d ed., 2012), 534.
45 Benne, *Paradoxical Vision*, 87.
46 Ibid., 95.
47 William H. Simon, "Moral Pluck: Legal Ethics in Popular Culture," *Columbia Law Review* 101, no. 1 (2001): 421.
48 Ibid., 421–422.
49 See Williams, "Professional Morality and Its Dispositions," 198–201.
50 Peters, in this volume, 89–96.
51 See John Witte Jr., *Law and Protestantism: The Legal Teachings of the Lutheran Reformation* (Cambridge: Cambridge University Press, 2002), 119.

Index of subjects

Index of proper names

www.ingramcontent.com/pod-product-compliance
Ingram Content Group UK Ltd.
Pitfield, Milton Keynes, MK11 3LW, UK
UKHW050754180926
475701UK00007B/1036
9780367591441